WORK LESS

WORK LESS

New Strategies for a Changing Workplace

JON PEIRCE

DUNDURN PRESS

Copyright © Jon Peirce, 2024

All rights reserved. No part of this publication may be reproduced, stored in a retrieval system, or transmitted in any form or by any means, electronic, mechanical, photocopying, recording, or otherwise (except for brief passages for purpose of review) without the prior permission of Dundurn Press. Permission to photocopy should be requested from Access Copyright.

Publisher and acquiring editor: Kwame Scott Fraser | Editor: Dominic Farrell
Cover designer: Laura Boyle
Cover image: istock.com/robbin0919

Library and Archives Canada Cataloguing in Publication

Title: Work less : new strategies for a changing workplace / Jon Peirce.
Names: Peirce, Jon (Jonathan Charles), author.
Description: Includes bibliographical references and index.
Identifiers: Canadiana (print) 20230538304 | Canadiana (ebook) 20230538312 | ISBN 9781459751316 (softcover) | ISBN 9781459751323 (PDF) | ISBN 9781459751330 (EPUB)
Subjects: LCSH: Hours of labor. | LCSH: Labor productivity. | LCSH: Employee morale. | LCSH: Quality of work life.
Classification: LCC HD5106 .P45 2024 | DDC 331.25/7—dc23

We acknowledge the support of the Canada Council for the Arts and the Ontario Arts Council for our publishing program. We also acknowledge the financial support of the Government of Ontario, through the Ontario Book Publishing Tax Credit and Ontario Creates, and the Government of Canada.

Care has been taken to trace the ownership of copyright material used in this book. The author and the publisher welcome any information enabling them to rectify any references or credits in subsequent editions.

The publisher is not responsible for websites or their content unless they are owned by the publisher.

Printed and bound in Canada.

Dundurn Press
1382 Queen Street East
Toronto, Ontario, Canada M4L 1C9
dundurn.com, @dundurnpress

This book is dedicated to the working people of Canada in the hope that it will contribute to their having a more rewarding and less stressful time at work than most have enjoyed up until now.

Contents

Introduction: Suddenly, the Time Is Now (Once Again) 1
1 Working Ourselves Sick 9
2 Historical Development of Work Hours I: The United States 21
3 Historical Development of Work Hours II: Canada 53
4 Historical Development of Work Hours III: Work Hours Around the World 63
5 A Special Decade: Work Hours and the 1920s 91
6 Technology, Work Intensification, Stress, and Distress 103
7 The "Great Resignation" and Its Effects on Work Hours 121
8 The Right to Disconnect 133
9 Hybrid Workplaces and Their Implications for Work Hours 159
10 What's Been Happening Lately on the Shorter Hours Scene? 179
11 Recommendations 203
Conclusion 211
Acknowledgements 213
Appendix A: Profile of Joe O'Connor: He Works so You Can Work Less 215
Appendix B: An Interview with Henry O'Loughlin 219
Appendix C: People and Organizations Working for Shorter Hours 225
Notes 229
Bibliography 263
Index 275
About the Author 288

INTRODUCTION

Suddenly, the Time Is Now (Once Again)

When one reaches a certain age and stage of life, bookshelf space is at a premium. With an eye to making more, I found myself, one raw January day early in 2022, looking over a bookcase beside my office desk, where I expected to find three or four likely candidates for the "Give a book/Take a book" wooden box down Gatineau's rue Jacques-Cartier from me. I needed space for a number of Christmas books still sitting in their gift bags, waiting for a more permanent home and for others I expected to be receiving shortly.

Half an hour's search having turned up nothing I was willing to part with, I was about to give up and switch to some more productive activity, when suddenly my eye was caught by a bright yellow binding. The binding alone made the book stand out on my generally sombre-looking shelves. Few of my books have ever had brightly-coloured covers, and even those few — Montaigne's *Essais* in the original French is one that comes to mind — have long since faded after decades in my possession. In contrast, this book had the bright, cheerful sheen of a new arrival.

Now my curiosity was piqued. I hadn't bought many books at all in recent years, and those I had bought typically had covers as drab as those adorning instruction manuals. What *could* this book possibly be, standing out as clearly from the rest of my collection as a yellow warbler amid a pack of slate-coloured juncos?

On taking the book down, I was surprised to discover it was none other than Bruce O'Hara's *Working Harder Isn't Working*, a book I'd eagerly purchased back in the 1990s when I was doing serious research into work hours but was not sure I still had in my possession. I remembered having read the book eagerly, pleased to discover a kindred spirit in my quest for shorter hours, which in those recessionary days was viewed primarily as a job-creation mechanism. O'Hara was an important source for the major study I did on work hours between 1997 and 2000. But once I'd finished that study,[1] my interests shifted, to the extent that I did no further research on the subject through the century's first two decades.

My first reaction was one of joy, as if I'd just run into a long-lost friend. Seeing the book took me back to the days, not *all* that long ago, when work hours had actually had a place on Canadian policy-makers' agendas, albeit not a very elevated place. (Its place on European policy-makers' agendas, as we'll see in a later chapter, was and still is a far loftier one.) But that initial joy soon gave way to sadness. Quite simply, it appeared that no one gave a damn about work hours anymore. It had been at least fifteen years since I'd even heard the subject mentioned. Meanwhile, people (other than retirees like me) seemed to be working harder than ever. Was this just another of the many windmills I'd tilted at in my youth and early middle age, to little lasting effect? If so, I would be keeping the book for purely sentimental reasons; self-discipline and a continuing need to declutter dictated I should probably cull it.

For twenty minutes, I sat wracked with indecision, forgetting the minor Victorian novels and obscure poetry collections that might also have been good candidates for culling. Finally, I decided to return the book to the shelf, at least for the time being. Whether or not I would ever read it again, its yellow binding lent a touch of colour to my otherwise drab book collection and might at least help cheer me up on dull, grey winter days. While many a book has been sold because of its cover, this could just have been the first recorded instance of a book's having been saved because of its cover.

Introduction: Suddenly, the Time Is Now (Once Again)

A few weeks later, having by this time again forgotten about O'Hara, and having satisfied my decluttering impulse by consigning half a dozen fourth-tier Victorian and contemporary novels to the little wooden box, I found myself thinking about work hours for the first time in many years. The reason for that was a piece I'd read on CBC News about a Toronto firm that, in the wake of the Covid-19 pandemic, had decided to go to a four-day week both as a recruitment incentive and to improve the health and job satisfaction of existing employees.

Intrigued and delighted, I recalled my earlier research on the subject and put together a CBC Opinion piece advocating for a more general adoption of shorter hours. To my amazement, the piece was accepted and then published on CBC's website within a week of my having conceived it.

Even the modest amount of research I did for the piece revealed that the four-day week, in particular, had once again become a hot-button topic. I discovered organizations in the United Kingdom and New Zealand as well as firms in Canada working for its adoption. I also found that an NDP member of Ontario's legislature and a Democratic member of the U.S. House of Representatives had, independently of each other, introduced legislation to enact the four-day week into law.[2]

But it was the response to the CBC Opinion piece that really suggested I was on to something big. Within two days after the piece's initial appearance, I had TV and radio interviews lined up. And the piece itself would garner one thousand comments before CBC closed off commenting altogether. Friends and colleagues who'd been made aware of my burgeoning interest in the subject began emailing me all manner of articles and research studies. And each day, the internet news seemed to include several more articles on the subject. Clearly, I'd made the right decision by keeping the O'Hara book. The rightness of that decision was confirmed when, less than a month after the publication of the CBC Opinion piece, I signed a contract with Dundurn Press to produce a book on work hours. And so here we are.

Where will we be going in this book? Because the connection between overwork and physical and mental health issues has become so clear since the onset of the Covid-19 pandemic, I begin with a chapter titled "Working Ourselves Sick," in which I lay out the current situation with regard to work hours and physical and mental health. The discussion then turns to the history of the struggle for shorter work hours. As students of the Canadian labour movement will be aware, that struggle was one of the key issues around which Canadian workers and the unions representing them organized in the late nineteenth century, establishing, among other things, "Nine-Hour Leagues" in Hamilton and Montreal.[3] It would continue to be a significant issue for the Trades and Labour Congress, Canada's first national labour confederation, through the earlier part of the twentieth century.[4] And it was an equally important issue throughout the early days of the American labour movement.

Accordingly, the next series of chapters is devoted to the history of the shorter work hours struggle. The series begins with chapters on the evolution of work hours in the United States and Canada, respectively. It will be followed by a chapter on the evolution of work hours in Europe and other countries around the world, including both long-industrialized countries such as France and the United Kingdom and newly industrializing countries such as South Korea and Singapore. The historical section closes with a chapter on the 1920s, a period that warrants special attention for a number of reasons — both because it was the one period when employers and their employees were often in agreement about the value of shorter hours, and because these were the years that saw the greatest reduction of work hours yet known. Beyond that, the 1920s also merit close study because of all the periods in relatively recent history, they most closely resemble our own period. Like the 2020s, the 1920s were ushered in with a global pandemic; both eras experienced major wars, as well, although the Russia-Ukraine conflict has not, as yet, attained global proportions. As was the case a century ago, the traumatic events of the present decade have inspired people of good will, including many in management, to seek to make workplaces more welcoming. Shorter work hours are a key part of that quest.

This chapter on the 1920s will serve as a bridge between past history and future possibilities, as it has close links to both. It is followed by a series of chapters that look at recent developments related to work hours. The first of those chapters will consider the intensification of work resulting

Introduction: Suddenly, the Time Is Now (Once Again)

from both conventional computer technology (in the 1980s) and more recent technologies, such as Zoom, that have facilitated the growth of off-site employment. This will be followed by a chapter titled "The Great Resignation," in which I lay out the dynamics of the post-pandemic labour market — one in which there are serious labour shortages for the first time in decades, and in which, having the upper hand for the first time in decades, workers worn to a frazzle by overwork are quitting their jobs with increasing frequency, confident that they can easily find other jobs if and when they need to.

The next chapter will deal with workers' "right to disconnect," a particularly important issue at a time when the distinction between work life and home life has become increasingly blurred, and many workers have come to believe they must respond immediately to all electronic communications from their employers, regardless of the inconvenience or cost to their personal lives. The issue, which some governments and employers had begun to address even prior to the pandemic, has taken on added importance since the onset of the pandemic, which saw many workers forced to work from their homes or from other remote sites.

A third chapter will address the rise of that off-site employment, a phenomenon that offers many opportunities for workers and employers but also poses many challenges. A key element of this chapter will be the rise of hybrid workplaces, or workplaces at which employees are physically present for part but not all of the work week, and the productivity issues arising from the growth of hybrid workplaces.

The book's final section will consider the current situation, both in Canada and in other countries, with respect to work hours, what shorter hours initiatives are currently underway, and what more needs to be done by different players, including employers, workers and their unions, and governments at all levels.

This section looks at shorter work hours initiatives currently underway and recently completed, including legislative initiatives such as those recently introduced in Ontario and the United States, and private-sector initiatives such as the shorter week trials just completed under the auspices of 4 Day Week Global, Work Time Reduction Center of Excellence, and other like-minded organizations. The section will also consider how such initiatives are progressing, what their likelihood of success appears to be, and which industrial sectors and jurisdictions appear to offer the most promising environment for adoption of a shorter work week. Included in this policy discussion will be the aforementioned "right to disconnect" initiatives, which are extremely important since shorter official hours won't mean much if employers can still contact employees outside of regular hours whenever they want. The section (and the book) will close with a series of recommendations directed variously at all the major players in the work hours game, from international bodies such as the International Labour Organization (ILO) to individual firms.

In connection with these recommendations, one important caveat is in order. While the recommendations are intended to apply as broadly as possible through the labour force, not everyone will benefit equally from them. A reduction in the maximum allowable weekly work hours will be of little benefit to part-timers and would likely have no applicability at all to those working in the gig economy. Shorter maximum hours are also unlikely to be of much benefit to temporary foreign agricultural workers, for whom enforcement of any sort of hours legislation has always been problematic. But this doesn't mean that the entire recommendation list is of no value whatever to members of the above groups. The right to disconnect, for example, would apply in all cases where workers are asked to communicate with their employers outside of their normal work hours — whatever those normal work hours might be. Similarly, prohibitions against electronic monitoring would apply to all workers, including part-timers and those working on a gig basis. And part-timers as well as full-timers would benefit from the increased vacation time I have proposed. Beyond that, it could fairly be argued that one of the benefits of shorter work hours and increased restrictions on overtime would likely be the creation of new full-time jobs. Instead of making staff work additional overtime to meet steady increases in demand, employers would have no choice other than to hire more people. With the creation of such jobs, at least a certain number of those now working part-time or in the gig economy would be able to move into more secure full-time jobs.

Introduction: Suddenly, the Time Is Now (Once Again)

Because the serious physical and mental health effects of overwork have been driving recent government policy initiatives, employer initiatives, and the set of employee behaviours summed up in the phrase the Great Resignation (described in detail in chapter 7), it's to these physical and mental health effects that the discussion now turns.

CHAPTER 1

Working Ourselves Sick

One of the truths hammered home by the Covid-19 pandemic is that we are working ourselves sick. Not that this is anything new. Writers as diverse as Bertrand Russell, John Maynard Keynes, Andrew Barnes, Bruce O'Hara, and Juliet Schor have been shining a spotlight on this issue for decades. As will be noted in more detail later in the chapter, individual workers are not the only victims; the health care systems and the environment have also been paying the price for all this overwork.

Writing in 1993, near the trough of a major recession, O'Hara said, "The health costs many of us pay are not Medicare premiums. Insomnia, eczema, digestive upsets, asthma, traffic accidents, back pain, and heart troubles are often the physical symptoms of over-stressed lives. The health crises of those dear to us — be they alcoholism, suicide, ulcers, or a nervous breakdown — may also have their roots in stress and overwork."[1]

Over a quarter of a century later, Barnes, in his *4 Day Week: How the Flexible Work Revolution Can Increase Productivity, Profitability, and Wellbeing, and Help Create a Sustainable Future*, would note, "In the UK, work-related stress, anxiety, or depression now accounts for 57 percent of all working days lost to ill health. The Society of Occupational Medicine reports that each year about 400,000 UK workers report illness that they attribute to work-related stress. Between 2017 and 2018, 15.4 million working days were lost to mental illness connected to work, up from 12.5 million the previous year."[2]

More succinctly, Barnes has noted, "When punishing work schedules become the norm, workers at every level pay the price with their physical and mental health."[3] And in the United States, it is much the same as in Canada and the United Kingdom. Economist Juliet Schor has noted that, due largely to overwork, "when we count not only our incomes but also trends in free time, public safety, environmental quality, income distribution, teen suicide, and child abuse, we find that things have been getting worse for more than twenty years, even though consumption has been rising."[4]

These statements by O'Hara, Barnes, and Schor mirror earlier findings by people like Johns Hopkins University epidemiologist Harvey Brenner, who found that increasing levels of overwork led to increased hospital admissions.[5]

One major reason for increasing levels of overwork over the past two decades is the spread of on-call work, once required only in life-and-death professions such as emergency medicine, firefighting, and midwifery, into most white-collar and professional fields.[6] If you are over fifty, perhaps you'll remember feeling sorry for the people required to carry huge cellphones or who had to wear pagers on their belts. These were the folks liable, at a moment's notice, to be called away from a gripping movie or an enjoyable restaurant dinner to attend to some emergency or other. If someone had conducted a survey in, say, 1995 asking people if they, too, would like to be able to connect instantly to the outside world in order to do their jobs better, I'm sure the positive response rate would have been below 5 percent. That notwithstanding, what with the internet and cellphones, we are in a very real sense almost all in the same position as the firefighters and emergency medical personnel of a generation ago — except that few of us receive the premium pay that many of those emergency workers of a generation ago would have received to compensate them, at least in part, for the disruption to their personal lives caused by their being on-call.[7]

It is, above all else, the internet that has, in Barnes's words, "made obsolete the rule of 'business hours' and replaced it with a state of permaworking," in which employees are tacitly expected to "focus solely on work, to the exclusion of family life and outside pursuits."[8] At least up until the Covid-19 pandemic, those unwilling to focus their lives entirely on work, such as women raising families or caring for aging relatives, were at serious risk of losing opportunities for career advancement, the assumption being that people unwilling to work at night or on weekends were insufficiently dedicated to the organization to warrant consideration for promotion, or perhaps to even continue holding their present positions.[9]

Such organizational cultures breed workaholism in the same way swamps breed mosquitoes. They have, indeed, turned workaholism from an occasional disease found mainly among troubled souls into a veritable epidemic. As Barnes has noted, while there have always been workaholics, "a compulsion to work was previously understood as a choice or, at worst, the product of a specific company's culture, not the manifestation of a larger cultural mandate."[10] At least until the Covid-19 pandemic arrived and caused many workers to start re-evaluating their entire work situations, workaholism simply "came with the territory" of professional work, particularly work with technology firms, although it's important to note, in this connection, that the technology industry is not monolithic and some high-tech firms have been in the vanguard of the shorter hours movement.[11] This has led not only to severe physical and mental health impacts on individual workers,[12] but as will be discussed in more detail later in the chapter, to added stress on already overburdened healthcare systems.

These physical and mental health impacts, along with the burden on healthcare systems, increased markedly during the pandemic. With many workers falling victim to Covid or unable to work because they couldn't obtain adequate child care, the burden increased on those continuing to work. For the year 2020, the Microsoft Work Trend Index reported an increase in the workday of 27 percent in the United Kingdom, 25 percent in the United States, and a whopping 45 percent in Australia. That index identified unmanageable workloads/work hours and a lack of separation between work and home life as two of four major stressors on remote workers. A Microsoft Index survey conducted in January of the following year found continued high productivity masking an exhausted workforce.[13] One in five global survey respondents said their employer didn't care about their work-life balance, while 54 percent reported feeling overworked and 39 percent, exhausted. No doubt these feelings of increased stress and the reality of overwork resulted at least in part from a substantial increase in the "digital intensity" of workers' days[14] — the result, in particular, of the greatly increased use of Zoom and other technologies enabling remote work. These technologies, whose effects will be discussed in greater detail in a later chapter, have brought with them specific physical and mental effects, such as headaches, stiff necks, and anxiety, going above and beyond the stress effects workers were experiencing prior to the pandemic.[15]

A question that might fairly be asked at this point is why, if overwork has such severe health impacts, it has been allowed to continue and even increase. One reason is that for decades prior to the pandemic, owing in large measure to economic developments such as globalization, competition from less developed countries, and the privatization of government-run enterprises, employers have held the whip hand in most Western countries. At the same time, the decline of unionization, driven in part by a structural economic shift away from manufacturing and in the direction of hard-to-organize service industries, has meant that employers have increasingly been free of any significant challenge to their workplace hegemony. Anthony Veal is but one of a number of recent commentators pointing to the significant decline in workers' collective bargaining power that has occurred in the late twentieth and early twenty-first centuries.[16] This long-term weakening of the labour movement has, among other things, had the effect of making it more difficult for workers seeking to challenge employers' demands on issues such as work hours without fear of reprisal.

The trend toward longer hours somehow endured, despite evidence accumulated over more than a century that longer hours wouldn't lead to increased productivity; as early as the 1890s, various European chemical industry firms (discussed in some detail in chapter 5) had found that *reducing* their work hours had led to increased productivity and lower absenteeism and sick rates, while in 1920, as is noted in chapter 2, prominent labour economist John R. Commons said the most important lesson the First World War had taught industry was that long hours don't pay. Closer to our time, a 2017 U.K. study of office workers showed that nearly 80 percent of respondents did *not* consider themselves to be productive throughout the entire working day, while over half (54 percent) said that distractions such as "social media and … news websites, making personal calls and texts, talking to co-workers about non-work-related matters, searching for new jobs, taking smoke breaks and preparing food and drinks" made the working day more bearable.[17] Even starker evidence is provided in an article in *The Economist* — the article that Andrew Barnes says gave rise to his work on the four-day week — that cites studies showing British workers to be productive for an average of two and a half hours per standard working day.[18] Without revealing any secrets from my own work history, I would hazard a guess that the studies just cited don't tell seasoned office workers much that they were not already well aware of.

Why, in the face of such strong evidence that longer hours were if anything making workers less productive rather than more, should the "long hours" culture have continued to hold sway for as long as it did? The answer, according to Barnes, is simple. Few employers actually know how to measure output. As a result, they gauge employees' value by the proxy measure of how many hours they spend at their desks, which leads to the immense waste of time characteristic of much office work.[19] It stands to reason that once employers learn how to measure output and understand the conditions that will maximize it, a significant shortening of work hours should be quite readily achievable.

Such a reduction can't come soon enough. In many Western countries, such as Canada, healthcare systems are nearing the point of total collapse. So, too, is the global ecosystem, which is threatened by climate change that has in large measure resulted from the burning of fossil fuels, such as those used to transport workers to and from their workplaces. Anything that can help reduce the burden on healthcare systems and cut down on the amount of fossil fuel needed for work-related transportation would be most welcome.

Just how serious is the situation with regard to health care? In Canada, the federal health minister has described the situation as a crisis and, as a result, has appointed a federal chief nursing officer to help deal with that crisis.[20] The announcement comes in the wake of a recent study commissioned by the Registered Practical Nurses Association of Ontario that found that half the province's registered practical nurses were considering leaving the profession, due to poor working conditions and a lack of resources to adequately treat patients.[21]

At the root of the crisis, which has been described as "a perfect storm of challenges that have resulted in emergency room closures and reduced health services in every province and territory,"[22] is a serious shortage of primary healthcare providers. According to Linda Silas, president of the Canadian Federation of Nurses Unions, five million Canadians don't have a primary healthcare provider.[23] Even before the pandemic, many healthcare professionals were stretched thin and were considering leaving their jobs.[24] The added stress brought on by working through the pandemic has caused many of those professionals to reduce their hours, leave the public healthcare system for work in private clinics or temporary agencies, or even to leave the profession altogether by retiring early.[25] Lack of primary-care providers has forced many to go to hospital emergency rooms with non-urgent problems,[26] which in turn has increased the already unacceptably long wait times in those facilities and the stress on already overburdened ER staff. Another consequence of the lack of primary care providers (also due in part to Covid-related closures) is that people have delayed seeking treatment for illnesses, with the result that when they do finally seek treatment they are sicker than they would otherwise have been and require more intensive treatment, which again adds to the workloads of already overburdened doctors and nurses.[27]

Finally, it's important to remember demographic factors, including most notably the retirement of large numbers of baby boomers from the work force. As the population ages, their healthcare needs increase. At the same time, many of the nurses currently working in the healthcare system are themselves reaching retirement age. While the effects of these retirements have been predicted for many years,[28] they appear not to have been taken sufficiently into account in planning for the healthcare system. At the very least, these demographic factors have aggravated staff shortages and burn-out caused by other factors such as the Covid-19 pandemic or the failure of many provinces, such as Ontario, to raise nurses' salaries enough even to keep up with inflation.

In the blunt words of Dr. Katharine Smart, past president of the Canadian Medical Association, Canada's healthcare system can no longer "provide basic health care needs to all Canadians."[29] Unfortunately, at least over the near term, the situation seems likely to get worse before it gets better, particularly with regard to wait times for scheduled care and discharge from hospitals to other facilities.[30] And the situation could get even worse should we be hit by another major new pandemic at some point in the future.

Canada is by no means alone in experiencing a crisis in its healthcare system. Such crises appear to be the norm, at least throughout the developed Western world. In Australia, the country's overall healthcare rating dropped significantly between March 2021 and June 2022, according to an Australian Healthcare Index survey. Major issues included a sharp decline in the availability of mental health services and longer waits for those needing such services, in addition to increasingly longer waits for elective surgery.[31] In Britain, the National Health Service, according to the chair of a parliamentary Health and Social Care Committee, is facing the worst staffing crisis in its seventy-four years of existence, at a time when there are some 6.5 million people on waiting lists for hospital treatment due to Covid-related backlogs.[32] And in the United States, a healthcare system described as having been in crisis as early as 2006, owing to escalating costs and threats to coverage for millions of people,[33] has more recently been termed an "unmitigated mess," with some twenty-seven million Americans lacking health insurance despite the Affordable Care Act. Even the insured often face "wildly expensive" costs for treatment, and many are forced to go into debt or even declare bankruptcy owing to medical debt.[34]

Things appear to be no better in continental Europe. In France, in hospitals along the Riviera, off-and-on nighttime emergency room closures have been commonplace, while many patients have been forced to wait in corridors next to other patients for up to forty-eight hours. As in Canada, staffing issues have been driving the decline in the quality of service. With the Covid-19 pandemic having "accelerated the departure" of doctors and nurses, there are now more doctors and nurses leaving the profession in France than entering it.[35] And in Italy, decades of budget cuts and privatization resulting from the government's adherence to the neoliberal "new public management" philosophy had already seriously weakened the healthcare system even before the Covid-19 pandemic, leaving it ill-equipped to deal with that pandemic.[36] Needless to say, things in Italy have only gotten worse since then. Italy would be the first country in Europe to be "overwhelmed" by Covid-19, and one of the first to impose a national lockdown.[37]

It isn't possible to isolate the specific reasons why any given individual seeks health care. But given the large number of people who have reported feeling physical and/or mental stress as a result of work, it stands to reason that overwork has caused a significant number of people to seek treatment in the healthcare system. It also stands to reason that dealing with that physical or mental stress at its source, by reducing work hours, would likely lead to a significant reduction in the number of people seeking medical treatment. While reducing work hours would clearly benefit the workers involved, it would thus also benefit society as a whole, by reducing the burden on the severely overstressed healthcare system.

Then there is the question of the environment. The impacts of overwork and in particular overproduction on the environment have been known for some time. Writing over a quarter of a century ago, leisure studies scholar Donald Reid warned of the possibility of "total environmental collapse" if the existing balance between work and leisure were not fundamentally changed. In Reid's words, "The environment cannot accommodate much longer an approach that rapidly depletes the earth's natural resources."[38] Given the severity and extent of the global climate change crisis, I would suggest that Reid was nothing short of prophetic. One can hardly open a newspaper or look at an internet news story these days without reading about severe flooding, prolonged heat waves and droughts, wildfires, and other cataclysmic results of climate change.

During the summer of 2022, as I was writing the first draft of this chapter, there was major flooding in Jackson, Mississippi. Earlier in the year, there had been serious floods in Alberta, the Northwest Territories, Manitoba, North Dakota, Minnesota, and British Columbia. And outside North America, the situation was if anything even worse, with nearly one thousand dead and thirty-three million homeless in Pakistan's worst flooding in a decade, and additional severe flooding, some of it leading to loss of life, in Nigeria, Sierra Leone, the Democratic Republic of the Congo, and the Philippines.[39]

With regard to wildfires, the situation was equally grave. On August 9, the province of Newfoundland and Labrador declared a province-wide emergency after nearly two weeks of unchecked fires burning in the centre of the province, driven by strong winds.[40] At the same time, numerous wildfires were burning out of control in British Columbia and the Northwest Territories.[41] Earlier in the summer, a number of Canada's western provinces had also been plagued by wildfires; these provinces included Manitoba as well as British Columbia.[42] And in the United States, wildfires were burning across the country, with a heavy concentration in the northwestern states of Idaho, Montana, Oregon, and Washington and a large number of fires in California.[43] And things were just as bad or worse in Europe, where destruction of land from wildfires centring on Spain, Portugal, and Romania reached record levels during the summer of 2022.

Far from improving, the situation had become even worse by June of 2023, as I was completing final revisions to this chapter. Indeed, there isn't space to chronicle all the natural disasters that occurred during the first six months of 2023. As of late June, wildfires were burning out of control in five provinces, including Nova Scotia, which had seldom seen large wildfires in the past, as well as Quebec, Ontario, Alberta, and British Columbia. One of the B.C. blazes, at Donnie Creek, had by June 18 consumed over 5,340 square kilometres of forest, making it the largest fire in the province's history.[44] Meanwhile, in my home area in the western part of Quebec, there has been a disaster a month through the spring of 2023, with an ice storm in April, major flooding of the Gatineau River in May, and in June, a series of wildfires that sent smoke billowing as far south as New York City and even beyond, at times making the local air quality so bad that residents were advised to stay indoors if at all possible and to wear masks if they did have to go outside.

With such a deluge of bad climate news coming at us almost constantly and from almost every part of the globe, it shouldn't be surprising that people's mental as well as physical health has begun to suffer. This is particularly true with young people, who will likely face the worst effects of the climate crisis since they will be around the longest.

In "Climate Change Is Worsening Youth Mental Health, Research Shows," M.A. Jacquemain notes that several recent studies have confirmed widespread mental health impacts resulting from worries about the climate crisis and frustration over how governments are dealing with that crisis.[45] One such study of young people, released in 2021, found nearly 60 percent of respondents either "very worried" or "extremely worried" about climate change, with the highest rates of serious concern occurring in countries, such as the Philippines and Portugal, that have recently endured major weather-related disasters (flooding in the case of the Philippines, wildfires in the case of Portugal). A full two-thirds of the respondents believed that governments were "failing young people." Young people's feelings of helplessness about the climate crisis are particularly noteworthy, with research conducted by the climate action and mental health organization Force of Nature finding over 70 percent of young people feeling helpless about the climate crisis, and only 26 percent feeling they knew how to help solve that crisis.

Given the severity and all-encompassing nature of the climate crisis, anything that can help mitigate it should be welcome. There is strong reason to believe that shorter work hours could be just such a mitigating factor. Over the years, there have been a number of studies showing a link between reduced work hours and lower emissions. One study looking at data from more than two dozen countries between 1970 and 2007 predicted that a 10 percent reduction in work hours could result in a 12 percent drop in the ecological footprint of humanity, a 15 percent drop in its carbon footprint, and a 4 percent drop in carbon dioxide emissions.[46] It stands to reason that a 20 percent reduction in work hours, as would result from a four-day work week, would likely have even greater positive impacts on the environment.

Just how would a shorter work week, and in particular a four-day work week, benefit the environment? At the most obvious level, having four round-trip commutes a week instead of five would mean 20 percent less fossil fuel being sent into the environment, at least for those driving to work.[47] Beyond that, people feeling less time pressure, as they would if they were working fewer hours, are more likely to make sustainable lifestyle choices outside of work. Both the Kellogg's workers of the 1930s, who as we will find out in succeeding chapters benefitted from a six-hour working day, and the contemporary workers surveyed in recent U.K. shorter week trials were more apt than others to engage in healthy pursuits such as gardening, walking, or biking to get to places, or preparing their own food rather than buying prepared foods.[48]

At the macro level, as noted by leisure studies writer Anthony Veal, a global work hours reduction could slow the rate of economic growth beyond what it would otherwise have been, thus easing environmental pressures, including global warming.[49] And a four-day work week could also reduce greenhouse gas emissions by reducing the amount of energy required to heat and cool office buildings, particularly if all workers took their day off on the same day.[50]

And of course, there is the recent rise in remote and hybrid work. The precise magnitude of energy savings that would be achieved through a switch to a hybrid workplace with fewer workers present at any one time is not yet clear since we have no realistic way of measuring just how many thermostats would be turned down and, therefore, how substantial the savings could be. Still, at the very least, the issue is one warranting further study.

Overall, while the precise size of the positive environmental impact that could be achieved through a switch to shorter work hours remains a matter of some debate, most would agree that the impact would be substantial. In the words of then 4 Day Week Global CEO Joe O'Connor,[51] while no one would argue that the four-day work week is "a silver bullet that will address all of our environmental concerns in one go,"[52] such a change has the potential to be "a very powerful enabler and a very powerful contributor" in the fight against climate change.[53] Added to the positive physical and mental health impacts that would result from a shift to a four-day work week, these environmental arguments should make the shift all but irresistible.

・・・・・・

Far from being new, the fight for shorter hours has been waged by workers, their unions, and many others, practically since the beginning of industrialization. Even though this history is long and occasionally tortuous, it's important to examine it in some detail. If we don't know where we have been, we'll find it a lot harder to know where we should be going. Accordingly, the next series of chapters is devoted to that history — first in the United States, then in Canada, and then in the larger world outside of North America. The series' final chapter focuses on the 1920s, a decade of particular importance in any study of work hours both because the great bulk of the twentieth century's work hours reductions occurred then, and because of all previous historical epochs, it most closely resembles our own.

CHAPTER 2

Historical Development of Work Hours I: The United States

American workers now work among the longest hours of workers in any industrialized country in the world (see Table 2.1, below), and have among the fewest paid days off (see Table 2.2, below). While faring somewhat better than their American counterparts in both categories, Canadian workers still rank well below most of their European counterparts.

It seems more than a little counterintuitive that workers in two of the world's most prosperous countries should be working such long hours, comparatively speaking. In general, long work hours are a sign of underdevelopment. As countries become more developed, they tend to modernize their industrial plants and work processes so that fewer hours are required to produce the same quantity of goods. A 2015 study found that countries where labour productivity, measured in GDP/hour, was lowest, such as Bangladesh, China, Peru, Mexico, and Indonesia, were generally those with the longest average annual work hours. On the other hand, countries where labour productivity was highest, such as Belgium, France, Norway, Germany, and Switzerland, generally had work hours ranking among the world's shortest. Norway's 1,384 average annual hours worked were more than one thousand below Bangladesh's 2,419, while the former country's labour productivity ($100.33/hr.) was over twenty times that of the latter country ($4.79)![1]

Admittedly, these are findings at the extreme. Still, it's worth noting that all the countries in the study with labour productivity of $60 or more per hour had average annual work hours below 1,800, while all those countries with two thousand or more average annual hours of work had labour productivity below $40 per hour.

Why, for the most part, American and Canadian workers have not benefitted from their increased productivity with shorter hours — and in particular, why the technological advances of the past four decades haven't resulted in shorter hours, unlike earlier waves of technological advance — will be the main business of the next two chapters, which deal with American and Canadian workers respectively.

. . . . . .

There's not much point attempting to compare work hours in different countries in the primarily agricultural economy that prevailed prior to about 1830, in that, as David Roediger and Philip Foner note in their book, *Our Own Time: A History of American Labor and the Working Day*, "The unit of labor was the task, not the hours, and a good working day was measured by the portion of field plowed or the number of rows harvested."[2] In such an economy, time measurements would remain, as Roediger and Foner put it, "impressionistic."[3] While serious time measurement did arrive with industrialization — with, in many cases, *longer* working days than had been the norm prior to industrialization[4] — there is also not much point in cross-national comparisons of work hours during industrialization's first few decades. With employers bent on extracting the maximum possible amount of labour from their employees, and little check on their power from either unions or protective government legislation, which to all intents and purposes did not exist until later in the nineteenth century,[5] workers everywhere put in hours that seem monstrous today.[6] Several of Roediger and Foner's earlier chapters are devoted to American workers' fight for a ten-hour day and six-day week during the middle of the nineteenth century. At the time, twelve-hour days were commonplace,[7] and some workers, such as tailors, street-railway workers, brewers, and bakers, were forced to work up to sixteen hours a day and, on occasion, seven days a week.[8]

By 1870, though hours remained horrendously long, there had begun to be some significant cross-national differences. A seven-country study by Huberman and Minns found about a 25 percent top-bottom difference, with Belgium leading the pack at 3,483 average annual hours worked and the United Kingdom having the shortest average annual hours at 2,755.[9] At 3,096 average annual hours worked — just under sixty per week — the United States was squarely in the middle of the pack.[10] As will become clear later, this pattern of significant cross-national variation has continued through to the present day, and even expanded. Factors explaining these cross-national differences include the relative strength of different countries' labour movements, those labour movements' willingness and ability to work in the political arena as well as on the shop floor, and the relative importance placed by unions on hours reduction compared to wage increases.

Writing in 1991, Susan Christopherson found Americans spending more hours and days at work than their counterparts in other industrialized countries, with the exception of the Japanese. This in itself is a shocking finding, given that in 1938 American workers enjoyed the *shortest* hours of any included in the Huberman-Minns study of work hours.[11] Even more shocking were Christopherson's findings that per capita work hours had *increased* by 14 percent between 1965 and 1986, that the number of people "moonlighting" with second jobs had jumped 20 percent between 1980 and 1987,[12] and that the number of women working more than forty-nine hours per week increased by 50 percent between 1979 and 1985.[13]

Have the intervening years brought any improvement? Not in the least. In 2021 the United States had the second-highest average annual hours in a group of ten OECD (Organisation for Economic Co-operation and Development) countries. Only Mexican workers put in more hours than American workers, whose hours significantly exceeded those of most of their European counterparts.

TABLE 2.1: AVERAGE ANNUAL HOURS OF WORK, SELECTED OECD COUNTRIES, 2021

Country	Average Annual Hours Worked
Mexico	2128
United States	1791
New Zealand	1730
OECD Average	1716
Australia	1694
Canada	1685
EU Average	1566
United Kingdom	1497
France	1490
Germany	1349

Source: OECD (2022), Hours Worked (indicator).

The difference is even greater when it comes to the minimum annual number of paid days off, taken as vacation leave or as paid holidays. The United States is the only country in the same group of eight OECD countries with no statutory requirement for vacation pay or paid holidays. While the vast majority of American employers (about 80 percent in each category) do provide their employees with paid vacation and holiday leave, the allowances provided fall far short of the statutory minima in the other countries in the study, again with the lone exception of Mexico. This grim story is told in Table 2.2 below.

How did this situation come about? To find out, it's necessary to consider the response of American workers and their unions to the growing pressure put upon workers by employers. It's also important to consider the role played by different levels of government, particularly state and federal government, in workers' long struggle for shorter hours. Also needing attention are social trends, such as the growth of an organized leisure movement in the late nineteenth century and of popular culture and workers' education in the early twentieth century,[14] which gave people some specific ideas as to what they would like to do with their spare time and thus spread support for shorter hours beyond the workplace and into the general population.

TABLE 2.2: MINIMUM STATUTORY VACATION LEAVE, PAID HOLIDAYS, AND TOTAL PAID LEAVE, VARIOUS DEVELOPED COUNTRIES, 2023

Country	Minimum Vacation Leave	Minimum Paid Holidays	Minimum Total Paid Leave
United States	0 (10)[a]	0 (8)[b]	0 (18)
Canada	10–25[c]	6–12[c]	16–32
Australia	20	10–13[d]	30–33
France	25[e]	11–13	36–38
Germany	20	10–13	30–33
Italy	20	12–22[f]	32–42
New Zealand	20	12	32[g]
United Kingdom	20	8–10	28–30

Source: Stefana Zaric, "Paid Annual Leave per Country: Global Guide." Deel, March 22, 2023, deel.com/blog/annual-leave-per-country.

[a] Figure in parentheses reflects the usual minimum amount of vacation provided by most employers.
[b] Figure in parentheses reflects the usual minimum number of paid holidays provided by most employers.
[c] Vacation and holiday minima are under provincial jurisdiction; different figures reflect different provincial minimum standards. For example, while the minimum vacation allotment is two weeks in most provinces, it is three weeks in Saskatchewan.
[d] Different holiday allotments reflect differing standards in different Australian states.
[e] At least five of the vacation days must be taken separately from the employee's main vacation period.
[f] Twelve national and up to ten regional holidays, depending on the location within Italy.
[g] Plus up to twelve additional regional holidays.

The Nineteenth Century

With industrialization came the precise measurement of work hours — of the length of time people spent in the workplace and on the job. While there continues to be debate about when average work hours changed from what they had been in the earlier, agricultural economy, and by how much,[15] much of the available evidence points to a lengthening of the workday, particularly during the first half of the century, and to an intensification of work, with workers expected to tend to more machines in the same period of time. Early industrialization brought longer hours to factory work in Massachusetts, with an average of fifteen minutes added to the workday between 1829 and 1841.[16] Not content to work their employees from sunrise to sunset, some employers went so far as to install primitive forms of artificial lighting, which allowed for an even longer workday, at the cost of overheated workplaces and significant fire risk.[17]

There aren't precise figures for the length of the workday in the nineteenth century. Most of those that exist come from the manufacturing sector, but even there the evidence is somewhat fragmentary since there was no detailed survey of manufacturing hours prior to the 1880 census. A survey prepared for that census by Joseph Weeks, and known as the Weeks Report, found that average weekly hours in manufacturing had declined from 69.1 in 1830 to 60.7 in 1880. A similar survey prepared for the U.S. Senate Committee on Finance in 1893, known as the Aldrich Report, found a steady decline in average weekly manufacturing hours, from 68.4 in 1840 to 60.0 in 1890.[18]

The Aldrich Report consistently found longer hours than the Weeks Report; in one case (1866), the difference was a full four hours. Despite these differences and a host of data problems, it's reasonable to conclude that nineteenth-century work hours in manufacturing were very long by contemporary standards but declined significantly during the latter part of the century.[19]

However long work hours may have been in fact, they were long enough to have been a major source of conflict between employers and workers almost from the outset of industrialization. Resenting both the longer hours and more intense pace of work, workers began agitating for a ten-hour day in major eastern cities such as Boston, New York, and Philadelphia as early as the 1820s.[20] As Roediger and Foner note, "The reduction of work hours constituted the prime demand in the class conflicts that spawned America's first industrial strikes, its first citywide trade union councils, its first labor party, its first general strikes,[21] its first organization uniting skilled and unskilled workers, its first strike by females, and its first attempts at regional

Historical Development of Work Hours I: The United States

and national labor organization."[22] The issue would have unique importance "because of its ability to unify workers across the lines of craft, race, sex, skill, age, and ethnicity."[23] All would have known in their bones what it was to be worked to near-total exhaustion by employers bent on extracting the last possible ounce of labour from them.[24]

Why wouldn't wage disputes have had the same ability to unify the entire work force? Unquestionably, almost all workers were severely underpaid, in addition to being grossly overworked. But employers could often end a wage dispute by "buying off" members of certain privileged groups (e.g., highly skilled workers) with a wage increase, thus allowing the employer to divide the work force. This would generally not have been possible in the case of hours disputes since "in any one workshop or factory it was usually impractical to allow part of the work force to leave long before the rest." The result was that all workers at any given site tended to work the same hours, and thus shorter hours became "a demand around which all could unite."[25]

And unite they did, fighting for a shorter workday both in the workplace and in the political arena. The early 1850s saw a proliferation of labour protests and ten-hour contracts in the East, with workers achieving such contracts in Baltimore as well as in the Massachusetts cities of Boston, Salem, Lynn, and Lowell.[26] Earlier, an average seventy-four-hour work week among Lowell's millworkers had led Sarah Bagley and the Lowell Female Labor Reform Association to petition the state legislature to intervene to reduce work hours. The effort proved unsuccessful, despite the country's first-ever examination of labour conditions by a government investigating committee. But similar complaints would lead to the passage of ten-hour laws in New Hampshire and Pennsylvania, although these laws would be of little practical value since they specified that contracts freely entered into by employers and employees could set any length for the work week. Of greater effect was an 1840 executive order signed by U.S. president Martin Van Buren limiting the workday for federal manual workers to ten hours.[27]

By the 1850s, some workers, anticipating the push for an eight-hour day that would begin with the Civil War, had begun agitating for a workday of less than ten hours. The decade's first two years saw steady agitation for an eight-hour day by both skilled and unskilled workers in Philadelphia, though this would ultimately prove unsuccessful. And in 1857, New Orleans ship carpenters and caulkers won a nine-hour day. Meanwhile, the demand for a ten-hour day had spread beyond the Northeast to the South, to San Francisco, and even to Midwestern farms.[28]

Finally, the 1850s saw the beginning of the theme, which would be much repeated in the early twentieth century, of shorter hours as something that would allow the interests of workers and employers to harmonize by increasing productivity. Many politicians would advance this theme in promoting ten-hour legislation, through which they sought to obtain the votes of workingmen.[29] (Of course, at the time, women couldn't vote, and so politicians had no need to curry their favour.)

The Civil War can be said to have marked a kind of watershed in the shorter hours struggle. No doubt in part due to wartime labour shortages, the Civil War saw renewed labour insurgency, with unions claiming 200,000 members by 1864. It was in this setting of a resurgent labour movement that the demand for an eight-hour day first became prominent,[30] with eight-hour advocates starting to urge for a national standard and a federal law to get around the limitations of disparate state actions.[31] It was perhaps not coincidental that the hub of the new eight-hour movement was Boston, which had previously been the hub of the abolitionist movement. As Roediger and Foner note, the identification of the eight-hour movement with the Civil War and the freeing of slaves gave shorter hours advocates the sense that they were "agitating a question of historical significance for the republic and the world," with organizers seeing participation in the movement as "part of an ongoing assault on oppression and misery."[32] Many of the country's leading abolitionists, such as William Lloyd Garrison, Charles Sumner, and Wendell Phillips, would lend their support to the shorter hours cause after the war, with Phillips seeing the defeat of the "slave power" as leading to a new pro-labour campaign. "No doubt," Phillips wrote in 1865, "the next great question for our country ... is the rights of the laboring class.... Eight hours to make a working day is the first rule to be observed."[33]

In response to this new movement, a new union, the National Labor Union, was created. Its aim was to unite workers of different trades, and shorter hours legislation was at the heart of its program. It first met in Baltimore, already a hub of shorter hours action, in 1867.[34]

By this time, agitation for shorter hours had moved beyond the industrial Northeast, with strong eight-hour movements operating in such cities as New Orleans and St. Louis.[35] The early postwar period also saw renewed legislative activity, with no fewer than eight states as well as the U.S. Congress adopting eight-hour laws.[36] But like the earlier ten-hour laws, these eight-hour laws foundered due to their lack of enforceability,[37] causing many to become disillusioned with the idea of achieving shorter hours through legislation and leading workers and their unions to again seek to achieve those shorter hours through strikes.[38] The year 1872, for example, would see scores of shorter-hour strikes, many of them successful, in such cities as Chicago, Buffalo, Philadelphia, Albany, and Jersey City. Other, less immediately successful strikes took place in New York, in several Rhode Island textile centres, and in sawmills in Michigan, Florida, and Pennsylvania.[39] Two years later, Massachusetts passed the country's first enforceable ten-hours law. Applicable only to female workers, it became fully effective in 1879.[40]

Clearly, the demand for an eight-hour day was not going away. As it had earlier, the shorter hours demand would prove a useful tool for organizing workers, including those who not only had no prior experience with unions but had "seldom even met in a common place."[41] With a new, stronger wave of unionization arising in the 1880s, owing to expanded industrialization, manufacturing sector growth, and even stricter "coercive drive" management controls on workers, the time seemed ripe for a new wave of action in support of shorter hours.[42]

While most workers enjoyed a ten-hour day and six-day week by 1883, there remained some glaring exceptions. Brewers, who had worked an average ninety-six-hour week as late as 1881, with shifts typically ranging from fourteen to eighteen hours, were still generally working a ninety-hour, seven-day week, while bakers and street-railway drivers in some locales were found working more than fifteen hours a day.[43] Later in the decade, in 1884 and 1885, a new wave of unemployment putting about one worker in eight out of work would lend particular urgency to shorter hours as a strategy for reducing the "itinerant mass of tens of thousands of chronically unemployed workers" travelling around the country in search of jobs.[44]

The eight-hour day would also become a pivotal issue for the Knights of Labor, a new kind of union that had started up in 1869 and grew quickly during the 1870s and early 1880s.[45] Unlike most craft unions, which focused their attention on improving terms and conditions at individual workplaces, the Knights aimed at nothing less than a moral and social transformation of industrial society.[46] As their leaders often said, they did not seek to make richer people; they sought to make better people.[47] The achievement of a substantially shorter workday was key to their overall program, since such a day would allow time for personal and social development. The push for the eight-hour day was a key factor in the Knights' mushrooming growth through the first half of the 1880s.[48]

That growth, and the American labour movement's belief that concerted strike action could bring about the eight-hour day, would come to a crashing end in May of 1886. On May 1, 1886, the date set two years earlier by the Federation of Organized Trades and Labor as the one past which workers would cease working more than eight hours per day,[49] an estimated 340,000–400,000[50] workers struck or demonstrated for shorter hours in actions all across the country.[51] While the largest actions appear to have been in New York and Cincinnati, there were strikes involving thousands of workers in Boston, Pittsburgh, Detroit, St. Louis, and Washington, as well as smaller actions in cities and towns as far-flung as Montclair, New Jersey; Duluth, Minnesota; South Gardner, Maine; Galveston, Texas; and Cedarburg, Wisconsin, to name but a few.[52] In New York City, a gathering of about ten thousand was addressed by no less than Samuel Gompers — the head of the American Federation of Labor (AFL) — Gompers's earlier opposition to the strike notwithstanding.[53]

Thanks to the use of roving pickets, the strike spread, with the second two days of the strike yielding at least seven thousand more participants in Milwaukee, and similar results occurring in Chicago, St. Louis, and Cincinnati.[54] It was the now-celebrated events at Chicago's Haymarket

Square, three days after the start of the strike, that would bring the apparently strong strike momentum to a halt.

The Haymarket protest, ironically, was not directly concerned with shorter hours but was a response to police brutality at a strike at a nearby McCormick Harvester plant, which had killed one demonstrator on the spot and probably three more later.[55] In response, workers were urged to "avenge this horrible murder" and to show up at a protest meeting at 7:30 the following evening, on Haymarket Square.[56] At this meeting, a surprisingly small crowd of no more than three thousand[57] heard orators such as Albert Parsons argue for socialism and urge workers to arm themselves. While doing so, they also warned workers to avoid individual terrorism. The storm-shortened meeting was about to come to a peaceful close when all of a sudden, acting on the order of inflammatory John Bonfield, chief inspector of the Chicago police department, 180 police waded into the crowd. Mere seconds later, a bomb allegedly thrown by an anarchist[58] exploded in front of the police officers, killing one and wounding fifty, whereupon the police fired at the protesters, killing one immediately and wounding about seventy. Seven more police would die later, mainly from gunfire wounds.[59]

The next day, in Milwaukee's Bay View suburb, nine strikers were killed by police gunfire as police tried to disperse roving pickets peacefully protesting in the wake of Haymarket.[60] A coroner's jury returned no murder indictments but praised the militia for ordering the firing to cease. At the same time, nearly fifty protesters were indicted, with some eventually serving six- to nine-month sentences for rioting and conspiracy. There would be only mild objections when the employers involved in the Bay View strike were found to have made cash gifts to the militias.[61]

In such a climate of hysteria, with the public traumatized by the violence, socialists, eight-hour advocates, and immigrants alike were branded as threats to public order, while the labour movement as a whole was put on the defensive.[62] It would have been well-nigh impossible for any of the Haymarket defendants to have received a fair trial. As Roediger and Foner wryly note, "The wheels of injustice turned swiftly."[63] The trial, they go on to suggest, was "openly an inquisition against the [anarcho-syndicalist] IWPA (International Working People's Association) rather than a murder investigation."[64] Just how fair a trial the defendants likely received can be deduced from the fact that, in discussing the cases seven years later, trial judge Joseph Gary suggested that the identity of the bomb-thrower "was not an important question."[65]

Massive police dragnets began operation immediately after the bombing, with hundreds of arrests of labour activists and scores of home searches, generally without warrants. Eventually, thirty-one people were indicted in connection with the murder. Of these, eight were selected for trial, and four would be executed on November 11.[66] While the jury issued its verdict and sentencing recommendations on August 20,[67] the press had made up its mind much sooner. By May 8, just four days after Haymarket, union leaders had been editorially convicted of murder by the *New York Tribune*, the *Chicago Inter-Ocean*, the *New York Times*, and *Harper's Weekly*.[68]

The debacle of the Haymarket Square bombing would change the character of both the American labour movement as a whole and the struggle for the eight-hour day. The strike wave itself had not been a total failure, however. Samuel Gompers himself, who had opposed the May 1 general strike as untimely,[69] would later estimate that the 1886 action cut the average American working day by an hour,[70] while federal statistics cited by Roediger and Foner[71] showed a three-hour decline in the average working week of all who struck in 1886, from about sixty-two hours to about fifty-nine hours. Nationally, it was estimated that nearly 200,000 workers earned shorter workdays, with the greatest improvements occurring in New York City (87,000 workers) and Cincinnati.[72]

Nonetheless, while labour historian Norman Ware's characterization of the eight-hour push as a "flop"[73] may be a slight overstatement, it can't be denied that the actions of May 1, 1886, and the days that followed both weakened and divided the American labour movement, particularly its more progressive elements, dampening the push for eight-hour days and changing the character of the struggle for decades to come. The Knights of Labor, badly divided because its leader, Terence Powderly, refused to support the strike — he would go so far as to try to block the mass action, issuing a "secret circular" condemning the use of strikes[74] — would never recover its former momentum and within a few decades would be defunct, having lost much of its credibility within the larger labour movement because of its failure to provide official support for the strike, a failure that seriously hurt the movement.[75] It is entirely possible that had the Knights thrown their support wholeheartedly behind the strike action that action would have achieved a different overall result.

Similarly, the public backlash in the wake of the Haymarket bombing would greatly weaken the labour movement's left wing and would mark the effective end of the mass strike as a strategy for achieving shorter hours. Lacking much in the way of an effective opposition, as the decline of the Knights of Labor would lead to a major decline in organizing women, Black workers, immigrants, and the unskilled, the conservative American Federation of Labor, dominated by white, male skilled craftsmen, assumed leadership of the American labour movement.[76] While it remained committed to the eight-hour day, even to the extent of briefly adopting an industry-by-industry strike strategy in 1890, it would soon abandon that strategy in the wake of other unions' unwillingness to follow the lead of that year's chosen union, the United Brotherhood of Carpenters and Joiners. After 1894, the AFL would not only avoid mass strikes, it would largely eschew political action as a means of achieving its objectives.[77] Leadership on the hours issue would pass from the labour movement to a coalition of middle-class professionals and reformers, who tended to view shorter working hours "not as a class issue but as a reform worthy of consideration on the grounds of efficiency, uplift, and safety."[78]

In the decades immediately following Haymarket, baseball and bicycles may well have had more to do with achieving shorter hours than labour actions such as strikes. The 1890s saw a rapid growth in organized leisure pursuits and "proplay movements for more parks, for school sports, and for organized childhood leisure."[79] The 1890s witnessed a veritable "bicycling craze," along with "the rise of modern baseball, a mania for college athletics (especially football), and the growth of popular cultural institutions like Coney Island,"[80] where both the middle class and ordinary working people could engage in a wide range of physical activities for just the cost of carfare. With many other, pleasanter things to do than work all the time, those same people, whether formally connected to the labour movement or not, would lend their support to the shorter hours cause.

Perhaps not coincidentally, the end of the nineteenth century and beginning of the twentieth also saw the growth of scientific types of management, which would use subtler methods than the old coercive drive approach of extracting every last ounce of strength from workers. The more enlightened sorts of employers began to be concerned with the total workplace environment, including the psychological as well as physical environment.[81] Of particular note was one group of scientific managers known as the behavioural school, who, in the words of management writer Claude George, sought to "recognize the centrality of the individual in any cooperative endeavour."[82] Such managers sought, by and large, positive ways of motivating workers. It was primarily under their auspices that large numbers of personnel departments were established in both American and Canadian firms, and organizational behaviour was established as an independent field of study.[83] These new, better-trained managers would prove receptive to the idea that long hours signified "the failure to adopt scientific, efficient management methods"[84] and were actually counterproductive to efforts to increase worker productivity.[85] It would be this argument that would eventually carry the day, leading to a fairly general adoption of the eight-hour day by the late 1920s.

The Twentieth Century

In 1900, the average American worker worked 2,938 hours, according to data from Huberman and Minns.[86] While there were certainly large variations among industries,[87] this figure, which breaks down to an average of about 56.5 hours per week,[88] would be consistent with a working day of ten hours Monday through Friday and a slightly shorter working day on Saturday, which it appears some workers had begun to achieve by that time. The American average placed it fifth out of eight industrial countries, squarely in the middle of a pack also including (from most hours worked to least), France, Canada, Belgium, Germany, Sweden, the United Kingdom, and Australia. Of note, the average number of hours worked in those eight countries ranged from 3,115 in France to 2,385 in Australia, a substantial variation of about 30 percent and a figure that points to significantly greater progress in achieving shorter hours in Australia and the United Kingdom than in most of the rest of the world.[89]

It appears that workers in manufacturing were putting in longer hours than those in many other industrial sectors. In 1900 the U.S. manufacturing sector census estimated weekly hours in that sector to be 59.6, a figure consistent with a ten-hour day and six-day week.[90] This figure is significantly greater than the 52.3 average weekly hours reported in railways, 50.3 in construction, 42.8 in bituminous coal mining, and 35.8 in anthracite coal mining. (In fairness, it should be noted that most construction workers would have had a significant number of days when they could not work due to inclement weather, and that many working days were lost annually in the mines owing to "overproduction, mismanagement, and seasonal unemployment"; thus, the average working day would very likely have been a good deal longer in construction and coal mining than the weekly figures cited above would suggest.[91])

Thirteen years later, in 1913, most American workers had achieved only marginally shorter hours than they'd had at the start of the century. By that point, the average American worker was putting in 2,900 hours per year, second only to France (2,933 hours) in the group of eight countries described earlier.[92] There continued to be substantial variation between countries, with Australian workers putting in an average of 2,214 hours, slightly more than 30 percent fewer than French or American workers. Average *weekly* hours (based on the data from Giattino et al.) were down only seven hours per week, to 55.8 hours, a figure that suggests no fundamental change in the workday or work week for most workers. The manufacturing sector did report a drop of slightly over four hours between 1900 and 1914, to 55.5 hours per week according to the manufacturing census,[93] a figure that would have brought it into line with the average in most other sectors. Construction dropped significantly, to an average of 45.2 hours in 1910[94] (the closest comparator year available for the Huberman-Minns 1913 data[95]). But railroads declined only slightly, to 51.5 hours, and anthracite coal actually saw a significantly *longer* workweek (43.3 hours) than it had had in 1900.[96]

For reasons not clear to me, Giattino et al. do not include any comparative data for 1920 in their study "Working Hours." But sectoral data from Robert Whaples's *Hours of Work* point toward a significant decline during the century's second decade, with manufacturing dropping from 57.3 hours in 1910 to 51.2 hours in 1920, and railroads dropping from 51.5 hours in the former year to 46.8 hours in the latter.[97] A similar story, albeit with somewhat different numbers, is told by Roediger and Foner, who note that between 1905 and 1920, the average working week of non-agricultural workers dropped from 57.2 to 50.6 hours.[98] In manufacturing, average hours plummeted from 54.5 to 48.1 hours, the latter figure being consistent with an eight-hour day and six-day week.[99] While in 1910, only 8 percent of U.S. workers had worked forty-eight or fewer hours per week, by 1919, that figure had increased to 48.6 percent — nearly a majority of the workforce. Similarly, the proportion working over fifty-four hours per week declined during the same period from 70 percent to 26 percent.

While by no means all workers enjoyed a forty-eight-hour week by 1920, that objective was well on its way to being achieved, though long hours (in some cases including a seven-day week) persisted "on the street railways, among operating engineers, in the oil fields, in canneries, in textile mills, and, most dramatically, in steel mills." The intervention of federal commerce secretary Herbert Hoover would eventually be needed to bring about an eight-hour day and six-day week in that industry[100] after the failure of a massive steel strike that began in September 1919[101] and a near-nationwide storm of protest against the steel industry's continuation of the twelve-hour day and seven-day week.[102]

One of the key factors in this large-scale shortening of hours was a renewed wave of strikes over hours in the years just prior to and during the First World War. As a result of those strikes, an estimated 340,000 workers gained an eight-hour day in 1916 and over 500,000 in the first half of 1917.[103] Beyond that, the severe labour shortages of the First World War suddenly put workers in a much stronger bargaining position, and thus they were better able to negotiate shorter hours than they had been.[104]

The First World War also saw significant federal legislation in support of the eight-hour day. Following on the heels of a 1912 Federal Public Works Act providing an eight-hour day for all work covered by federal contracts and a 1915 bill establishing maximum hours for maritime workers, Congress passed the Adamson Act in 1916 in order to avert a threatened nationwide rail strike. The act established eight hours as the basic workday, with overtime pay required for longer hours.[105] These federal measures came on top of a steady stream of state hours legislation, which began with the Massachusetts law first passed in 1874 establishing a legal maximum of sixty hours per week for women. By 1911, that maximum had dropped to fifty-four hours, and the percentage of states with maximum hours laws (aimed mainly but not entirely at women and children) had risen to fifty-eight, a figure that would reach 76 percent in 1920 and 84 percent in 1930. Clearly, the principle of state intervention in hours legislation had been firmly established.

Meanwhile, for the first time, driven by the need to maintain wartime production, the federal government began to intervene directly in labour disputes; its National War Labor Board would "almost invariably" award the eight-hour day in hours disputes.[106] Observing the effects of this shorter day on productivity, many scientifically trained managers found that workers continued to produce as much in a shorter day as they had working a longer day, with the result that most major American employers brought in the shorter day during the 1920s.[107]

By 1929, the work hours picture was radically different than it had been in 1913, or even 1920. Canada led the eight-country "pack," with 2,354 average annual hours, the United States being close behind at 2,316. But the top-bottom variation was small, with Canada's figure only about 10 percent higher than that of Germany (2,128 hours.[108]) The figures would be consistent with a five-and-a-half-day week of eight-hour days, with some time off for holidays, which by then were being more widely granted. Some reduction in the number of days worked per week was achieved: five-day weeks had been granted by certain employers. (According to Roediger and Foner, the first such week was granted in 1908 by a New England spinning firm wishing to allow its employees to observe the Jewish Sabbath.[109]) Most notably, Henry Ford, a pioneer of the eight-hour day, moved to a five-day week in 1926,[110] and there was also pressure to adopt a five-day week in industries, such as garment manufacturing, whose workers were mainly Jewish.[111]

During the 1920s, the five-day week was also achieved by enough AFL craft unions (painters, bricklayers, carpenters, electrical workers, and plasterers) to allow the AFL to boast, at its 1928 convention, that 165,000 of its members were working such a week.[112] By 1927, at least 262 large establishments had established the five-day week, compared to just thirty-two in 1920.[113] But the five-day week would remain, for most, an elusive target, harder to achieve than the eight-hour day had been.[114] As late as 1932, a federal Bureau of Labor Statistics survey found that only 5.4 percent of 44,025 establishments had adopted a five-day week for all or even some of their employees.[115]

The character of the shorter hours movement would change as much during the 1920s as did the hours worked themselves. After the defeat of a giant steel strike in 1920, the unions for the most part remained quiescent on the hours issue, although there were a few exceptions here and there.[116] Leadership of the shorter hours coalition passed from the labour movement to a reform coalition comprised of religious humanitarians and the previously mentioned corporate/engineering experts who emphasized productivity and profit. As Roediger and Foner note, "That the ideas of the corporate/engineering group came to dominate the coalition speaks to the weakness of the post-1919 labor movement."[117] (As will be shown in the next chapter, the same was equally true if not more so for the Canadian labour movement, whose radical wing was decimated in the wake of the failed Winnipeg General Strike.)

In their quest for shorter hours, the scientific management/capitalist reformers appeared to be motivated by a mix of genuine concern for workers' health, much like the concern that would motivate the Kellogg Company's six-hour day, launched at the end of the decade,[118] a desire to increase productivity and "machine longevity," and a desire to "defuse union protest."[119] (In introducing the eight-hour and five-dollar day, Henry Ford had reportedly boasted to an associate that he would "lick the IWW" (the radical International Workers of the World) by doing what he was doing.[120] Nor was he by any means alone in his view that paying high wages and offering short hours would be a good way to keep unions out; few of the "welfare capitalist" managers of the 1920s made any bones about their anti-union animus.[121]

Through the 1920s, productivity-based arguments in favour of the shorter working day came thick and fast. In 1920 John R. Commons and John

Historical Development of Work Hours I: The United States

B. Andrews wrote, "Of the many lessons that the world war taught industry, none is more clear-cut than that long hours do not pay."[122] By 1924, "a growing body of literature linked shorter hours with decreased absenteeism due to illness or disability and enabled the economist P. Sargent Florence to argue that 'about one-quarter' of the right-hour difference between a fifty-two hour and a sixty-hour working week was simply given back in increased lost time due to sickness."[123] Others would stress that many disputes at work resulted from fatigue, which would mean that reducing work hours (and hence fatigue) would be a good way to reduce workplace conflict.

Chief among the business-oriented shorter hours reformers was Commerce Secretary Herbert Hoover, who, as noted earlier, was instrumental in forcing the steel industry to move from a twelve-hour to an eight-hour day.[124] But Hoover was also instrumental in developing and preaching what Benjamin Hunnicutt in his book *Free Time: The Forgotten American Dream* has termed "the gospel of consumption" — a vision of progress that replaced the goal of more leisure time with the goal of more things to buy.[125] Shorter hours pioneer Henry Ford himself was fully aware of this gospel when, as a rationale for granting his workers shorter hours, he noted that he wanted them to have the time to be able to drive the cars they were making. As for Hoover, the Committee on Recent Economic Changes, which he chaired, concluded that American business had discovered during the 1920s that "the leisure that results from an increasing man-hours productivity helps to create new needs and new and broader markets."[126]

The gospel of consumption was seen as business's response to "the threat of leisure," posed by the ever-decreasing hours that seemed likely as a result of continuing adoption of labour-saving technology. With economists such as Harvard's Thomas Nixon Carver warning that what was then called "The Higher Progress" (i.e., continued increase in leisure) would likely lead to a significant *decrease* in overall demand for material goods,[127] worried businessmen increasingly felt compelled to push consumers to buy things — including, in at least some instances, things they neither really wanted nor needed — simply in order to keep themselves in business. While the gospel of consumption would be temporarily shelved during the early years of the Depression, as workers, employers, and politicians alike turned to the problems resulting from acute scarcity, it would start to return during the Depression's later years and come back with a vengeance after the Second World War. In Hunnicutt's view, it would be workers' buying in to the gospel of consumption that would lead them to oppose further reductions in the work week, as material goods came to hold higher priority with them than additional leisure.[128]

For the most part, this has continued to be the case right through to this very day!

The Depression and Its Aftermath

The Depression, which caused so much misery to so many, not just in the United States but all around the world, would be the spur to some of the most creative thinking ever engaged in around the issue of work hours. Much of that thinking was a product of the new administration of U.S. president Franklin D. Roosevelt, who had swept to power in 1932 with the broad mandate to deal with the Depression by any means possible — and to get Americans back to work as quickly as possible. The Republican administration defeated by Roosevelt in that election was none other than that of Herbert Hoover, whose voluntaristic approach to economic issues,[129] while it may have worked at a micro level when dealing with the hours issues of the 1920s, was clearly not up to the task of rebuilding a shattered national economy and assuring terrified citizens that better times were truly just around the corner.

It is not fair to suggest, as some progressives do even today, that Hoover essentially did nothing to deal with the Depression — that he simply sat idly by, throwing up his hands and loudly proclaiming to all comers his constitutional inability to act. The man who as America's food relief czar had arranged to feed many millions of hungry Europeans after the First World War, and who would help feed millions more after the Second World War,[130] would never have sat idly by in the midst of such a crisis. But he may not have understood the full magnitude of the crisis he was dealing with.

Historical Development of Work Hours I: The United States

From the outset of the Depression, labour leaders pushed for shorter hours, seeing the sharing of the available work as the only way out of the massive unemployment — at times as high as 25 percent — gripping the American economy. Among other things, the train brotherhoods in 1930 began to push for a six-hour day, while the metal trades began a drive for a five-hour day, introducing a motion to that effect at the 1930 AFL convention.[131] Essentially agreeing with the labour movement's prescription for a healthier economy, Hoover called on the business community to bring in shorter hours voluntarily as a more humane alternative to massive layoffs,[132] to this end creating a work-sharing commission, chaired by Walter Teagle, the president of Standard Oil, to promote work-sharing at the firm level.[133] While the best-known examples of the commission's positive results were the changes made by the Kellogg Company in Battle Creek, Michigan, and Goodyear Tire in Akron, Ohio, both of which adopted six-hour days with five-day weeks,[134] many other firms, such as Sears, Standard Oil, and General Motors, reduced their work weeks. The commission had strong public support and enjoyed significant cooperation from business. It would claim to have created three to five million additional jobs, while in 1933, the Department of Labor estimated that 25 percent of the nation's workforce was employed due to work-sharing.[135] Both parties would adopt work-sharing planks in their 1932 campaign platforms, with Hoover and Roosevelt "claiming to be the original and stronger advocates of the measure."[136] Adding urgency to the issue was the AFL Executive Committee's call for a legislated thirty-hour week, which took the form of a bill providing severe penalties for overtime hours worked in excess of that.[137]

Continued high unemployment, despite the Hoover administration's best efforts, along with Roosevelt's pledge to end Prohibition, pretty well guaranteed Hoover's defeat in the 1932 election.[138] That election offered proof positive that the limits to voluntary action against the Depression had been passed. Clearly, the Depression was, by this time, a crisis of such magnitude and duration that direct federal government intervention — the very thing that had always been anathema to Hoover — was not just permissible but essential. The election of FDR ensured that such strong government intervention would indeed come — and sooner rather than later.

Even before FDR's March 4 inauguration, Congressional leaders were at work drafting shorter-hours legislation.[139] During the first month of FDR's administration, the U.S. Senate passed, by a solid 53–30 margin, a bill essentially enacting the AFL proposal into law. Sponsored by Alabama senator Hugo Black, the bill provided for a legislated six-hour day and five-day week, with overtime penalties for work performed in excess of that, and barred from both interstate and foreign commerce goods produced in establishments where longer hours were permitted.[140] So eager was Black to get the legislation passed that he actually introduced it on December 21, 1932 — just three weeks after the AFL resolution giving rise to it and more than two months before Roosevelt's inauguration.[141]

Having passed the Senate by a comfortable margin, Black's bill was sent to the House of Representatives, where it received the strong support of Labor Committee chairman William Connery.[142] Supported, initially, by Roosevelt himself, by Labor Secretary Frances Perkins, and by many Congressional Democrats, the bill seemed assured of passage.[143] By all appearances, the United States seemed poised to enter into the new world long dreamed of by labour and its reformist professional allies — one of progressively shorter work hours and progressively greater quantities of leisure time.

But within a few months, the shorter hours movement was turned on its head. Government policy would move in an entirely different direction, not just for the duration of the Depression but afterward as well. Never again would the shorter hours movement enjoy such broad popular support (from the business community as well as the labour movement) or have such strong political clout. As Hunnicutt says, ruefully, "Rare were those prescient enough to foresee that the century-long shorter hours movement had come to an end and that 1933 would prove to be its political high-water mark."[144] The tragic irony was that on this issue, American working people would be done in by their "friends" (the progressive Roosevelt New Dealers) rather than by their "enemies" (the conservative Republicans philosophically opposed to any federal government intervention on work hours).

How did it happen that the new Roosevelt administration, which had initially strongly supported Black's bill, to the extent that Labor Secretary Frances Perkins went before the House Labor Committee to give the bill the administration's stamp of approval,[145] came so quickly to oppose it? Hunnicutt says "it is far from clear" what motivated Roosevelt's advisors, such as Rexford Tugwell and Harry Hopkins, whose influence on Roosevelt appears to have been strongest.[146]

One area of concern, surely, was the bill's provision forbidding importation of goods produced by workers working longer than thirty hours per week.[147] More generally, much of the business community appears to have been opposed to the legislation as such. Senator Black himself — the bill's sponsor — conceded as much, allowing that most of industry, including the National Association of Manufacturers, opposed the bill as being both ineffective and unconstitutional.[148] While the business community's opposition couldn't prevent its passage by the Senate, it did find more fertile territory in the House, where by this time Roosevelt himself, whom the business community had clearly "gotten to," was opposing the bill and declaring it unconstitutional, just as the National Association of Manufacturers had. The bill was then bottled up in the Rules Committee, where it would die.[149] To all intents and purposes, the battle for the legislated six-hour day had been lost, though Black would make another (this time completely futile) attempt to pass a similar bill through the Senate two years later.[150]

What the Roosevelt administration did offer was a National Industrial Recovery Act (NIRA), which promised to create many jobs through public works projects. In a bid to placate labour's thirty-hour advocates, the legislation creating the NIRA stipulated that hours on those public works projects, commonly known as the WPA (Works Progress Administration), would be limited to thirty per week "so far as practicable and feasible."[151] But the stipulation would be far more often honoured in the breach than in the observance, with about 85 percent of all codes covered by NIRA specifying a forty-hour week, and nearly as many providing for weeks longer than forty hours than weeks shorter than that.[152]

Perhaps of more lasting value to American workers was NIRA's Sec. 7(a), which declared that every industrial code must among other things provide that "employees shall have the right to organize and bargain collectively through representatives of their own choosing, and shall be free from interference, restraint, or coercion of employees ... in the designation of such representatives."[153] These principles, embodied in the 1935 National Labor Relations Act, more commonly known as the Wagner Act in honour of its chief sponsor, New York senator Robert Wagner, would for the first time provide American workers a firm legal basis for collective bargaining. With standards of unfair labour practice written into the act and a National Labor Relations Board established to enforce the act, American workers could organize freely, which they did, signing up hundreds of thousands of new workers in the years immediately following the act's passage. Of particular significance was the way in which the act facilitated the organization of unskilled and semi-skilled workers who would otherwise have had difficulty forming unions, "since they lacked the scarce skills needed to withstand employer anti-union initiatives."[154]

But although the Wagner Act definitely stimulated American union growth, it turned out not to be of much help in the shorter hours battle. By 1935, as part of its New Deal, the Roosevelt administration had embarked on a very different path for addressing unemployment. This path would be one of perpetual economic growth and "Full-Time, Full Employment," with "full-time" now defined as a forty-hour week. To this end, Roosevelt committed government to do "whatever it would take to create enough work in the public and private sectors ... to replace the work taken by new technology."[155] Using stimulus spending to finance this new role, the government would now be the "employer of last resort" whenever the private sector failed to generate enough jobs. During the 1930s, many thousands of Americans would be put to work on major public works projects such as the Tennessee Valley Authority and Hoover Dam, which helped bring electricity to thousands of rural Americans.[156] During and after the Second World War, in a climate of what Hunnicutt has described as "perpetual military mobilization," more and more of these government-created jobs would be related to the military.[157] Hunnicutt sums up the nature of the Roosevelt administration's policy shift when he says, "Instead of opting for expanding the realm of freedom and facing the autotelic challenge that generations of Americans, beginning with the eighteenth-century American theologian Jonathan Edwards, had struggled with, Roosevelt, and then the nation, chose the perpetual creation of needs and eternal expansion of necessity, accepting the new, daunting challenge to create sufficient work for all to have 'full-time' jobs, forevermore."[158]

With the Roosevelt administration having to all intents and purposes abandoned the thirty-hour week cause, despite FDR's subsequent admission of regret that he had not got his administration behind Black-Connery[159] — the bill was co-sponsored by William Connery, a Massachusetts congressman — average weekly hours started to rise from a low reached in 1934, at the depth of the Depression.[160] But this doesn't mean that the government was idle on the hours front. The decade would see the passage of several hours-shortening federal initiatives (most stipulating a forty-hour rather than a thirty-hour week). These included the Motor Carrier Act, which as a safety measure set hours maxima for workers engaged in interstate transportation, the Postal Act, which set a forty-hour week for most postal employees, the Bituminous Coal Conservation Act regulating hours in coal mines, the Maritime Hours Law Act of 1936, which placed crews of vessels under the Maritime Commission on eight-hour days, and the Sugar Act of 1937, which set a maximum eight-hour day for children fourteen to sixteen working in sugar, except when they were working for their families.[161] The two most important pieces of federal hours legislation passed during the decade were the Public Contracts Act, which set a maximum eight-hour day and forty-hour week for work on all government contracts of $10,000 or more, and the Fair Labor Standards Act (FLSA) of 1938, which to this day has remained the major legislation dealing with work hours in the United States.[162]

Not a new departure, the FLSA "embodied," in the words of labour historian Jeremy Felt, what had become the conventional wisdom, among social reformers, on the issues of minimum wages, maximum hours, and child labour.[163] Despite its less than radical nature, the bill was passed only after considerable manoeuvring between the two houses of Congress.[164]

The FLSA set a minimum wage, for employment affecting interstate commerce, of twenty-five cents per hour for the bill's first year. For the next six years, that figure would rise to thirty cents per hour; thereafter, the minimum would be forty cents per hour. Lower wages were allowed for learners, apprentices, messengers, or aged or physically disabled workers.[165] Weekly hours of work were limited to forty-four in the bill's first year of operation, forty-two in its second year, and forty thereafter, except when overtime at time and a half was paid. The bill was silent on daily hours of work. This omission would be criticized by the labour movement, as was the weak language on child labour.[166] And there were a large number of exclusions, including for those engaged in administrative, professional, and executive work, retail, fishing, packing, marketing, and processing of aquatic products, as well as seamen, transport, farm, and agricultural cannery workers, and workers involved in making cheese and butter. But unlike much earlier state hours legislation, the FLSA would punish willful violations with a fine of up to $10,000 or six months' imprisonment, or both, imprisonment being applied only to second offenders. And within the Department of Labor, the act created a Wage and Hour Division, with an administrator appointed by the president.

Despite its many loopholes, the FLSA does appear to have brought about substantial progress in reducing work hours between its passage in 1938 and the United States' entry into the Second World War, with a number of cities adopting six-hour and seven-hour days for their workers.[167]

The forty-hour week, which it was as much as anything responsible for, was an improvement over the hours enjoyed by many American workers at the time, and a significant improvement over the hours enjoyed by workers in most other countries. It would also serve as an inspiration and a model for similar legislation passed in France by the social democratic Popular Front government of Léon Blum.

The Second World War would mark the effective end of the shorter hours movement in the United States. There would be some continued progress on the hours front in Canada and in a number of European and Pacific Rim countries, but in the United States, the passage of the Fair Labor Standards Act would mark the end of any serious legislative effort to reduce working hours, though there would be a brief flurry of renewed interest in 1977 when Michigan representative John Conyers introduced an amendment to the FLSA mandating a thirty-five-hour week.

While Conyers's bill never made it to the House floor, it did progress to the point of public hearings before the Subcommittee on Labor Standards of the House Committee on Education and Labor in 1979, hearings that would generate significant public interest in the work hours issue for the first time in many years.[168] In addition to expressing his delight over the Conyers proposal, incoming United Auto Workers president Douglas Fraser somewhat optimistically told his convention that a four-day week was "inevitable."[169] Alas, it was not to be. By 1981, not only had the Conyers bill been permanently shelved, but the entire American labour movement, already badly weakened by reactionary AFL-CIO president (the AFL merged with its rival, the Congress of Industrial Organizations, in 1955) George Meany's unwillingness to organize the unorganized and severing of ties with progressive Congressional allies over such issues as Vietnam and major weapons systems,[170] was fighting for its very survival.

The 1980 election of Ronald Reagan, one of whose first acts as president was to decertify the striking Professional Air Traffic Controllers Organization (now the National Air Traffic Controllers Association), would serve as a sort of open sesame for anti-union employers who under previous administrations might have thought it wiser to keep such sentiments under wraps. Now, with the president himself leading the way, U.S. employers openly launched a massive offensive against unions. Particularly following the 1982 recession, union concessions and givebacks, among which were shorter hours provisions, became the order of the day. Whether or not, as Jane Slaughter, the co-founder of *Labor Notes*, has suggested, "union gains on shortening work time ... [were] among the first to go during the concessions offensive,"[171] some such gains were indeed lost, if only in order to maintain weekly wages at existing levels. At the same time, public spending cutbacks would lead, often, to longer hours for the smaller number of public sector workers who remained.[172] While the deep 1982 recession did lead a number of unions and unionists to once again propose hours reductions as a remedy for high unemployment,[173] such reductions were not widely adopted, at least not in the United States. (In Canada, there was much more of an effort to promote work-sharing to help alleviate the unemployment resulting from this recession.)

But the end of the shorter hours movement goes back much further, to the war years and even before. Understandably, work hours increased during the war, as companies and workers were pressed to maintain adequate civil production while feeding the huge American war machine. For a time, however, it was thought that those longer hours would cease with the war's end. Some, including the AFL, feared a post-war recession, such as had occurred to a degree in both the United States and Canada following the First World War. To this end, the AFL at its 1944 convention passed a resolution calling for a six-hour day and five-day week immediately upon cessation of hostilities.[174]

Shortly after the war's end, however, it became apparent that there would in fact be no postwar recession. Instead, the postwar baby boom fuelled much construction and development. Whole new towns arose in the outskirts of big cities such as New York and Los Angeles. Highways were built *en masse* for travel both within the new suburban towns and between them and their metropolitan centres. As baby boom children matured, schools were built in record numbers to provide for their education. Even churches experienced a modest construction boom, particularly in the new suburban communities.[175] And quite naturally, the auto industry boomed as well, as car ownership shifted from being a luxury to being a necessity, and as millions of new postwar families suddenly needed cars — or additional cars — to get themselves around. No longer were shorter hours needed to help spread around the available employment. If anything, the demand for labour had begun to exceed the supply.

In this booming economy, the longest sustained period of economic growth that the United States would ever know, the labour movement's priorities shifted dramatically. The AFL's committee on shorter work hours lapsed, while liberal labour leaders like the United Auto Workers' Walter Reuther began to focus on guaranteed annual wages and stimulative Keynesian economics. In coalition with liberal Democrats in the House and Senate, labour leaders joined forces to pass the Employment Act of 1946, with labour leaders agreeing with the liberal Democrats that the bill's full employment objectives would be best achieved through stimulative fiscal policy, high military spending, and expansion of overseas markets — not through shorter work hours.[176]

Even through a sharp recession in 1958, there would be no significant challenge to the new conventional wisdom of "guns *and* butter" until

Historical Development of Work Hours I: The United States

1968, when Eugene McCarthy, in his campaign for the Democratic presidential nomination, reminded Americans that resources were indeed finite, and that it would be necessary to start choosing between continued high military spending and continued social programs. In the meantime, the watchword was spend, spend, and spend some more, as Americans started to take longer vacations, sometimes involving significant travel, and to buy things like powerboats, fishing cabins, and fancy sporting equipment, which their parents had only dreamed of owning, if they had ever thought about them at all. Those who questioned the cycle of everlasting spending (much of it, now, on credit) into which most Americans appeared to have been drawn tended to be viewed as eccentric. Those still pressing for "30 for 40" (thirty hours' work at forty hours' pay) were attacked by labour leaders like the UAW's Walter Reuther for their ill-timed, even subversive demand — this despite the fact that the UAW had during the mid-1940s itself passed a resolution in favour of "30 for 40"![177] (Evidently a well-developed case of amnesia is a useful thing to possess if one wishes to succeed as a labour leader.)

While the shorter hours forces might not have been completely routed, they were, by the mid-1950s, certainly in retreat. At the 1956 AFL-CIO convention, the newly merged confederation's first joint one, despite a strong shorter hours pitch from the confederation's president, George Meany,[178] the issue was officially characterized as a marginal one by Otto Pragan of the International Chemical Workers' Union.[179] Noting that the "movement to reduce hours below forty did not enjoy the support from reformers nor the union solidarity which earlier campaigns for a shorter day had elicited," Pragan went on to conclude that the push for shorter hours was no longer a "nationwide movement," but rather an issue affecting only a few selected industries.[180]

As if to confirm Pragan's rather cynical remarks, at the following year's AFL-CIO convention, Meany did not even mention work hours in his keynote address. Roediger and Foner cite this as an example of the postwar labour movement's lack of follow-up on the issue and also of its tendency to "blow hot and cold" — not a useful strategy in their view.[181] Forty hours did indeed appear, in the words of Roediger and Foner, to have become "almost sacrosanct" as a lower bound for the work week, with any extra time reductions taking the form of vacations, long weekends, and earlier retirement. Increasingly, reductions in working hours had come to be seen not as victories for labour but as signs that the economy was in trouble.[182] By 1963, there were signs that rank-and-file union members had come to agree with leaders like Reuther on the hours issue. A Gallup poll taken in that year found only 42 percent of union members supporting a thirty-five-hour week.[183]

The labour movement had been seriously weakened earlier by the passage of the 1947 Taft-Hartley Act, which amended the Wagner Act, prohibiting some union activities and limiting others, as well as by certain amendments to the Fair Labor Standards Act that significantly loosened standards for the measurement of working hours, particularly standards relating to travel time to and from work.[184] Most notably, these amendments allowed any state wishing to do so to opt out of union security provisions. The existence of such "right-to-work" states soon made it easier for employers wishing to remove their unions to do so.[185] Almost certainly the existence of "right-to-work" states has been a major factor in the decline of the U.S. labour movement, from a density rate of 32.5 percent in 1953 to less than one-third of that (10.3 percent) in 2021.[186] Effectively, these laws weaken unions by depriving them of a national financial base.[187] More specifically, Taft-Hartley weakened the labour movement by stalling white-collar organization and guaranteeing the failure of the Operation Dixie campaign, which had sought to organize the South during the early postwar years.[188]

Given its increasingly weakened state, even if the labour movement had wanted to push for shorter hours and had united in such a way so as to maximize the possibility of achieving that end, it is unlikely that, by the 1970s, it would have possessed either the numerical strength or political clout to have done so. Perhaps the clearest sign of the American labour movement's weakness by the twenty-first century was the fact that in 2012 the Democrats held their presidential nominating convention in North Carolina, a long-time right-to-work state that then had the lowest union membership rates in the entire country.[189] It would have been impossible to imagine such a thing's happening during the Roosevelt or Truman administrations, or even during those of John F. Kennedy or Lyndon B. Johnson. The labour movement would have protested mightily until the decision was reversed. If the labour movement ever protested the choice of venue for the 2012 nominating convention, I am not aware of any such protest. All the scuttlebutt appeared to be about how the convention location decision was a savvy one that might help put North Carolina, a marginal state politically, into the Democratic column on election day.[190]

With a gravely weakened labour movement focused on its own survival, the shorter hours movement in the United States was left without any effective leadership. There would, at least until after the Covid-19 pandemic, be little effective opposition to employers who, in the name of meeting growing foreign competition, were seeking to work their employees ever longer and harder.

Has the work hours situation been any different in Canada? Is it really much different today? The next chapter will seek to answer these questions, with an eye to pointing out both the convergence and divergence of the two countries' work hours paths and the reasons for their divergence at particular points.

CHAPTER 3

Historical Development of Work Hours II: Canada

As is shown below in Table 3.1, Canadian workers currently put in on average about one hundred hours less per year than their American counterparts — a relatively minor difference as a percentage of total hours worked. As the annual average hours worked in this table are not broken down into regular hours and hours taken off for vacation and holidays, it is not possible to identify precisely the reason for the slightly fewer hours worked by Canadian employees. But given that Canadian workers, as we saw in Table 2.2 in the previous chapter, enjoy significantly more in the way of vacation and holiday entitlements than their American counterparts, albeit less than workers in most other industrialized Western countries, it seems likely that longer vacations and a greater number of holidays account for most or even all of the difference. To give just one example, almost all Canadian workers get Good Friday off, and a great many also get Boxing Day and Easter Monday. None of these days is normally given as a holiday in the United States.

Whatever the reasons for the relatively small difference between average Canadian and American hours worked, workers in both countries generally work quite long hours by world standards, and have for some time, despite the fact that their countries are among the world's most prosperous. Only with the pandemic and the Great Resignation that has arisen in its aftermath has there been any real hope for improvement in either country.

Initially the struggle for shorter work hours in Canada mirrored to a significant extent what was unfolding in the United States, though for reasons noted below it was somewhat slower getting started. Through the pre-industrial eighteenth and early nineteenth centuries, in Canada as in the United States, the pace of work was based on the job needing to be done rather than on the clock.[1] With the beginning of industrialization in Canada and the launching of large-scale construction projects, such as the building of canals and railways, serious labour strife ensued. On the canals, for the building of which large numbers of labourers were brought in from Ireland, fourteen-hour workdays were a major cause of such strife, as were the grossly inadequate wages and long waits between paydays.[2] If Canada did not see the large number of struggles for shorter hours that, say, the northeastern United States did early on, it was chiefly because large-scale industrialization was slower to come to Canada, and there were simply not all that many factories in the country prior to the middle of the nineteenth century — not because Canadian employers were by nature any more beneficent than their fellow employers south of the border!

Another reason the shorter hours struggle appears to have taken longer to come to full fruition in Canada than it did south of the border was the slow development of an independent organized labour movement. In addition to the country's later industrialization, development of an independent organized Canadian labour movement was slowed for a variety of reasons, including the fragmentation of Canadian labour into separate English-Canadian and French-Canadian movements, heavy waves of out-migration of Canadian workers to the United States, especially New England, and a degree of economic underdevelopment that kept many Canadian industries seasonal well into the nineteenth century, a fact that forced the employees of those industries to move to the United States to find work during the industries' "off" months.[3] Another reason was the tendency — often for economic reasons — of Canadian workers to affiliate with the American-based "international" unions rather than independent Canadian ones.[4]

Historical Development of Work Hours II: Canada

The different patterns of industrialization and unionization are reflected in the work hours cited below (Table 3.1) for Canada and the United States. This table reveals that despite a general similarity in the overall trend of work hours in the two countries, there were a number of specific points at which the two countries' trends diverged, sometimes quite markedly.

TABLE 3.1: AVERAGE ANNUAL HOURS OF WORK, VARIOUS YEARS

Year	Average Hours (Canada)	Average Hours (United States)
1870	2845	3076
1880	2934	3044
1890	3017	2983
1900	3102	2938
1913	2868	2900
1929	2354	2316
1938	2212	1756
1950	2209	1989
1959	2104	1953
1966	1995	1962
1980	1827	1801
1990	1797	1796
2000	1779	1845
2010	1703	1736
2017	1696	1757

Sources: Huberman & Minns (2007) and PWI 9, no. 1 (2019), cited in Giattino, et al., 2020.

The first of these points came between 1870 and 1913. With regard to the first of those periods, it's worth noting that Giattino et al. have identified three distinct periods in the development of work hours in the industrialized countries they have charted. The first of those periods is from 1870–1913, when in most countries there was a relatively slow decline in hours worked. But while this is true for the United States, as can be seen in the above table, and is also true for other countries such as the United Kingdom, whose work hours development will be discussed in detail in the next chapter, it is *not* true for Canada, where average annual work hours *rose* each decade between 1870 and 1900, going from 2,845 in the former year to 3,102 in the latter year, before dropping to 2,868 — still slightly higher than the 1870 figure — over a decade later in 1913.

While a full explanation for this apparent anomaly is not immediately available, most likely Canada's late industrialization, mentioned above, is an important factor here. This late industrialization, along with other factors such as the country's harsh climate and sparse population, meant that many industries remained seasonal well into the closing decades of the nineteenth century. This would have resulted in an artificial shortening of average Canadian work hours, when in fact a good many Canadian workers would have been putting in significant hours in the United States, where they would have been forced to move for at least part of the year due to Canada's seasonal unemployment. The increase in average hours seen through the century's three final decades points toward increasing industrialization and, in particular, a decline in purely seasonal work, rather than the Canadian labour movement's lack of action on the shorter hours front.

For even as the average annual hours of work continued to rise through the 1870s and beyond, due to increasing Canadian industrialization, a shorter hours movement was in full swing north of the border as well as south of it. The search for shorter hours was a key issue in the now burgeoning Canadian labour movement, as it was in labour movements around the world, Indeed, nine-hour leagues in Hamilton and Montreal marked the beginning of broader workers' solidarity in Canada,[5] with the leagues' strategy based on a series of strikes to support shorter hours demands.[6] The quest for shorter hours was also a key element of the strategy of the Knights of Labor, whose aim, as was often said, was not to make richer people, but better people.[7] Work schedules that would allow more time for reading, recreation, and family and community life would be critical in achieving the "better" lives the Knights were seeking.

A strategic blunder on the part of the printers' unions likely delayed the actual achievement of a nine-hour day in Canada. What happened was that the unions struck George Brown's *Globe* newspaper ahead of schedule in 1872, which caused Brown to charge the strikers with conspiracy.[8] But in the longer term, the strike was not a total loss, as it provided politicians with evidence of working people's political power and may well have been responsible for the Macdonald government's enactment, later that same year, of a Trade Unions Act removing peaceful picketing from criminal prosecution.[9]

Like the American labour movement, the Canadian labour movement, which at that point was composed mainly of international (i.e., American) unions in any case, did the best it could over the next half century to achieve shorter hours. But its ability to achieve any sort of major or lasting gain was limited by its own inherent weakness, including the lack of the legal right to bargain collectively, as well as by strong employer resistance, of the sort displayed by the employer delegation at first National Industrial Conference in Ottawa in 1919.

At the tripartite conference, both the employees' group and the neutral public group expressed strong support for adoption of the eight-hour day. But the employers' group was adamantly opposed, declaring the proposal not opportune at a time when "Canada needs increased productivity to pay the war debt and to maintain competition against other countries," and saying also that the then-current average of fifty hours a week across Canada provided workers with "an adequate standard of health and recreation." Perhaps not coincidentally, the employers' group was also opposed to providing full collective bargaining rights to unions,[10] a right that, as is noted in more detail later, Canadian workers would gain only in 1944.

Would an eight-hour day proposal have met the same degree of resistance among a group of American employers and managers as it did in Canada? Perhaps the fact that since foreign companies controlled large parts of the economy, Canadian managers weren't really "masters in their own house" had something to do with their reluctance to embrace a change that by this time was beginning to be widely adopted in the United States. Another possibility is that Frederick Taylor's scientific management philosophy, which undergirded the adoption of shorter hours in many countries, was not as widely disseminated in Canada as it was south of the border, or for that matter in European countries such as the United Kingdom and Germany. It was this philosophy, whose guiding principle was that work methods should be determined by objective data rather than by past practice or rule of thumb,[11] that led to the conducting of experiments involving the detailed measurement of productivity in many American industries, including, most notably, shipbuilding, during the First World War. The experiments' key finding was that shorter hours resulted in little or no drop in productivity. This understanding persuaded many American employers to adopt the eight-hour day during the 1920s.[12] Whatever the answers to the above questions, there was, by 1929, a remarkable convergence between Canadian and American work hours, with the former at an annual average of 2,354, just about three-quarters of a week longer than the latter, at an annual average of 2,315. By 1929, the top-bottom differences in work hours throughout the Western world were of the order of just 10 percent — a degree of convergence not experienced before, or since. The combined influence of Henry Ford and other enlightened industrialists who had adopted the eight-hour day and the International Labour Organization's international standard on the eight-hour day are likely the strongest factors explaining such a degree of convergence.

Less than a decade later, however, in 1938, Canadian and American work hours had come to diverge dramatically. What one notices in studying a list of eight countries drawn from Giattino et al. is that there is little variation among the top six countries (headed by Canada at 2,212 average annual hours, and including the United Kingdom at 2,200 hours, Belgium at 2,196 hours, Germany at 2,187, Sweden at 2,131, and Australia at 2,109). All of these countries' hours patterns would be consistent with a general eight-hour day and five-and-a-half-day week. None of these six countries had changed that much since the end of the 1920s. The gradual, long-term reduction in hours had continued, but there were no dramatic changes in any of those six countries.

In the larger group of eight, the two outliers are clearly the United States, at 1,756 hours, and France, at 1,760 hours. The seemingly anomalous position of these two countries demonstrates the significance of government action in the shorter hours struggle. By 1938, the United States had passed the Fair Labor Standards Act, guaranteeing workers a five-day, forty-hour week. France had taken a similar path following the election of the social democratic Popular Front government of Léon Blum in 1936. Prior to this government's election, many French workers had been forced to work up to sixty hours per week. Blum's government set the maximum number of hours at forty, for forty-eight hours' pay, and also provided workers with two weeks of paid annual leave. The lower number of average annual hours for French workers, which virtually parallels the American situation, would be consistent with a five-day week and eight-hour day, with some time off for vacation and holidays.[13]

Why, given the historically close connection between the two countries' economies as well as their geographic proximity to one another, didn't Canada follow a similar path with regard to work hours? Again, the divergence can readily be explained as resulting from political and institutional factors. Unlike the United States, which from 1933 on enjoyed one of the world's most progressive governments, Canada spent the decade of the 1930s under the sway of governments best described as centre-right. In 1935 the overtly reactionary Conservative government of R.B. Bennett was defeated. Replacing it was the subtler but in some ways nearly as reactionary Liberal government of Mackenzie King. While Canadians had suffered just as much from the Depression as had Americans, there was, under King, no spate of humanitarian social legislation, and none of the hours laws that marked Roosevelt's second term.

Perhaps most important of all, Canadian workers still, even as late as the start of the Second World War, did not enjoy the right to form unions and bargain collectively with employers, a right that American workers had received in 1935. Insisting on the perfection of the thoroughly outmoded Industrial Disputes Investigation (IDI) Act he had been instrumental in enacting in 1907, King steadfastly refused to move beyond it, even in the face of bitter wartime strikes that were essentially over union recognition rights.[14] Only in 1944, confronted simultaneously by a National War Labour Board report concluding that labour strife would continue until Canadian workers were granted the same bargaining rights as their American counterparts enjoyed and a growing political threat from the left, in the shape of the social democratic Co-operative Commonwealth Federation, or CCF, did King finally yield and grant Canadian workers basic bargaining rights.[15] Canada would be the last significant industrialized country to grant its workers such rights.

Not surprisingly, given that in 1939 Canada's workers didn't enjoy basic bargaining rights whereas those in the United States did, union membership rates were far lower in Canada than in the United States. In his book *Industrial Relations: The Economy and Society*, John Godard[16] reported a Canadian union density rate of 17 percent for 1939. For the United States, where workers had by then been able to bargain collectively for four years, the comparable figure was 28.6 percent.[17] With no legal protection for bargaining rights, and with union membership rates just over half those in the United States, Canadian workers would have had much more difficulty in negotiating favourable hours provisions than their American counterparts. And the smaller, weaker Canadian labour movement had far less political clout than did the American movement of the day, which was regularly consulted by presidents Roosevelt and Truman[18] and which had been so instrumental in the introduction and passage of hours legislation in the United States. Overall, given the sharp disparities in the size and strength of the two countries' labour movements, it's perhaps surprising that the differences in average hours worked were not greater than they were.

A third point of divergence in Canadian and American work hours came in the years immediately following the Second World War. As Table 3.1 illustrates, Canadian average annual hours in 1950 were virtually unchanged, at 2,209, from what they had been in 1938. It appears that the five-and-a-half-day week continued to be the norm in Canada through the 1950s; it would not be until the 1960s that a forty-hour week was legislated.[19] In the United States, average annual work hours over this same period *increased* substantially, from 1,756 to 1,989 — a rise of more than 10 percent. Such an increase seems a clear sign of the labour movement's abandonment of the shorter hours fight, as described in the previous chapter. While most workers did not go back to the five-and-a-half or six-day week,[20] many (including my architect father) worked plenty of overtime. In the wake of the postwar baby boom, the demand for new houses, schools, roads, hospitals, and recreational facilities, not to mention churches (my father's specialty), seemed well-nigh endless. International Chemical Workers' Union official Otto Pragan, cited earlier, may have been charitable in effectively characterizing shorter hours as a boutique issue. Not once during my boyhood, adolescence, or young manhood, which included two periods when I myself was a union member, did I hear shorter hours referred to.

After 1950, as Table 3.1 again shows, work hours in Canada and the United States came, gradually, to converge. In both countries, average work hours dropped steadily after 1950, the drop being sharper in Canada, where most workers in 1950 had yet to achieve a forty-hour week. By 1990, Canadian and American workers were both putting in an average of just under 1,800 hours per year. After 1990, a gradual decline in hours continued in Canada; in the United States, hours effectively plateaued. By 2017, the last year of the study period documented in Table 3.1, Canadians were working an average of about sixty hours per year less than Americans. Very possibly the addition of new holidays accounts for much if not all of this difference, as there was no general statutory reduction in work hours in Canada at this point, but the period did see the addition of new holidays, such as Family Day. Perhaps the biggest difference between the two countries was Canada's use of work-sharing (involving reducing hours for all rather than laying off the newest hires) as a means of coping with high unemployment during the Great Recession of the early 1980s.[21] This difference may be more broadly related to Canada's generally more collective economy.

It would be interesting to contemplate what an hours comparison between Canada and the United States might look like in 2030, after nearly a decade of experimentation with various forms of shorter work week. While that is obviously not possible now, a look at work hours from around the world is instructive. A survey of global work hours is interesting both in and of itself, and also allows for a comparison of the Canadian and American hours just discussed with the situation in other countries around the world.

CHAPTER 4

Historical Development of Work Hours III: Work Hours Around the World

In general, as noted by Charlie Giattino et al.,[1] workers through the nineteenth century worked horrendous hours, by contemporary standards, no matter where they lived. In industrialized countries, weeks of sixty to seventy hours (corresponding to six days of ten to twelve hours) were the norm. In some cases, as discussed in the U.S. chapter, workers were even forced to work up to fourteen or more hours per day, or on Sundays, as in the case of the steel industry. While there were variations both by industry and by country, one may get some sense of just how bad things were in France from the fact that workers in that country considered the achievement of a twelve-hour day after the Revolution of 1848 to be a victory.[2]

The period from 1870 through 1913 (the beginning of the First World War) saw a gradual decline in hours worked, resulting from the efforts of the labour movement and a certain amount of protective legislation, often aimed specifically at working women and/or children.[3] From 1913 through 1929, the decline in hours was much steeper. It resulted from what became something close to a global consensus in favour of an eight-hour workday (albeit with a continuation, in most cases, of a six-day week), a consensus signified by, among other things, the passage of significant eight-hour legislation in the United States and the signing, in 1919, of an International Labour Organization convention on the eight-hour workday, a convention that would eventually be ratified by more than fifty countries worldwide.[4] After a bit of an uptick during the Second World War, which can likely be explained as a result of increased demand for labour needed for war production, hours resumed their long-term decline, but more slowly, after the war. The early postwar period saw most European countries as well as Australia and Canada adopt a five-day week — something the United States had already adopted before the war, as noted earlier — and by the 1970s and 1980s, quite a few European countries were moving to work weeks of less than forty hours, while many had also instituted far longer vacation entitlements than workers are used to in North America, often through employment standards legislation.[5]

Even with the growing differences in vacation entitlement, the big picture with regard to hours across the industrialized Western world, comprising Europe, the United States, Canada, and Australia — for which hours data can be traced back to 1870 — has remained remarkably similar for a group of thirteen countries. Information on developing countries in Asia, Africa, and Latin America has not been included because of an almost total lack of data from such countries for the period prior to 1950, which would make any comparisons between them and developed countries meaningless for the period considered here. The developing countries' work hour patterns will be discussed in some detail later in the chapter. While many of those countries have achieved some success in shortening work hours, for the most part they tend to feature significantly longer hours than those generally worked in industrialized Western countries.

Table 4.1 compares work hours for the aforementioned group of thirteen industrialized Western countries in three different years: 1870, 1929, 2017. The first year, 1870, was a sort of peak year of early industrialization, while 1929 represents the point at which most of the dramatic early shortening of work hours had been carried out, and 2017 is the last year for which there is full comparative data.

Historical Development of Work Hours III: Work Hours Around the World

TABLE 4.1: WORK HOURS, VACATION DAYS, AND PAID HOLIDAYS, SELECTED YEARS, VARIOUS DEVELOPED COUNTRIES

Country	1870	1929	2017	Days of Vacation	Paid Holidays
Australia	2792	2186	1731	20	7
Belgium	3483	2229	1584	20	10[a]
Canada	2845	2354	1696	10–15[b]	6–12[b]
Denmark	3434	2301	1400	25	11
France	3168	2198	1514	25	11–13
Germany	3284	2128	1354	20	9–17[c]
Italy	3000	2153	1723	20	12–22
Netherlands	3274	2253	1430	20–25	11
Spain	2968	2342	1686	23	8–14
Sweden	3436	2152	1609	25	13
Switzerland	3195	2281	1590	25	7–15[d]
United Kingdom	2755	2257	1670	20	8–10
United States	3076	2316	1796	0 (10)	0(8)[e]

Sources: Hours for 1870 and 1929: Huberman and Minns (2007). Hours for 2017: PWI 9.1 (2019), both as cited by Giattino, et al., 2020. For vacation and holiday entitlements, Zaric, "Paid Annual Leave per Country: Global Guide."

[a] Plus various regional holidays.
[b] Jurisdiction over vacation and holiday entitlement is provincial. All provinces require at least two weeks (ten days) of paid vacation per year. In Saskatchewan, the minimum is three weeks (15 days). Holiday entitlements vary significantly by province.
[c] Germany mandates nine national holidays and up to eight regional ones, depending on the state in which the employee works.
[d] Varies by canton.
[e] In the United States, there are no statutory minima for vacation and holiday entitlements at either state or federal level. Most employers grant a minimum of two weeks (ten days) of paid vacation, and eight paid holidays.

Table 4.1 shows that in most countries workers were working over three thousand hours a year in 1870. In some cases (e.g., Belgium, Denmark, and Sweden), they were working significantly more than that. The relatively shorter Canadian hours, which would increase during the century's final decades, were, as noted in the previous chapter, likely the result of delayed industrialization. For the shorter hours in the United Kingdom and Australia, a more positive explanation appears likely. In England, women and children had been granted a ten-hour day legislatively in 1847,[6] while in Australia as well as New Zealand, skilled workers had had some success in achieving an eight-hour day as early as the 1840s and 1850s.[7]

By 1929, the hours worked in the thirteen countries under study had become remarkably uniform, with only about two hundred hours — less than 10 percent — separating the countries with the highest and lowest average annual hours (Canada and Sweden, respectively). The number of hours worked would have been consistent with an eight-hour day and a work week of somewhere between five and one half and six days. The next chapter, on the 1920s, will offer more detail on how that decade brought about such uniform working hours around the world.

The figures for 2017 show significantly more variation than did those for 1929. In all cases, hours worked in the later year were significantly shorter than they had been in the earlier one. But now the thirteen countries cluster into three distinct groups: those with over 1,650 average annual hours, headed by the United States, whose 1,796 hours are actually more than the average for 1938, noted previously, and also including Australia (1,731), Italy (1,723), Canada (1,696), Spain (1,686), and the United Kingdom (1,670). In the middle are countries with between 1,500 and 1,650 average annual hours, including Sweden (1,609 hours), Switzerland (1,590), Belgium (1,584), and France (1,514). The countries with the fewest average annual hours include the Netherlands (1,430), Denmark (1,400), and Germany (1,354).

While the standard work week through the entire group of countries has remained relatively uniform, at somewhere between seven and eight hours per day for a five-day week, there are now important variations in the amount of paid vacation and holiday time. (See two right-hand columns of Table 4.1.) These variations likely have a significant effect, particularly at the top and bottom ends of the hours scale. For example, it should not come as a surprise that the United States, which has no statutory vacation and holiday minima at all, and where even those employers that do provide paid vacation time provide very little, by European standards, has

Historical Development of Work Hours III: Work Hours Around the World

the longest average hours of any country in the sample. It should also not come as a surprise that Canada, where the statutory minima for vacations (except in Saskatchewan) are half what they are in most European countries, also ranks relatively high on the list. At the other end of the scale, Denmark's minimum of twenty-five days (five weeks) of vacation, high even by European standards, undoubtedly helps explain why it ranks near the bottom in average annual hours worked.

· · · · · ·

The movement toward shorter hours has been underway for longer than most people realize. As early as 1594, King Philip II of Spain issued an edict establishing an eight-hour day for factory and fortification workers, with seven hours the maximum for mine workers. By the early nineteenth century, there were calls for an eight-hour day in England, and later in the nineteenth century that country passed legislation limiting the hours of work for women and children. The latter part of the nineteenth century saw select groups of skilled workers in Australia and New Zealand achieve the eight-hour day. By the 1920s, the eight-hour day had become the norm throughout the developed Western world, thanks to an International Labour Organization convention passed in 1919 and eventually adopted by more than fifty countries. The five-day week (including a two-day weekend) and significant vacation and holiday entitlements would not come until later in the twentieth century.

Table 4.2, below, lists some of the major landmarks of the move to shorter work hours in the developed world, outside of the United States and Canada. It will be useful to compare this list of landmarks to the list of landmarks in the developing world, which will be found later in the chapter.

TABLE 4.2: MAJOR LANDMARKS IN THE ESTABLISHMENT OF SHORTER WORK HOURS IN DEVELOPED COUNTRIES

1594	King Philip II of Spain issues a royal edict limiting daily hours of work to eight for workers in factories and on fortifications. The same conditions apply to Indigenous factory and fortification workers in Spanish America. Mine workers are limited to a daily maximum of seven hours.
1810	English industrialist Robert Owen raises the demand for a ten-hour day and institutes such a day in his "socialist" enterprise at New Lanark.
1817	Owen first promotes the goal of an eight-hour day.
1833	The British Factory Act limits work hours for children employed in factories. Those between nine and thirteen years of age can work only eight hours a day; those between fourteen and eighteen years of age are limited to twelve hours. Children under nine are required to attend school.
1841	The French "Monarchy Law" prohibits the employment of children under age eight at any time, and of those under thirteen for night-time work. (Admittedly, the law is routinely flouted.)
Early nineteenth century	British factory owners in the industrial north of the country start allowing their workers to leave at 2 p.m. Saturday, on the understanding that they will report for work sober and refreshed on Monday morning. Previously, many workers had spent much of their one day of rest (Sunday) drinking, leaving them unfit for work on Monday. This marks the beginning of the weekend as it exists today.
1847	England passes legislation limiting the workday for women and children to ten hours.
1848	Following the revolution of 1848, French workers achieve a twelve-hour day.
1856	Stonemasons in Melbourne strike over working hours, eventually winning an eight-hour day.
1857	Building trades workers in New Zealand achieve an eight-hour day.
1866	The International Workingmen's Association takes up the demand for an eight-hour day at its congress in Geneva.

Historical Development of Work Hours III: Work Hours Around the World

1879	First recorded use of the term "weekend," in the British magazine *Notes and Queries*.[8]
1882	The first Eight Hours Day holiday is granted by the South Australia government; it is celebrated the following year on September 9. A similar holiday will be established in New Zealand in 1899.
1889	Beckton (East London) gas workers achieve an eight-hour day after a strike against compulsory eighteen-hour shifts.
1910	German *Kurzarbeit* (shorter work hours compensation) plan is introduced in the potash mining and fertilizer industries, as a means of reducing unemployment in those industries. It will become fully established in 1924. Similar plans are now in effect in Austria and the Czech Republic.
1919	Passage of the International Labour Organization's Hours of Work (Industry) Convention at the organization's conference in Philadelphia. This convention, which proposed the application of the principle of the eight-hour day or of the forty-eight-hour week, will eventually be ratified by more than fifty countries, though, ironically, it is never ratified by the United States, the host country for the conference. Most countries will ratify the convention within the first five years after its passage, though there are a few laggards.
1936	French president Léon Blum introduces a forty-hour week and a requirement of two weeks' paid vacation. The French learn how to "do vacations," proving extremely apt students! Surprisingly, the vacation entitlement is left in place under the Vichy regime of Marshal Pétain despite Pétain's personal opposition to the idea.
1938	Passage of the Danish Holiday Act, outlining laws businesses must adhere to, to protect their employees' rights to vacation and paid holidays.
1947	The eight-hour day takes effect in Japan, with the passage of that country's Labour Standards Act.
1950s and 1960s	General move to a five-day week across Europe.
c. 1970	German businessman and social entrepreneur Wilhelm (Willi) Haller starts developing time-recording equipment, which measures the actual length of time an employee has worked and allows for the development of flexible and variable hours work schedules. By the late 1970s, the concept of flextime (*Gleitzeit*) has become immensely popular throughout the country, to the point where it is often seen on bumper stickers.

1982	The Socialist government of French president François Mitterrand increases vacation leave to five weeks and cuts the work week from forty to thirty-nine hours. It wished to cut the work week to thirty-five hours but was deterred from doing so by the parlous state of the economy.
1984	IG Metall, Germany's largest union and a national trendsetter on work hours, stages a successful seven-week strike for a thirty-five-hour work week (down from thirty-seven) in the states of Baden-Württemberg and Hesse.
1986	Norway shifts to a seven-and-a-half-hour day.
1993	A European Union Working Time Directive requires that employees in all EU member states receive at least twenty days of paid vacation per year.
2000	The Netherlands passes a law allowing workers to shift to a part-time work schedule while retaining their job, hourly pay, health care, and pro-rated benefits.
2000	France introduces a thirty-five-hour week through the Aubry Law, named after the country's labour minister, Martine Aubry.
2018	Successful IG Metall strike in Germany earns workers of both sexes a two-year, twenty-eight-hour work week during their period of parental leave, with the right to return to full-time employment on conclusion of that leave.
2020	Revisions to the Danish Holiday Act come into force. These revisions require employers to give their employees a minimum of five weeks' paid vacation per year.

The work hours developments listed above are but a small sample of the developments that have taken place in the industrialized Western world over the past two centuries. Unfortunately, there isn't space here to comment on these developments in the detail they deserve, let alone to list other, perhaps equally noteworthy developments in the shorter hours movement.

A few general tendencies are worth brief mention. As the first part of Table 4.2 shows, governments not infrequently granted shorter hours to women and children before granting them to the labour force as a whole. (The same tendency often applied in the United States, as well.) It's also worth noting that quite a number of the early shorter hours "victories" were won by strong unions of skilled workers, generally workers possessed of relatively scarce skills, and that it would typically require several decades for the gains won by these workers to be applied to the work force as a whole. Finally, most of the recent shorter hours gains have been the result of legislation passed by sympathetic socialist or otherwise left-oriented governments, such as those in many Scandinavian countries or the French governments of Léon Blum and François Mitterrand.

Germany would appear to be an exception. There, major gains have been achieved as a result of strike action by IG Metall. But IG Metall is not the same kind of union as were the Australian, British, and New Zealand craft unions that first won shorter hours for their members in the nineteenth century. This broad-based industrial union is a conglomerate, boasting members from many different industrial sectors. As a result of the German system of concertation (co-determination), it typically works closely with German governments, particularly those of a social democratic persuasion, and over the years, its strikes have been relatively rare. It has assumed a national leadership role on the issue of work hours, tending to be a trendsetter for other unions. Its goal has long been the achievement of shorter work hours for all of German society, not just for the fortunate few who happen to be its members.

With the exception of the United States and, to a lesser extent, Canada, most developed countries in the industrialized Western world have continued to move toward a shorter work week. In most, a shorter work week is considered desirable, at least in principle. Outside of the developed Western world, there is no consensus regarding the desirability of shorter hours. There are countries, particularly in the Pacific Rim of Asia, where many workers are forced to put in the kind of hours not generally seen in North America since before the First World War. While these countries typically have some kind of protective labour law in place to limit work hours and mandatory overtime, such laws may more often be honoured in the breach than in the observance, as government agencies look the other way, fearful of offending the giant tech companies that routinely flout those laws. In Latin America, which in other respects shows considerable inter-country variation in its hours laws, a six-day week remains the norm, as it was a century ago. And in much of Eastern Europe (including Russia), hours laws are relatively progressive, more or less along the lines of Western European laws, and tend to offer workers reasonable protection against exploitative overwork. A feature found in several Eastern European laws is some form of "time banking," which allows workers the right to accumulate overtime and receive it, sometimes in big enough chunks that they could be called "sabbaticals," in the form of compensatory time off rather than money. Time banking will be discussed in more detail later; it is a concept that has promise in the North American as well as European context.

To say that progress at achieving shorter hours has not been uniform would be to understate things considerably. That many people continue to work longer hours than they should, even well into the twenty-first century, is a fact of life. In 2007, nearly ninety years after the International Labour Organization's convention calling for an eight-hour day, one of the ILO's own studies found that at least 614.2 million people around the world worked "excessive" hours, by which the ILO meant hours in excess of forty-eight per week — the norm in 1919.[9] One can only imagine what this figure would have been had the norm been forty hours per week — the standard in the developed world at least since the 1960s.

A detailed look at the development of work hours between 1951 and 2017 in countries outside of Europe and North America (see Table 4.3) confirms the existence of an extremely varied pattern.

Through 1971, in most of the countries for which there exist data, workers were working quite long hours by contemporary standards. As late as 1971, three countries — South Korea, Hong Kong, and Thailand — had an average of more than 2,400 annual work hours, a figure consistent with at least an eight-hour day and six-day week, or a longer day if all or part of Saturday was a rest day. While 1980 brought modest hours reductions to work hours in Chile, Colombia, Brazil, Hong Kong, and Singapore, there were increases — in the case of South Korea and Thailand, large ones of the order of 10 percent — in several other countries. The increases brought

TABLE 4.3: WORK HOURS, VARIOUS ASIAN, LATIN AMERICAN, AND EASTERN EUROPEAN COUNTRIES, SELECTED YEARS 1951-2017

Country	1951	1960	1971	1980	1990	2000	2010	2017
Chile	2655	2480	2393	2366	2422	2263	2070	1974
Taiwan	2372	2354	2331	2314	2231	2180	2063	1990
Greece	2303	2228	2100	2112	2112	2108	2020	2017
Columbia	2302	2218	2168	2074	1969	1956	2039	1998
Venezuela	2147	2024	1956	1997	1889	1897	—	—
Brazil	2051	2134	2129	1985	1879	1838	1780	1703
Hong Kong	—	2722	2527	2479	2677	2509	2157	2063
Singapore	—	2297	2246	2183	2327	2463	2373	2238
South Korea	—	2453	2625	2864	2677	2509	2157	2063
Thailand	—	—	2455	2710	2580	2503	2349	2185
Bangladesh	—	—	2075	2099	2122	2217	2250	2232
China	—	—	1976	1971	1975	2090	2173	2174
Sri Lanka	—	—	1894	1962	1981	2001	1872	1934
Hungary	—	—	—	2193	1945	2033	1956	1937
Vietnam	—	—	—	2630	2643	2394	2300	2170
Costa Rica	—	—	—	—	2364	2368	2249	2212
Slovakia	—	—	—	—	1828	1816	1805	1745
Uruguay	—	—	—	—	1788	1704	1590	1552
Jamaica	—	—	—	—	1938	1963	1966[a]	—
Bulgaria	—	—	—	—	—	1640	1645	1644
Russia	—	—	—	—	1933[b]	1982	1976	1974

Sources: Huberman and Minns (2007) and PWI 9.1 (2019), both as cited by Giattino, et al., 2020.

[a] = Data are for 2012.
[b] = Data are for 1992.
A blank line in any given cell indicates there are no data available for that year and country.

South Korea to an average of 2,864 hours and Thailand to one of 2,710, with newcomer Vietnam joining them in the long-hours club, with an average of 2,630. The figures for South Korea and Thailand would have been consistent with a nine-and-a-half or even ten-hour day and a six-day week, or even longer hours if Saturday were made a full or partial day of rest. All three of these countries had hours significantly longer than those worked in 1929 by any of the countries in the group of thirteen developed, largely Western European and North American countries listed in Table 4.1, and only slightly below the 2,900 worked by the average American worker in 1900 (see chapter 2).

The year 1990 would see some reduction in the hours worked in South Korea, Thailand, and Taiwan, as well as in the Latin American countries of Venezuela and Brazil. But hours rose in Singapore, Hong Kong, and Chile, and were pretty much unchanged in Bangladesh, China, Vietnam, and Sri Lanka. There were still five countries (Hong Kong, Thailand, South Korea, Vietnam, and Chile) where workers were putting in an average of more than 2,400 hours per year. Overall, the situation was something close to a wash, as compared to 1980.

Would the new millennium bring about nirvana for the workers of the world? Not exactly. While there were worthwhile (defined as at least 3 percent) hours reductions in Chile, Taiwan, Hong Kong, South Korea, and Thailand, as well as 1990 newcomer Uruguay, hours increased in Singapore, Bangladesh, China, and Hungary. In many other countries, they remained basically unchanged. At the turn of the millennium, Hong Kong (2,509 hours), South Korea (2,509), Thailand (2,503), and Singapore (2,463) all maintained national annual averages in excess of 2,400 hours — a figure, once again, greater than that found in any of the developed countries surveyed in 1929.

The year 2010 is the first in which overall progress toward shorter hours is observable in the sample as a whole. That year saw large drops (of the order of 15 percent) in average hours worked in South Korea and Hong Kong, and smaller but still worthwhile drops in Taiwan, Chile, Greece, Brazil, Costa Rica, Uruguay, Singapore, and Sri Lanka. Hours did increase by a non-trivial amount (more than 3 percent) in Colombia and China, but the

Historical Development of Work Hours III: Work Hours Around the World

trend overall was positive. Eight countries, including some in Latin America as well as Eastern Europe, had, by that point, an average of fewer than two thousand annual work hours, no country had an average over 2,400 hours, and only three (Singapore at 2,373, Thailand at 2,349, and Vietnam at an even 2,300) had averages of 2,300 or more.

The positive trend would continue through 2017, the last year considered in this study. This time, a single country (Sri Lanka) showed an increase over the previous period, and it was a relatively modest one, from 1,872 to 1,934 average annual hours. There were continued declines in high-hours havens Vietnam, Thailand, South Korea, and Singapore. And there were now even more (nine) countries with averages below two thousand hours, despite the removal from the sample of two countries that in 2010 had had averages below two thousand. Best of all, peak hours had continued to drop; there were just three countries with annual averages over 2,200 hours (Singapore, 2,238; Bangladesh, 2,232; and Costa Rica, 2,212). No country had an annual average over 2,250 hours; no country was averaging more annual hours than the developed countries in the sample had in 1929. While this might seem like a modest milestone, and progress toward it had been slow, the figures for 2017 do represent a major improvement over those for 1951, or even those for 1980 or 1990.

For a better understanding of this, it is useful to focus in more detail on a few countries that, for better or for worse, have been trendsetters with regard to work hours. The discussion starts with Asia, generally acknowledged to have some of the world's longest work hours.

Asia

As Table 4.3 notes, as late as 2000, four Asian countries had average annual working hours in excess of 2,400; in three of them, the figure was over 2,500. Such long hours are characteristic of countries in the early stages of industrialization. South Korea, for example, only began transforming itself from an agricultural to an industrial, high-tech, and service-oriented economy in the 1960s.[10] A feature of early industrial legislation that has survived to the present day in some Asian countries is special protective legislation for women workers. In Bangladesh, for instance, women cannot be required to work between 10 p.m. and 6 a.m.[11] Similarly, in Sri Lanka, night work is banned for all female workers; for male workers, on the other hand, this ban only applies to those between the ages of fourteen and eighteen. With regard to limiting the number of work hours, a similar distinction between male and female workers is found. All females working in shops or offices are barred from working more than nine hours in a day (including breaks), but this restriction applies only to those male workers in shops and offices under eighteen years of age.[12] Readers will recall that in North America work hours restrictions for women (and children) came into effect well before restrictions covering all workers.

Table 4.3 shows that South Korea's hours increased steadily (by about two hundred hours per decade) between 1960 and 1980. Even in 2000, South Korean workers were putting in longer hours, on average, than they had in 1960. While the country's Labor Standards Act sets a statutory maximum of forty hours, up to fifty-two hours is legal with overtime. In any case, enforcement of the act is weak and violations are routinely ignored. South Korean workplaces can be particularly difficult places for women workers, who often face the double burden of extra family responsibilities at home and of having to conform to a traditional, male-dominated hierarchical culture at work.

To call the country a "high-hours haven" is to understate the situation. In 2022, incoming president Yoon Suk Yeol criticized outgoing president Moon Jae-in's fifty-two-hour limitation, saying that people should be allowed to work 120 hours a week and then take a good rest.[13] Such a comment hardly seems appropriate in a country in which there were already reports of delivery workers dying from overwork.[14] Since then, Yoon has formalized his desire to see Koreans work longer hours, in March 2023 introducing a policy that would increase the maximum allowable work week by about one-third, to sixty-nine hours.[15] While the plan puts monthly, quarterly, and yearly caps on the number of working hours, it nonetheless increases the likelihood of overwork-related deaths, in the view of a Samsung-affiliated employee. The opposition Democratic Party, which brought in the fifty-two-hour week during its time in office in 2018, has also noted that the plan risks increasing unemployment "as it could allow employers to lay off workers and ask those who stay to work longer."

Having long ranked among the world's leaders in hours worked, South Korea continued to do so in 2020, placing fourth in an OECD member survey behind only Mexico, Costa Rica, and Colombia. While South Korea has achieved major progress in work hours reduction since 1980, dropping its average annual hours by nearly 40 percent, to a 2017 figure of 2,063, the election of a flamboyantly workaholic president like Yoon doesn't augur well for its future progress in hours reduction. And neither, certainly, does the new longer work week plan proposed by Yoon.

Singapore is (like China, to be discussed shortly) a country in which the promise of seemingly reasonable statutory regulation of work hours is belied by the realities of a profoundly work-obsessed culture.[16] There is a statutory maximum of eight hours of work per day and forty-four per week in the country's Employment Act. But the act applies only to workers earning below a certain income threshold. There are no hours restrictions at all on those earning a salary above that threshold. It also doesn't apply to domestics, sailors, and most government staff, or to managers, executives, and professionals such as lawyers, doctors, dentists, and accountants.[17] Indeed, the Singapore act is more distinguished by those it excludes from coverage than by those it includes. As a result, it is not uncommon for Singapore employees to work nine to ten hours a day on weekdays and half-days on Saturdays, which adds up to fifty to fifty-five hours per week; as a general rule, office employees work from 9 a.m. until 6 or 7 p.m., depending on industry and company policies.[18]

An Instant Group study, which found Singapore the most overworked country in the Asia-Pacific region, noted that the average Singapore worker was putting in an average of forty-five hours per week and received only seven days of annual leave, which is well below the minimum in any country with a minimum standard annual leave entitlement. The same study found levels of burnout and stated intention to leave one's job very high. Over three-quarters (76 percent) of respondents wanted a four-day week to reduce overwork.[19]

Unlike Singapore, Hong Kong doesn't even pretend to have reasonable hours regulations. For the most part, it has no hours regulations at all. Except for certain specific classes of workers, notably bus drivers and security personnel,[20] Hong Kong has no statutory work week, maximum hours, or overtime regulations for adult workers, and it doesn't appear likely to get any anytime soon. [21] Perhaps not surprisingly, given its near-total lack of hours regulation, Hong Kong was recently named the world's most overworked city in a Work-Life Balance Cities Ranking by BDO, with 30 percent of its workers putting in more than forty-eight hours per week.[22] In the city's service sector, the six-day week still dominates, and intense social pressure combined with an overtime culture sees many employees working late as well as on weekends.

Hong Kong also quite transparently condones child labour, although it does go to the extent of regulating the number of hours children can work, which is more than it generally does with adults. Children under thirteen cannot work during school hours on school days but are permitted to work two hours on school days or four on non-school days during the term. Outside of the school term, they can't work more than eight hours per day (including breaks). Children between thirteen and fifteen can't work more than eight hours per day, including breaks, or at night between 7 p.m. and 7 a.m. There is no requirement that they be in school. Children between fifteen and eighteen are limited to a weekly maximum of forty-eight hours and are also barred from night work. [23]

Some of the most spectacular examples of abusive work hours have come from China, although there have recently been signs that, as noted in a BBC article by Yip Wai-yee,[24] a "tipping point" has been reached, and the government is finally prepared to act to halt egregious violations of its hours legislation. In principle, that legislation is quite reasonable. Chapter 4 of the Labour Law of the People's Republic of China stipulates a maximum normal working day of eight hours and working week of forty-four hours. Overtime is permitted but is limited, with premiums ranging from 50 to 200 percent of workers' wages depending on whether the overtime is worked on an ordinary workday, a day of rest, or a public holiday.[25]

All of this sounds quite reasonable — in theory. But again, as in many other developing countries, the eminently reasonable labour law is more often honoured in the breach than in the observance. In reality, hours, particularly in the technology sector, have generally been set by people like tech tycoon Jack Ma, who notoriously declared it a blessing for workers to be part of the "996" work culture, meaning they work from 9 a.m. to 9 p.m. six days a week.[26] There are a variety of other "long hours" cultures in place in China, some even more intensive than 996. At least forty companies have adopted 996 or some similar system.[27]

The extremely deleterious effects of 996 and its kindred systems, which included some workers actually dropping dead "in harness" from overwork and others committing suicide, did not go unnoticed by either Chinese workers or the general public.[28] Among other things, the "lying flat" movement to be discussed in more detail in chapter 7 was a direct response to the 996 culture, with its spokesperson Luo Huazhong publicly and pointedly asking, "Do we have to work twelve hours a day in a sweatshop, and is that justice?" Nor has Luo been the only Chinese worker to protest against long hours. In 2019 a group of programmers made headlines when they launched a campaign on code-sharing platform Github, banning start-ups that overworked staff from using their open-source code.[29] Still, the Chinese government maintained a largely hands-off attitude to these flagrant violations of the Labour Law — until August of 2021. Then, in a joint statement, China's top court and labour ministry detailed ten court decisions related to labour disputes, many involving workers being forced to work overtime. The cases covered various scenarios across a wide range of sectors, from tech to the media and construction. What they all had in common was that the employers lost, every time. "Legally, workers have the right to corresponding compensation and rest times or holidays. Complying with national working hours is the obligation of employers," the government warned, adding that further guidelines would be developed to resolve future labour disputes.[30]

The extent to which the threat of further government action will put a stop to the country's longstanding tradition of abusive, exploitive work hours remains to be seen, although initial signs are hopeful. For example, in August 2021, smartphone maker Vivo said it would scrap its "big/small weeks" practice of alternating five- and six-day weeks in favour of five day weeks for all.[31] Yip suggests that the court decisions will make it likelier that in the future workers will feel more emboldened to take their employers to court for hours violations.[32] It also remains to be seen whether a new pattern of government enforcement of hours laws will emerge in the countries close to China, now that such a pattern has apparently been started in the region's largest and most powerful country.

Other Asian countries may not have gone quite as far as China has in exploiting its workers, but long hours are still the norm throughout most of the region. In Vietnam, for example, the Labour Code sets maxima of eight hours a day and forty-eight hours a week, with a reduction to six hours a day for those "working in heavy, noxious, or dangerous conditions."[33] However, the ILO, in one of its discussion papers,[34] found Vietnamese workers putting in long hours, hours virtually unchanged — from an average of 47.5 to 47.4 hours — between 2013 and 2018.[35] The study found some 61.4 percent of workers putting in between forty-five and fifty-four hours per week, while just 18.6 percent worked forty hours.

A more recent study[36] came up with a slightly more precise formulation of the average Vietnamese working week. This study suggests that a normal working day starts between 7 and 8:30 a.m. and ends between 4 and 6 p.m., with long lunch breaks of at least one and a half hours and a 12:00 noon quitting time on Saturday. While the lunch break may make the long working hours slightly more tolerable, these still seem like extremely long hours by Western standards.

Thailand has a maximum work week of forty-eight hours (eight six-hour days), or forty-two hours if the work is hazardous; it also features a steep premium for overtime work. On the other hand, the minimum annual leave is just six days for Thais — an extremely low figure by any standard.[37] Like Singapore and South Korea, Thailand has regularly ranked among the world leaders in hours worked (see Table 4.3 for details).

Bangladesh has, in principle, a more reasonable law regulating hours;[38] there are, however, questions about how thoroughly that law is enforced.[39] Bangladesh labour law sets normal hours of work at eight per day with a maximum of forty-eight per week for adult workers. Work beyond normal hours is subject to an overtime premium of 100 percent. It appears that the six-day week is normal, and workers are permitted to work up to a maximum

Historical Development of Work Hours III: Work Hours Around the World

of ten hours per day (including overtime) with a maximum of ten hours per week of overtime. Like a number of other Asian countries, Bangladesh has special regulations governing women, who may not be required to work between 10 p.m. and 6 a.m. Significantly, it does not allow anyone to work in more than one establishment on the same day.

Sri Lanka's hours regulations include a number of features found elsewhere in the region, such as special hours for women and young workers. According to the regulations, normal hours of work cannot be more than eight in a day or forty-five in a week, again suggesting that at least some Saturday work is normal. Also, employers cannot require employees to work more than twelve hours in any day. However, daily hours limits don't apply to anyone holding a managerial or executive position in a public institution or who has a salary above a given threshold. Night work is illegal for male workers aged fourteen to eighteen and all female workers in shops and offices, and males under eighteen and females of any age cannot be required to work more than nine hours a day (including breaks) in shops and offices.[40]

Somewhat surprisingly, given the generally long hours allowed under the country's labour law, Sri Lanka recently made headlines when it provided a four-day week to the country's public sector workers.[41] However, this was not a standard four-day week, designed to allow workers more time for rest and recreation with their families and to pursue hobbies. The purpose of this week, at a time of serious food shortages across the country, was to allow public sector workers to spend the day growing food. Whether the experiment will be a success is an open question, given that many Sri Lanka public sector workers do not own land, while others must travel long distances to reach land suitable for growing crops, which would be of questionable efficacy. It is also possible that the provision could become a source of resentment for other workers not qualifying for a four-day week.

Latin America

Latin American countries offer a wide variety of approaches to work hours, ranging from Mexico, where recent newspaper articles have boasted of the benefits of the six-day week, to Jamaica, where work on Sunday earns no more of an overtime premium than work on any other day, and to Uruguay, which has both a daily and a weekly limit on permissible total hours and where there are special gynecological and blood donation leaves. The one thing that most of the region's countries have in common is a six-day (or at least five-and-a-half day) work week.

Like much of the world, Mexico officially adopted an eight-hour day and six-day week early in the twentieth century. In 1931 Article 131 of the Mexican Constitution, originally written during the Mexican Revolution of 1910–1920, came into force. This article provided (among other things) for an eight-hour day.[42] Unlike most other countries, however, Mexico has seen no further reduction in its work week in the intervening ninety years. The country, unlike any other that I have researched, publishes articles boasting of its long-hours status. An undated Centris article on the benefits of the six-day week, making an implicit comparison between Mexico and the United States, where the five-day week became the norm before the Second World War, says, "Although our work week is longer, we have the benefit of enjoying a generous vacation schedule that provides the rest and rejuvenation needed after many weeks of hard work."

What exactly is that vacation schedule? It provides for a minimum of six days' annual leave after one year — comparable to the leave allotments found in such workers' paradises as Singapore and Thailand — increasing by two days per year up to four years, after which it increases by two days every five years. The Centris article also refers to the "generous" number of paid holidays (eight) allowed under Mexican law. Again, this is fewer than would be found in most other countries; it is only generous in comparison with the United States, which as noted earlier has no statutory minimum for annual leave or paid holidays. Employers do, however, grant annual leave and paid holidays; the average figure, as noted in Table 2.2 above, is ten days' leave and eight paid holidays. (I would invite the reader to consider whether these "generous" holiday and vacation benefits, minimal even by typical American standards, really make up for an extra day of work every week.)

Another recent article on Mexican work hours and labour law, while stopping short of offering outright praise for long hours, did extol the fact that "Mexican labour laws allow the flexibility for employers to adopt work shifts and weeks to ensure maximum productivity and take advantage of the savings Mexico's labor rates offer."[43] Put nicely, this would appear to be acknowledgment of the fact that Mexico has become a low-wage haven.

Another Latin American country whose workers routinely put in long hours is Costa Rica. There, as in Mexico, the normal work week consists of six eight-hour days. Overtime is permitted to a maximum of four additional hours (more in case of emergency) and is subject to a premium of 50 percent of the worker's regular wage. Those who work on their usual day of rest receive twice their regular rate of pay.[44] A 2017 OECD study found that Costa Rican workers achieved the unenviable distinction of working the second longest hours of those in any country in the organization, with an average of 2,112 annual hours. Only Mexican workers were putting in more hours.[45] To date, there are no signs that Costa Rica plans to shorten its working hours.

At the other end of the spectrum is Uruguay, which in 1915 became the first country in the world to adopt the eight-hour day, even in advance of the ILO Convention.[46] To be sure, the forty-eight-hour week is the norm, with a standard work week of forty-eight hours in industry and forty-four in commerce.[47] In both, a weekly thirty-six-hour rest period is required, which strongly suggests that a five-and-a-half-day work week (with a half day on Saturday) is the norm, as it was in North America during the years immediately prior to the Second World War. Child labour is quite strictly regulated, with an outright prohibition on labour for children under fourteen, and the stipulation that even those sixteen and over can only work if they have completed nine years of school — a clear statement that education comes first in Uruguay.

Leaving aside the absence of a five-day work week, which appears to be found almost nowhere in Latin America, Uruguay offers a progressive slate of benefits, in many ways more closely comparable to those found in Europe than to those found in the rest of the region. There is a minimum annual leave requirement of four weeks, with additional leave for workers with more than five years' seniority, and the country has in addition fifteen annual public holidays. Overtime is governed by a "double maximum" threshold of eight hours per day and forty-eight per week, and there is a steep premium for overtime work. Beyond that, Uruguayan law provides one of the world's broadest range of benefits, including study leave, gynecological leave, and blood donation leave.[48]

In between come countries such as Brazil, Colombia, and Chile. Brazil has what is, for the region, fairly standard hours maxima of eight hours per day and forty-four per week, with shorter hours prescribed for members of certain occupational groups. Regular bank employees and telemarketing operators can work only six hours a day, while musicians are limited to five. Employees may be required to work only up to a maximum of two hours a day overtime, at a premium of 50 percent of their regular wage, or 70 percent for night work. Overtime beyond two hours in a day requires labour ministry approval.[49]

As for Colombia, through 2021 it had the longest statutory hours in the OECD, with norms of eight hours per day and forty-eight per week. But in 2021 it passed a law providing for a phased reduction in weekly hours, to forty-two hours per week between 2023 and 2026, the idea being to allow employers plenty of time to adapt to the new legislation. A flexible hours provision has made it possible for work to be done over five or six days, and this provision remains in force. However, the maximum daily number of hours that can be worked under this provision has been reduced from ten to nine. Special hours restrictions apply to adolescent workers. Those aged fifteen to seventeen can only work a maximum of six hours per day and thirty per week, and not after 6 p.m. Those aged over seventeen can only work a maximum of eight hours per day and forty per week, and not after 8 p.m.[50]

Chile's situation is similar to that of Colombia. Currently, it has long working hours but is in the process of shortening them legislatively. Under Chile's current regime, the weekly norm for work hours is forty-five per week, which can be worked in either five or six days. But legislation first introduced in 2017 (and then stalled in the country's Congress) and reintroduced in 2022 by newly elected socialist president Gabriel Boric would shorten the work week to forty hours in phased reductions of one hour per year over five years. The bill, which fulfills one of Boric's campaign promises,

Historical Development of Work Hours III: Work Hours Around the World

has now become law following an overwhelming vote in favour by Chile's Congress on April 11, 2023.[51]

Jamaica is of considerable interest because it has had in place for some eight years a flexible hours system, of the sort that many hours reformers would advocate. At the same time, the system illustrates some of the potential pitfalls of flexibility. The Jamaican law, the Employment (Flexible Work Arrangements) (Miscellaneous) Provisions Bill, came into effect in November 2014.

Under the Jamaican system, work hours remain forty per week, as they were prior to the new legislation, but instead of fixed schedules, an employee can negotiate with their employer a starting and quitting time, the number of hours to be worked each day, the number of days to be worked each week, and the days on which the employee is expected to work. Telecommuting is also explicitly permitted under the new law. Perhaps most importantly, there are no limitations as to the hours when work can be performed. Shops, for instance, can remain open twenty-four hours a day if they wish, though workers cannot be required to work more than twelve hours a day in those shops.

Overtime in excess of forty hours per week still requires a premium payment of 50 percent of the employee's regular wage. But overtime in excess of eight hours a day (up to a maximum of twelve) only draws straight pay, so long as the weekly maximum has not been reached. Importantly, Sunday, for which employers previously had to pay workers double their normal wages, is no longer a special day with regard to overtime. While workers must still receive double pay for working on a holiday or vacation day, work on Sunday is paid at the same rate as work on a weekday. The 2014 legislation also got rid of provisions barring women from night work.

It remains to be seen whether the Jamaican model is one that North American employers and workers would care to adopt, but it is certainly different from most other models, and in my view warrants careful study at a time when we are looking to improve productivity and reduce stress on workers.

Other Countries

Overall, the work hours in countries in Eastern Europe and Africa fall somewhere in between the moderate hours worked in most Western European countries and the very long ones worked in most Asian countries, with countries in the northern part of Eastern Europe coming closer to the Western European regimes, while those in Africa and the southern part of Eastern Europe are closer to the Asian regimes.

Slovakia has a fairly progressive but, in most respects, unremarkable work hours regime. There is a standard eight-hour day and forty-hour week; employees' average working time including overtime cannot exceed forty-eight hours. There are fifteen public holidays and a minimum annual leave entitlement of four weeks. The most notable feature of Slovakia's work hours regulation is its "working time" account, which allows for compensation (in paid time off) for accumulated overtime. An employer can introduce such an account only through a collective agreement or an agreement with employees' representatives. Such "time banking," which as noted earlier was initially introduced in certain German industries early in the twentieth century, is a distinctive feature of several Eastern European work hours regimes.[52]

Hungary's work hours regime is generally similar to Slovakia's, though it appears to give employers a few additional options for increasing hours. Normal work time is eight hours per day or forty-eight per week, inclusive of overtime. Employers and employees can agree to increase daily working hours to a maximum of twelve per day for employees working on-call or who are close relatives of the employer. (This last is *not* a provision I think Canada should replicate!)

Like workers in Slovakia, those in Hungary get a minimum of four weeks' annual leave. And as in Slovakia, overtime hours can be banked. A working time bank allows employees to save and combine their working time, earned time off, or monetary benefits converted to time off and also allows them to accumulate longer periods of time off in the bank, which they can then use for purposes such as travel or study sabbaticals. Under the time-banking system, employers have considerable flexibility to adjust hours

Historical Development of Work Hours III: Work Hours Around the World

to meet demand (by asking workers to work more overtime). But even under this provision, a twelve-hour day is the maximum allowable.[53]

Bulgaria has the same basic work week structure as Slovakia and Hungary, but like Hungary allows employers a number of ways to increase regular hours. Its standard week is five eight-hour days. Employees can be made to work a maximum of twelve hours in a shift or fifty-six per week; in addition, there is normally a maximum of 150 overtime hours per year, although this can be extended, via a collective agreement, to three hundred hours per year. Extended workdays are allowed, up to a maximum of ten hours per day, but only up to a maximum of twenty consecutive working days or sixty days in a calendar year. The time worked during these extended days must be made up, in the form of reduced hours, within four months of the date when the extended hours were worked. Thus, while the Bulgarian regime grants employers some flexibility to accommodate hours to demand, it also seeks to ensure that the cumulative effect of overwork is not too great, by insisting on repayment in the form of time off.[54]

Russia was among the first countries in the world to introduce an eight-hour day, having done so just four days after its October Revolution in 1917. It would re-introduce the eight-hour day on a number of occasions between 1928 and 1957.[55] Its work hours are currently regulated by the Labor Code of 2001.[56]

The standard Russian work week is forty hours. There are fourteen paid holidays per year, and employees receive a minimum of twenty-eight days' annual leave, with an additional seven days' paid holidays for those working under hazardous conditions or in the Far North or other equivalent regions.

Overtime cannot exceed four hours in two consecutive days or 120 hours per year for each employee. It is payable at one and a half times the employee's regular rate of pay for the first two hours, and double that rate for any subsequent hours. At the employee's request, overtime may be "paid" as time off rather than in money, and the amount of time off provided under this arrangement cannot be less than the overtime hours worked. Night shifts are one hour shorter than day shifts. Each employee's work week must include a rest period of at least forty-two hours (this suggests that a certain amount of Saturday work is contemplated, or at least condoned). That said, those working on a weekend must receive at least double their regular rate of pay, though the "payment" can be made in the form of time as well as money.

The four remaining countries studied, Israel, Greece, Turkey, and South Africa, all have tougher work hours regimes than any of the Eastern European countries just discussed. Of these, the most moderate is that of Israel, which as of 2018 has a forty-two-hour work week. Many Israelis work five days of 8.4 hours; some work a five-and-a-half-day week, with a half day on Friday morning. Workers must have at least thirty-six hours of consecutive rest each week.[57]

The lot of Turkish workers is a good deal harder. There, forty-five hours is a standard work week and those hours are divided equally among the days of the week. Saturday work is common. A special feature of the Turkish regime is that those working in radiological clinics are entitled to an additional half day of leave. Night shifts are limited to seven and a half hours.

Overtime, which should only be given with the employee's consent, should not exceed 270 hours per year, and is subject to a premium of 50 percent of the employee's hourly wage. Sundays are considered weekly holidays. The weekly holiday must begin no later than 1 p.m. Saturday and last at least thirty-five hours. There are nine official religious and public holidays; those working on such holidays must receive double pay. Vacation leave is on a sliding scale, ranging from a minimum of fourteen days to a maximum of twenty-six days. For employees under age twenty or over fifty, twenty days is the minimum.[58]

There appear to be a number of significant issues associated with working in Turkey.[59] Among other things, an OECD wellbeing survey based on data compiled in May 2017 found 39 percent of Turkish employees working what the OECD describes as "very long" hours (fifty or more per week), which was three times the organization's average of 13 percent. At the same time, overall labour force participation was low in Turkey, at just 50 percent of those aged fifteen to sixty-four, compared to an OECD average of 66 percent. There were also large gender gaps in women's participation, pay, and job quality, with many more women than men working in the informal sector. Given the above data, it seems worth considering whether bringing

Historical Development of Work Hours III: Work Hours Around the World

more women into the labour force might help reduce hours for all Turkish workers, by increasing the available supply of labour.

Like Turkey, South Africa is a long way from being a workers' paradise. Its work week is a maximum of forty-five hours, which can be worked in five nine-hour days, or in eight-hour days if the employee works more than five days per week. The daily lunch hour is not counted in hours of work, and hours and overtime regulations are applicable only to those earning below a given income threshold.[60] In this last respect, South Africa's regime is similar to some of the work regimes in Asia discussed earlier in the chapter, with an hours law more distinguished by who is excluded from coverage than by who is actually covered.

Greece is another country where workers typically work quite long hours. In 2015 Greeks were working the longest hours in Europe, at 42.0 average hours per week, well ahead of Portugal and Spain, which came next.[61] This trend continued into 2018, when Greeks were found working the longest average hours in the European Union, at 42.3 hours per week.[62] The standard Greek work week is eight hours a day, Monday through Friday, but the forty hours may be spread over five or six days. Premiums for work beyond those hours are very low. What is called "overwork," which means work up to forty-five hours in a week for those working five-day weeks and forty-eight hours for those working six-day weeks, draws a premium of just 20 percent of the employee's hourly wage. Overtime for work beyond the "overwork" hours is permitted, up to three hours in a day or 150 in a year. For these extra hours, the wage premium is 40 percent, or 60 percent in the case of work deemed "urgent." Those working at night receive a 25 percent shift premium, and an additional 25 percent for any overtime hours a week. There are nine paid public holidays per year, and Greek workers receive a minimum of four weeks' paid annual leave after one year, which amounts to twenty days for those working five-day weeks and twenty-four days for those on a six-day schedule. While this annual leave provision is quite generous, the low overtime premiums — among the lowest I have seen anywhere — would almost certainly encourage employers to make liberal use of overtime rather than bringing on additional workers to meet extra demand. The case of Greece illustrates the importance of examining all aspects of a country's work hours legislation in attempting to determine the reasons why some countries have longer work hours than others — in particular, those laws dealing with overtime compensation.

・・・・・・

This review of international work hours has shown the widely varying progress in achieving shorter work hours made around the world. Some countries, particularly those in Europe, have moved far beyond the norms established by the International Labour Organization and national governments during the 1920s. Other countries (e.g., Mexico) achieved those norms early on, but have made little if any subsequent progress in shortening work hours. Still others, including most notably the newly industrializing countries of the Pacific Rim, remain far short of achieving the norm first established over a century ago.

All of this is to suggest that the 1920s have been, and remain, both a watershed and a benchmark in the global fight for shorter hours. The decade is of such significance, both internationally and within North America, that it deserves special attention — at least partly in the hope that today's business and union leaders and policy-makers can benefit from the lessons learned during the 1920s. It is to this remarkable decade that the discussion now turns.

CHAPTER 5

A Special Decade: Work Hours and the 1920s

The 1920s are of special interest and importance to students of work hours, first, because the eight-hour workday that is still the norm in most countries was established then, and second, because it was a decade similar in many ways to the current one and offers many examples that might be used to good advantage today by those seeking to reduce work hours.

What made the 1920s so special? To begin with, in the wake of the bloodiest conflict the world had yet known, there was an overwhelming, nearly universal desire for peace, for an end to conflict. This desire led political leaders to establish institutions they believed would prevent any future conflict like the First World War (then known as "the Great War") from recurring. Chief among those institutions was the League of Nations, launched in 1919. Close on the League's heels came the International Labour Organization, whose primary aim was (and still is) to advance social and economic justice by setting international labour standards.[1] These standards are aimed at ensuring accessible, productive, and sustainable work worldwide "in conditions of freedom, equity, security, and dignity."

As the Wikipedia article on the founding of the ILO suggests, "In the post-World-War I euphoria, the idea of a 'makeable society' was an important catalyst behind the social engineering of the ILO architects. As a new discipline, international labour law became a useful instrument for putting social reforms into practice."

Though shorter hours had previously been granted in individual firms, and through legislation in certain jurisdictions, the adoption of the ILO convention on hours of work in 1919 marked the world's first large-scale use of a rights-based approach to the issue of work hours. In the conclusion of his article "The Road to the Eight-Hour Day" Swiss political economist Stephan Bauer suggests that the introduction of the eight-hour day required concerted international action.

> [International action] has certain advantages over extraordinary national procedure that should not be underestimated. An international treaty, unlike a law, cannot be provided with loopholes in the shape of technically unjustified exemptions and special privileges. The national honor becomes more involved through the charge of having broken a treaty than through violations of the law by a fellow citizen. For this reason, the enforcement of a protective labor treaty encounters less resistance from local interests, crowned and uncrowned local magnates, than a law. The international treaty increases the national state power and strengthens the feeling of the masses that they are defending a common human right.[2]

Unfortunately, Bauer's logic never really took hold in the United States, where resistance to any surrender of national power to international bodies was (and still is) particularly strong. It did, however, provide a solid basis for the move to the eight-hour day in most of the rest of the industrialized world.

The farsighted leaders involved in establishing the ILO clearly recognized the need to reduce conflict in workplaces and on the shop floor, as well as on the battlefield. To this end, they were vitally interested in hours of work, an interest that made (and makes) perfect sense, since as has been noted in previous chapters, ever since the start of industrialization a large proportion of the conflict arising between labour and management had been around the subject of work hours. Stephan Bauer makes the connection between shorter hours and future peace explicit when he says, "The securing of eight hours devoted to cultivation of the mind and recreation, the creation of the equal right of all peoples to internal and external progress, is the safest pledge of common resistance against a repetition of the crime of 1914."[3]

It's noteworthy that three of the first six ILO conventions adopted by the ILO at its first conference in Washington, D.C., dealt with work hours. As noted earlier, the conventions dealt with hours of work in industry, which established the eight-hour day as an international norm and would eventually be ratified by more than fifty countries; night work for women; and hours for young persons in industry.

At the same time as the ILO was developing a rights-based approach to establish the form of the eight-hour workday, scientifically trained managers and their political allies were, as noted earlier, using a knowledge-based approach derived from their study of management process to try to achieve the same end. The basic idea behind the knowledge-based approach is that shorter hours are, quite simply, more efficient. Among other things, workers who are less fatigued make fewer errors and are less likely to be injured on the job or to miss time due to illness. This approach was particularly prominent in the United States, where scientific management reached its zenith during the early twentieth century — it took hold to a lesser degree in Britain, France, and various other European countries. (Another reason why the knowledge-based approach played such a prominent role in the United States was that that country never signed on to the ILO Convention and its rights-based approach, not being a member of the League of Nations and therefore not being a member of the ILO.) A plant- or industry-based approach to work hours was arguably better suited to the United States' longstanding culture of political voluntarism than the ILO's rights-based approach, which presupposed a significant degree of government involvement in industrial relations.

Even before the formal launch of the scientific management movement, with the 1911 publication of F.W. Taylor's *Principles of Scientific Management*, farsighted employers around the world had begun to recognize the connection between shorter hours and increased productivity. As early as

1893, a move from twelve-hour to eight-hour shifts in Belgian zinc smelters had resulted in a 10 percent increase in hourly output. Within six months of the changes, workers were producing as much in seven and a half hours as they had previously produced in ten hours. The establishment sick fund, which had run a deficit in 1892, was in surplus. In addition, "Alcoholism disappeared, while self-respect and discipline increased."[4] Likewise, the Swiss chemical industry had discovered that the shorter the hours of work in their factories, the lower employee accident and sickness rates were.[5] In 1895 the firm Brunner Mond and Company, reporting on the success of its new eight-hour shift system, attributed productivity improvements to the fact that "employees work more steadily and more intensively" than under the old system of longer shifts. Most notably, the proportion of chemical workers qualifying for an attendance bonus more than doubled, from 43 percent to 92 percent, with the introduction of the shorter shifts.[6] Similar results were obtained by factories in England, France, and Germany.[7]

While there were by the start of the First World War a not insignificant number of such individual "success stories" involving shorter hours, it would be the combination of Taylor's scientific management system, which spread rapidly to progressive firms like DuPont,[8] and the First World War that would create an irresistible push for shorter hours. The significance of the First World War was that it posed logistical challenges of such magnitude that they could not be met using traditional management methods. In the words of business management professor David Ahlstrom, the war helped to "jump-start and accelerate the diffusion of ... key management innovations" such as human resource management, strategic management, and high-performance work systems.[9]

The widespread application of scientific management principles would "lead directly to the study of human resource management,"[10] a key tenet of which was the need to use positive rather than negative means of motivating workers. The link to shorter hours was a direct one. After a number of scientific management experiments conducted during the war, including some conducted in the United States[11] and others in England,[12] found little or no drop in productivity associated with shorter hours, the eight-hour day came to be quite widely adopted in the United States.[13] Though the

A Special Decade: Work Hours and the 1920s

forty-eight-hour week remained common, by 1920 a forty-four-hour week with a half-day on Saturday had become "almost universal" among skilled trade workers represented by unions. And virtually all workers, including even those working more than forty-eight hours per week, "had the short Saturday as a feature of their regular work."[14] The institution we now know as the weekend, and to which many of us scarcely give a thought anymore, was on its way to being established in American business.

Many Canadian workers were also seeing their hours reduced, though not to the same extent.[15] One reason for the slower diffusion of shorter hours may well have been the determined opposition of many Canadian employers, as expressed at the National Industrial Conference in Ottawa in 1919. As mentioned earlier in the book, at the tripartite conference, both the employees' group and the neutral public group expressed strong support for adoption of the eight-hour day. But the employers' group was adamantly opposed, declaring the proposal not opportune at a time when "Canada needs increased productivity to pay the war debt and to maintain competition against other countries," and saying also that the then-current average of fifty hours a week across Canada provided workers with "an adequate standard of health and recreation." Perhaps not coincidentally, the employers' group was also opposed to providing full collective bargaining rights to unions.[16] That said, as the tables presented earlier show, even Canadian workers did achieve significantly shorter hours during the 1920s.

Again, looking at the 1920s from a global perspective, there was a strong desire to achieve shorter hours, both as a way to reduce workplace conflict and as a way of rewarding the working classes for their support of the war.[17] Thanks to scientific management, there was an understanding of the link between shorter hours and increased productivity and knowledge of how to achieve shorter hours in the workplace. The third, essential ingredient for a general shortening of hours was the people needed to actually bring about the change. In the international arena, those people were, by and large, the political and intellectual leaders involved in creating the League of Nations and the ILO. In the United States, those people were primarily engineers and industrialists aided by the occasional politician, such as Herbert Hoover, who had been an engineer himself, with the ability to translate the results of the industrial engineers' work into tangible workplace improvements.

In the United States, the single most important individual in the shorter hours movement was automaker Henry Ford, who adopted an eight-hour day in 1914 and a five-day week in 1926. As noted earlier, Ford recognized early on that if best use were to be made of the period's new, highly efficient production technology, work hours would have to be reduced substantially. It would simply not be possible for people to work the same hours with the new, far more labour-intensive machinery as they had with the older, less efficient machines of the past, which offered more opportunities for pauses during the working day. Ford was also perceptive enough to recognize that shorter hours could be of significant help in recruitment and retention of top-quality workers in a tight postwar labour market. Finally, at the macroeconomic level, Ford recognized that shorter hours and higher wages could help stimulate the national economy, by providing workers with the means to buy the cars they were making and the time to enjoy those cars. But this link between shorter hours and increased consumption would soon prove to be a two-edged sword.

The second major figure in the American shorter hours movement was cereal-maker William K. Kellogg, who, with his plant manager Lewis Brown, used shorter hours (in this case, a six-hour day) to help motivate workers,[18] as well as a recruitment and retention tool. Another, not insignificant, benefit of Kellogg's approach to labour management was that it created hundreds of new jobs in the Depression-battered town of Battle Creek, Michigan, through the addition of a fourth daily shift.

In Kellogg's case, devotion to the shorter hours cause was the product of personal experience. As a young man, he had been worked half to death by his older brother, John Harvey, a prodigious workaholic, often having to work on holidays; at one point, he'd had to spend 120 hours of a single week on duty.[19] Needless to say, working such horrific hours had taken a severe toll on both his physical and mental health and his family life. "I never learned to play" was a frequent lament. A psychiatrist friend allowed that he had never seen "a more lonely, isolated individual."[20] Having experienced the sickness of workaholism at first hand, Kellogg was determined not to let others, whether they were kin like his grandson or his plant employees, have the same fate visited on them.[21]

But while Kellogg's push for shorter work hours may have had a basis in his personal experience, it was also soundly rooted in observed fact, with much of the evidence being provided by plant manager Lewis Brown, a serious student of scientific management. The results of the first five years of "Kellogg's Experiment" bear this out; the experiment benefitted the company just as much as the workers. Its burden (or overhead) unit cost was down by 25 percent, labour unit costs were down by 10 percent, accidents had been reduced by 41 percent, the severity of accidents (in days lost per accident) had improved by 51 percent, and there were 39 percent more employees at the plant than there had been at the start of the experiment. As a result, Kellogg proudly proclaimed, "we can afford to pay as much for six hours as we formerly paid for eight."[22] Other businesses, such as Goodyear Tire & Rubber Company, brought in their own six-hour shift systems, and in 1931 Kellogg was invited to Washington to meet with President Hoover, the third major figure in the shorter hours triumvirate.[23]

Hoover is remembered today, to the extent that he is remembered at all, as a sort of stick figure reactionary who as president stood in the way of the reforms needed to bring the United States out of the Depression because of his unwavering opposition to federal government intervention in the economy. This depiction of him, as was noted earlier, is ungenerous and lacking in nuance. While it's true that he was opposed to many types of federal government economic intervention, and that such opposition likely prevented him from dealing with the Depression as effectively as he otherwise might, he was not opposed to all such intervention; the stereotype of Hoover many Americans (especially those raised as Democrats) learned at an early age was at the very least an oversimplification.[24] Within his own party, he rated as a progressive, at least prior to his presidency;[25] the truly reactionary Calvin Coolidge once characterized Hoover as a thorn in the side.[26] Much more important, though, is that the primary focus on the failures of Hoover's presidencies tends to obscure his immense earlier successes, both overseas, as administrator of an immensely successful food relief effort following the

First World War,[27] and at home as the man who brought the eight-hour day to the American steel industry and sought to apply his engineering know-how to the creation of safe, humane workplaces for all American workers.[28] In many ways, Hoover's belief that rational, humane personnel policies could reduce conflict both in the workplace and in society at large mirrored the beliefs of the ILO's shorter hours architects.[29]

The tragedy for Hoover is that he even ran for president at all, instead of following the lead of his predecessor, Calvin Coolidge, and opting out of the 1928 presidential race. Had he never served as president, he would today be remembered, not as some sort of failed reactionary, but as one of the great humanitarians not just of his time but of all time. In this, he has much in common with Jimmy Carter, another engineer-turned-politician whose single term in the White House is not generally regarded as a great success, but whose humanitarian achievements, through the foundation he and his wife, Rosalynn, set up after he left office, have been of world class. Hoover's belief in scientific management and the importance of engineers in shaping public policy never wavered. In his view, engineers were in a "unique position to make the 'sane' analysis of weakness and sober proposal of remedy" that were the necessary first steps in any program of social and economic reform.[30]

In addition to the fact that it possessed the desire, the knowledge, and the people needed to achieve shorter work hours, one other factor made the 1920s a decade ideally suited to the achievement of this goal. This was the fact that (with a few notable exceptions), it was a period of relative harmony between management and labour. In part, this was a function of the labour movement's overall weakness, both in Canada and the United States. After its defeat in radical action at the end of the First World War, the labour movement, weakened both numerically and politically, was in steady retreat throughout the 1920s.[31] In other words, the labour movement wouldn't have had the resources to carry on a major battle over work hours even if it had — it didn't. As we shall soon see, it didn't have to.

It's also worth noting that many managers and engineers believed, with Taylor, in a fundamental community of interest between management and labour.[32] As the decade progressed, this harmony applied in particular to

A Special Decade: Work Hours and the 1920s

the issue of work hours. To Hoover, long work hours were anathema — both bad for productivity and in total opposition to the kind of humane, enlightened society he and other progressive social engineers were seeking to create.[33]

While Hoover's may have been among the most powerful voices in support of shorter working hours, his was far from the only voice. After Kellogg's launched its six-hour day "experiment," it wasn't long before *Forbes*, *Business Week*, and *Factory and Industrial Management* were singing its praises, as was the *New York Times*.[34] As Benjamin Hunnicutt has noted, "Most business and financial publications agreed that Kellogg's scheme offered a permanent solution to technological unemployment based on 'elimination of the work, not the worker,'" a solution that provided "shorter hours for men and longer hours for machines."[35] T.R. Darrow of the Harvard Business School even used Kellogg's as a case study in his graduate classes after visiting the Kellogg plant.[36]

The labour movement, meanwhile, was almost completely on board. William Green, president of the American Federation of Labor, which in 1926 had committed itself to the "progressive shortening of the hours of labor,"[37] praised the Kellogg scheme for its job-creation possibilities, noting that the increase in hourly wages it provided would "enable workers to maintain a relatively high purchasing power."[38] To AFL vice-president Matthew Woll, the increased leisure enabled by a shorter work day was a useful "restraining influence" on the "materialistic spirit of production" that he saw as dominating modern society. To him, "constructive recreation" for physical, social, cultural, and spiritual purposes was the valuable alternative to "work and more work."[39]

All in all, the conditions seemed right for a general adoption of the six-hour day as the law of the land in the United States, to be followed by a continued progressive shortening of work hours after that. The United States, as noted earlier, came very close to general adoption of that shorter day through the Black-Connery Act, which would have established such a day legislatively.

Why didn't that more general adoption take place? In a word, because of what Hunnicutt refers to as the "gospel of consumption," a philosophy that dictated that the acquisition of material goods should take priority over increased leisure, both for individuals and for society as a whole. The seeds for this new gospel had been planted even by some of the leaders of the shorter hours movement, such as Henry Ford and Herbert Hoover, whose Committee on Recent Industrial Changes concluded that American business had discovered during the 1920s that "the leisure that results from an increasing man-hours productivity helps to create new needs and new and broader markets."[40]

The new gospel of consumption would come to full fruition after the Second World War, with the postwar baby boom driving a huge demand for labour in most sectors of the economy. At the bargaining table, unions emphasized wage increases over hours reductions. Though many unions retained a theoretical commitment to a thirty-hour week through the early postwar period, it was becoming increasingly clear that most of them weren't prepared to do very much to help achieve that shorter week. Perhaps the clearest indication of how low the shorter hours issue had fallen on labour's agenda was the 1949 admission by the AFL's Committee on a Shorter Work Day that its work had lapsed during the previous years.[41] Thereafter, it would receive only sporadic attention,[42] and then not with any great hope of success.

As noted, the consequences of that gospel of consumption are still with us today. People are working themselves sick in order to acquire goods they often don't need or, in many cases, even really want. The question now is whether the situation has reached the point, as it had at the end of the First World War, that the demand for change will be irresistible, even if it entails some risk on the part of employers and workers.

Before closing this chapter, let's take a quick look at the similarities and differences between this decade, the 2020s, and the decade of the 1920s. To begin with, both of these "'20s" decades were ushered in with global trauma. In the case of the 1920s, that trauma was the First World War, compounded by a worldwide flu epidemic that began just as the war was ending.[43] In the case of the 2020s, that trauma is the Covid-19 pandemic we are still having to deal with, compounded by the ongoing and worsening effects of global climate change. In both cases, the global trauma provided a strong impetus for change; it made it clear that things simply could not go on as they had been.

A Special Decade: Work Hours and the 1920s

In both cases, as well, there is the knowledge needed to bring about the necessary changes — the knowledge of the relationship between shorter hours and increased productivity, acquired through the scientific management experiments conducted in the United States and Britain during the First World War, as noted above, and currently, through the experiments with a four-day week conducted in Australia, as described by Andrew Barnes,[44] as well as in Iceland, New Zealand, Scotland, Spain, and the United Kingdom, to name but a few.[45] While most of the recent trials have involved four-day work weeks of thirty to thirty-two hours, other types of reduced work weeks have been and are still being tried out, as well.[46] Clearly, as was the case a century ago, there is no dearth of supporting evidence to back up claims that a shorter work week can increase or at least not reduce productivity.

Yet another similarity between the two periods is that the primary drivers of change today are those outside the organized labour movement, as was the case a century ago. The major impetus today appears to be coming from employers and, to a lesser extent, governments; the same was true in the 1920s. In both cases, the comparative weakness of the labour movement was (and is) likely the main reason why the labour movement isn't doing more on the issue.[47] (On a world scale, Germany's IG Metall has long been, and remains, an important exception here. Its ability to achieve shorter work weeks is based to a large extent on its longstanding habit of cultivating and maintaining close relationships with centre-left governments headed by the Social Democratic Party.)

A major difference between the two periods is the lack, today, of leaders — whether those leaders come from the business community, government, the labour movement, or the academic world — of sufficient stature and charisma to influence others to support the shorter hours cause and possessed of sufficient resources and energy to be willing and able to work on that cause over the long haul. In the United States in the 1920s, those leaders included engineer-politicians like Herbert Hoover and businessmen such as Henry Ford, W.K. Kellogg, and Lewis Brown. In England, key figures included Lord Leverhulme, whose vision of a six-hour day and a garden-filled industrial community was an inspiration for Brown in the work he did with

Kellogg's.[48] Thus far, no one of the stature of any of the four individuals just named has emerged. Whether such a person will appear in the near future is an open question. Society is generally reluctant to create heroes of any kind, and even more reluctant to allow them to continue to succeed over a long period.

Despite the lack of comparable leadership figures today, the present situation is similar enough to that existing in the 1920s that useful lessons can be drawn from the shorter hours work done then, chief among them the importance of having available solid evidence to back up claims of increased productivity resulting from reduced work hours. Further discussion of this will be found in the concluding chapters, but before that, it is important to take a look at some of the central features of today's workplaces, starting with the extreme intensification of work many of them impose through various types of computer technology.

CHAPTER 6

Technology, Work Intensification, Stress, and Distress

Technology has been a source of increased workplace stress since the start of industrialization, particularly since the introduction of the automated assembly line in auto plants in the early twentieth century. As was noted in chapter 5, Henry Ford compensated his auto plant workers for the assembly line's increased stress by shortening their work hours dramatically, doing so in order to reduce the staggering quit rates initially induced by the assembly line, which workers loathed.

By and large, this did not happen following the next big wave of technological innovation in the 1980s, which saw typewriters replaced by computers for most office work and automation increased in manufacturing processes.[1] Not only did most workers receive no hours reduction to compensate for the added stress brought to their jobs by the new technology, many began to fear for their jobs, as that new technology was significantly more efficient than the previous generation had been. For others, that new technology would have a significant "de-skilling "effect, making their work less interesting. Sadly, it would be, at least at first, much the same with the "second generation" of technological advance, involving

Zoom and other video conferencing technologies. Until the Covid-19 pandemic and the subsequent "Great Resignation" (discussed in the next chapter) caused employers to realize they would have to rethink their approach to work hours if they wanted to stay in business, workers were expected to put in the same hours on Zoom as they had face-to-face. The results were often disastrous.

All of this is to say that the number of hours worked is not the only variable to be considered when looking at the overall amount of stress felt by workers. Not all work hours are created equal. In order to determine the total amount of stress felt by workers, we need to look at the *intensity* of the work they do as well as its duration.

Generally, each new wave of technological change involves a ramping up of the intensity of work. Just as many Ford assembly workers reported feeling as tired or more so after eight hours on a Ford assembly line as they had after ten- or eleven-hour days using the previous technology, many office workers affected by the widespread introduction of computers in the 1980s and 1990s found six hours working on a computer as fatiguing, if not more, as eight hours working on a typewriter. (Today, the situation is even worse. Staring at a screen all day definitely takes its toll, as most readers will know all too well. And of course, dealing with email, chats, texts, and a multitude of programs only increases the intensity of work.)

The major difference between the early period of automation and the introduction of computers in the 1980s and 1990s (and the much wider use of computers today) is that while Henry Ford compensated his workers with shorter hours and higher wages for the greater stress of their work on the new assembly line, employers in the 1980s and 1990s rarely did so. (The same is, if possible, even more true today.) Indeed, late twentieth-century workers were at real risk of losing their jobs altogether to the new, more productive machines being introduced then, or of having their jobs "de-skilled" and made far less interesting, due to the new machines' simplification of work processes.[2]

A similar conclusion about the importance of considering work intensity as well as duration was reached by Erich Fein et al. at the conclusion of "Work Intensification, Work-Life Interference, Stress, and Well-Being in Australian

Technology, Work Intensification, Stress, and Distress

Workers," a major study of the effects of technology on Australian workers, who wrote, "The findings of this study are an important reminder that work intensification should be monitored along with total working hours as a strong predictor of work-life interference,"[3,4] and by Francis Green, who finds "computerized or automated equipment in jobs ... associated with higher levels of employee effort."[5]

For their part, in their study "How Work Intensification Relates to Organization-Level Safety Performance: The Mediating Roles of Safety Climate, Safety Motivation, and Safety Knowledge," Johanna Bunner et al. found that increased automation, which in their view inevitably leads to work intensification, results in adverse effects on both individual and organizational occupational safety, as workers increase their speed of work, reduce their breaks, or do both in order to meet production quotas.[6] Part of the increase in speed, Bunner et al. find, is achieved through reduced compliance with safety measures; under the stress of strict production quotas, complying with those measures may require more effort than ignoring them. Among other things, especially in production industries, work intensification can be linked to a "rise in musculoskeletal disorders and other psychosocial risks." Additionally, note the authors, "Work intensification has been linked to poor communication at work, leading to a subsequent loss of values and respect for colleagues." In extreme cases, the consequences can include outright harassment and bullying. Such findings aren't likely to come as much of a surprise to anyone who has ever worked in a situation in which fewer people are expected to achieve more in a shorter period of time.[7]

For the most part, work intensification has resulted from the computerized technology that has been in use in workplaces for the past four decades. And there's no doubt that this technology, particularly in its most recent incarnations (e.g., Zoom and its ilk), is a major source of stress — and distress — for those who must work with it.

Again, as was noted earlier in the chapter, it's important to note that work intensification was an ongoing phenomenon long before the first personal computer was even a gleam in its inventor's eye. Its history extends back for more than a century, dating from Henry Ford's introduction of the automobile assembly line in 1913. To describe the assembly line's effects merely as revolutionary is to understate those effects. In a single, bold stroke, Ford transformed the entire American industrial landscape.

From assembling entire cars, workers went to assembling only a small number of parts. The pace of work increased greatly, and work became far more monotonous than it had been. At the same time, the role of skilled workers was greatly reduced.

The introduction of the assembly line was not initially a popular move; indeed, as science journalist Kat Eschner succinctly puts it in the title of her *Smithsonian Magazine* article, "Workers hated it."[8] They hated it enough that they voted with their feet, leaving Ford in droves. Through the assembly line's first year, the company's turnover was a staggering 380 percent. It was in response to this completely untenable labour situation, rather than from any inherent feelings of benevolence toward his workers, that Ford came up with the idea of paying the then-unheard-of wage of $5 a day for an eight-hour day — a wage over twice what rival automakers were paying for a longer day. Turnover all but ceased, and Ford became the employer of choice in the auto industry.

The new assembly line model cut the time required to produce a Model T from twelve hours to just over an hour and a half. This led to a dramatic increase in production and an equally dramatic reduction in price, from $850 to $300.[9] Now the car was affordable for average Americans, including most notably Ford's own workers. "When I'm through, about everyone will have one," boasted Ford.[10] And who could say he was wrong? His own workers could not only afford to buy the cars they were making, with their eight-hour day (as of 1926), they had the time to drive those cars.

That isn't to say that a job with Ford was ever a walk on the beach. As a 1920s-era Ford worker told a journalist, "The machine I'm on goes at such a terrific speed that I can't help stepping on it in order to keep up with the machine. It's my boss."[11] Many years later, a college student assembly-line worker quoted by technology historian David Nye would say, "You've got to work like hell in Ford's. From the time you become a number in the morning until the bell rings for quitting time you have to keep at it. You can't let up. You've got to get out the production and if you can't get it out, you get out."[12] Summing up the various benefits and drawbacks of the assembly line, Nye concludes, "Workers benefited from the short hours, higher wages, and falling consumer prices, but they worried about the loss of freedom on the shop floor, about endless repetition of the same movements for eight hours, and about jobs that deadened the soul."[13]

Despite the many undeniable drawbacks of his assembly line system, Henry Ford must be given credit for being among the first to recognize that workers needed to be compensated in time off, through significantly reduced work hours, for the added intensification brought to their jobs by the assembly line. It would be this recognition that, as noted in chapter 5, guided the Kellogg Company in its experiment with a shorter week during the Depression. Sadly, such a recognition is far too rare in current discussions of work hours — even in many of the most enlightened and best-informed of those discussions. To consider work hours without considering work intensification is to look at but one side of the coin.

Computer Technology: The First Wave

The 1980s was the decade that saw the first large-scale introduction of computers into North American workplaces. I personally first became aware of computers around 1982, when an editor of the *Kingston Whig-Standard*, the paper for which I was a regular freelancer, started complaining about a crash of the "system" during a break in our tennis game. After hearing him hold forth on the "system's" many drawbacks for the better part of five minutes, I said, "It sounds perfectly ghastly. Why on earth would you subject yourself to such a thing?"

"It's the wave of the future," he replied. "Like it or not, it's how newspapers will be produced from here on in." At this point, we resumed our tennis game. The two of us would never exchange another word on the subject of computer technology. And I would, at least for the next three years, keep on producing my work on a manual typewriter, as I had since grade 7 — apparently without incident. Computers were for other people — people a lot wealthier[14] and more technologically hip than I. Having precisely zero interest in the machines, I simply ignored them through the rest of my time in Kingston.

Three years later, it would be quite a different story. By that time, I had left English and "re-invented" myself in industrial relations, doing a Master's degree in my new field at Queen's. With my new credentials in hand, I got a job with the Economic Council of Canada, working as a researcher on the Labour Markets and Technological Change project team. In that position, I wouldn't just become acquainted with technology; I would have an up-close-and-personal sort of involvement with it. My job would be to examine Canadian collective agreements to determine what sort of protection unionized Canadian workers enjoyed against the adverse effects of technological change. In addition, I would be looking at relevant labour board and arbitration cases to see if existing legislative arrangements offered workers any real protection, and, if not, how those legislative arrangements might be improved. Given what I already knew about the Canadian industrial relations system, I didn't expect to find much in the way of substantial protection, either in collective agreements or in the labour board and arbitration cases. Still, I was excited at the thought of undertaking a serious investigation of the subject.

By 1985, the use of computer technology was far more widespread than it had been just three years earlier. It had, indeed, become sufficiently widespread and its effects had become recognized to an extent that American psychotherapist Craig Brod had coined the term "technostress," which he defined as a "modern disease of adaptation caused by an inability to cope with the new computer technologies in a healthy manner."[15]

In his pioneering book, Brod identified two distinct though related manifestations of technostress: the inability to accept computer technology, and overidentification with that technology.[16] The symptoms of this new disease included a broad range of both physical and mental health effects. Physical impacts, especially for those working all or most of the day at the terminal, such as keypunchers, typists, and cashiers, included pain in the shoulders, forehead, neck and arms, as well as eye strain.[17] Mental health effects, for those unable fully to adapt to the new technology, included depression and a broad range of fears, some of which even resulted in nightmares.[18]

Technology, Work Intensification, Stress, and Distress

As for those who in Brod's view had entered a "techno-centred" state by becoming "too successfully identified" with the new technology, the biggest single effect was loss of the capacity to feel and to relate to others.[19] Brod found that individuals who had come to march to the computer's drumbeat rather than their own were often short with spouses, professional clients, and others whom they saw as wasting their time by not moving or coming to the point quickly enough.[20] This "internal speed-up" also took its toll on workers themselves, as did failure to adapt fully. While these techno-centered individuals, including many computer professionals, might on the surface have seemed well-adjusted, Brod found them to be emotionally debilitated and often on the verge of exhaustion.[21] They had, in fact, "sacrificed their psychological well-being for the predictable, rational, logical safety of a computerized environment."[22]

There were also growing concerns about the potential use of new technology for surveillance of workers.[23] In addition to allowing employers to expect far more quantitative production from workers than had been the case with typewriters, the new machines allowed for far more detailed monitoring of employees' work. By the mid-1980s, notes Brod, companies could "calculate such minute statistics as how many pieces of a paper a typist might use to type a letter, or how long it took an employee to read two reports and six memos."[24] Such monitoring would itself become a significant source of strain and stress, making "the already-resented time clock, which after all measures only one's physical presence," seem benign in comparison.[25] Worse still, in the new electronic workspace, workers were more cut off from co-workers than ever before, making it harder even to find sympathetic souls with whom to commiserate.[26]

Yet another source of stress were the increased standards of perfection expected as a result of the new technology. Prior to the introduction of computers, a boss might well allow a letter with one or two white-out corrections to be sent out. Not so with the advent of computers. Even the most minor mistake would demand reprinting of the entire document; worse still, bosses could keep making minor editorial changes *ad infinitum*, since all the secretary had to do "was print out a new version, as if the computer were doing all the additional work by itself."[27] In a classic understatement,

Brod concludes, "One has to wonder how much the electronic printer, like the Xerox machine that created new mounds of paperwork to read and store, actually advances the cause of office efficiency."[28]

Were workers being recompensed, either through higher wages or shorter hours, for having to work harder and faster than ever before, and under less pleasant conditions? For the most part, the answer was no. Indeed, many women, including some who had initially welcomed the opportunity to learn word processing as a "new skill they felt might enhance their career potential," saw their salaries drop as "jobs [were] divided into a series of easily automated 'subroutines.'"[29]

Why, in fact, didn't workers share in the many economic benefits of the new technology, as they had following the introduction of the assembly line early in the twentieth century?

A complete answer to the above question would require a book all by itself. But it may be possible to offer a few preliminary hypotheses. One reason, surely, was the lack, in late-twentieth century North America, of a Henry Ford–style visionary figure, someone able to put the various political economy pieces together and see the bigger picture. (Wilhelm [Willi] Haller, mentioned earlier, in Table 4.2, was such a figure in Germany. Regrettably, Haller died quite young; even more regrettably, his influence didn't extend far beyond his native country, although he did make a number of foreign trips, including at least one to Canada, where I met him, in an attempt to "spread the gospel.") Another was the intense foreign competition characteristic of the late twentieth century, which (rightly or wrongly) caused many employers to feel they had to extract the maximum amount of labour from their employees in order to keep up with competition from lower-wage countries all around the world. At the time Henry Ford launched his technological and organizational innovations, he faced little in the way of competition from automakers even in Europe, let alone those in developing countries.

In addition, as noted in chapters 2 and 3, the labour movement in both the United States and Canada, especially the former, was a good deal weaker in 1984 than it had been in 1914. In the earlier year, the threat of a major auto strike was real, as was the threat (already realized) of wholesale quitting to protest conditions. By the 1980s, most of those still working in the auto industry considered themselves lucky to have a regular job with benefits. Even the most militant union would have been reluctant to take proactive action to address issues involving technological change. Even had such a union done so, it might well not have been successful. Canadian labour boards, whose work I examined in detail for my Economic Council study, tended to treat tech change as a management right, even in cases where its effect on employment levels, wages, and skills was clear.

Yet another reason why unions didn't do more to work for shorter hours in compensation for the increased stress involved in working with computers is that as discussed in chapter 2, the labour movement had long since (with very occasional exceptions) opted for higher wages rather than shorter hours. For most unions, the latter had simply fallen off the radar screen. Indeed, the consumer-oriented lifestyle adopted by most union members as well as other workers demanded that workers earn as much as they possibly could in order to pay for all their fancy consumer goods. By the twentieth century's final two decades, the average worker in both Canada and the United States was locked into a spiral of deep debt.[30] Many had to work overtime just to keep up with the mortgage and credit card payments that would allow them to live the style of life to which they felt they were entitled.

Tech Change and the Industrial Relations System

To the extent that Canadian unions were addressing technological change at all, through the 1980s, their major focus had been on protection against the adverse economic effects of tech change through provisions requiring advance notice or consultation prior to such change being effected, training or retraining related to the change in question, guaranteed employment or the monetary equivalent, and notice of any layoff related to such change, as well as complete or partial prohibition of contracting out of work following such a change.[31] Even on these bread-and-butter issues, unions were by no means universally successful. The three most common provisions, those relating to advance notice, tech-change-related training, and contracting out prohibitions, were found in only 30 to 40 percent of the agreements in

Labour Canada's "large agreement" pool composed of agreements covering five hundred or more workers.[32] For agreements covering fewer than five hundred workers, the figures were significantly lower, ranging from 18 to 28 percent of my personal sample of 183 "small agreements."[33] In no case were as many as half of all workers covered by any single tech change provision, the highest rate of coverage, 43 percent, being for advance notice provisions in the "large agreement" pool.[34]

For their part, American unions had been even less successful in addressing tech-change-related issues. A 1983 study by Dennis Chamot and Kevin Murphy[35] of American "large agreements" (those covering one thousand or more workers) found that fewer than 20 percent of those agreements contained any technological change provision at all, and only about 10 percent contained an advance notice provision. These figures suggest that on average, tech change provisions were at least twice as frequent in Canadian agreements as in American ones, if not three or four times greater.[36]

If the 1980s' tech change provisions on bread-and-butter issues such as advance notice and contracting out were spotty, they were extremely rare in areas related to health and safety or worker privacy, even though such issues had been on organized labour's agenda for some time.[37] My analysis of my "small agreement" pool, which allowed for an individual investigation of issues like VDT (video display terminal)-related health and safety and surveillance cameras in the workplace, found only just over 2 percent of agreements with any VDT-related provision, and no provisions at all related to surveillance cameras or any other kind of electronic monitoring equipment.[38]

A similar analysis conducted by the Research and Planning branch of Manitoba's Labour Division, based on some 640 agreements in force as of January 1, 1983, yielded virtually identical results. For instance, only eleven of those agreements contained provisions for paid eye examinations for VDT operators, as those using computers were then called. Most of the employees covered by the VDT provision were in the Manitoba Government Employees' Association, which had recently negotiated such a provision (including a paid annual eye exam) with the provincial government. Eighteen, or 2.8 percent of the agreements, guaranteed pregnant VDT operators the right to transfer to alternate work. And ten (1.6 percent) of the agreements contained a provision guaranteeing that a worker who had spent two consecutive hours operating a VDT would be assigned to alternate duties as a break from the intense eye work necessitated by the computer, while no agreements at all contained provisions covering the selection, installation, inspection, and maintenance of VDT equipment. The extremely low incidence of VDT provisions led the authors of the report to conclude, "The collective bargaining process, at least in Manitoba, has not been a successful vehicle for guaranteeing workers a safe and healthy work environment."[39]

By the mid-1980s, a limited number of VDT provisions do appear to have made their way into Canadian agreements, particularly those involving the telephone industry and government workers. Where these provisions existed, as in the case of Canadian Pacific, they often focused on the right of pregnant workers to transfer away from the machines.[40] Very occasionally, as in the case of Denison Mines, a provision would give workers using one of the new machines for much of their workday (four hours in the case of Denison) the right to a break of ten minutes an hour away from the machine, during which time the employee could be assigned other duties if the employer wished.[41] The Denison provision, along with a comprehensive VDT provision negotiated into their agreement by the Carleton University support staff establishing an eight-member parity committee to address all "matters of concern related to the installation and use of the VDTs," including testing, transferring employees away from VDT areas for health-related reasons, and the plan for dealing with VDT-related health issues,[42] is among the very few I've seen from the period recognizing in any way the greater intensity of work on computers as compared to work on the previous technology (typewriters), and the need for specific regulations recognizing the qualitatively as well as quantitatively different nature of work with computers.

Meanwhile, if health-related VDT provisions remained rare, provisions relating to surveillance cameras and other forms of workplace monitoring and the protection of workers' privacy in the face of such monitoring were rarer yet, despite the frequency with which surveillance and monitoring issues were discussed in the management and industrial relations literature of the day.[43] Throughout my research on tech change provisions, I became aware of just two dealing with surveillance cameras. The first of these, in a 1981 agreement between the federal government and the inside postal workers represented by the Canadian Union of Postal Workers (CUPW) stipulated that no new closed-circuit TV units would be added and that the use of existing ones would be restricted.[44] The second, a much stronger provision in a 1984 agreement between Carleton University and its support staff, represented by Canadian Union of Public Employees (CUPE) Local 2424, barred surveillance cameras from employee-occupied areas during normal working hours without the knowledge of the employees concerned and of the CUPE local, if the employees in question were union members. The employer was not permitted to use the cameras for monitoring of work, and no information obtained by means of the cameras was ever to be used against employees unless such information constituted evidence of criminal behaviour, such as theft.[45] The Carleton provision was the only provision I saw during my time at the Economic Council that appeared to recognize the considerable potential for abuse of privacy represented by surveillance cameras, and the need for strict regulation to guard against such abuse.

Strict surveillance of workers, prisoners, and others deemed inferior is, of course, far from new. As far back as the eighteenth century, the British philosopher and reformer Jeremy Bentham envisaged a structure called a panopticon, intended for use in prisons. As the name suggests, the structure would have consisted of a ring of cells built around a single tower, where prisoners, who were expected to work a fourteen-hour day, would suspect they were being watched all the time.[46]

Even Solzhenitsyn's gulag didn't go *quite* this far. Fortunately, Bentham's monstrous idea has almost never been put into practice — one was built in the United States and another in Cuba. But detailed work monitoring is an idea that never died. As Jenny Odell notes in *Saving Time: Discovering a Life Beyond the Clock*, it was common in the early twentieth century, courtesy of scientific management specialists such as F.W. Taylor and Frank Gilbreth. The widespread adoption of computers and surveillance cameras in the 1980s facilitated more detailed monitoring and surveillance of workers. Since then, even more detailed monitoring and surveillance systems have come into effect in many

Technology, Work Intensification, Stress, and Distress

workplaces. Along with surveillance cameras, including webcams in worker computers, some companies now monitor the keystrokes of employees.

Even in the 1980s, it seemed that most employers and even many workers and unions really didn't understand the magnitude or significance of the changes wrought in work by the first generation of computer technology. My overall conclusion, after noting the extreme rarity of such forward-looking tech change provisions as protection of workers' skills, the involvement of workers in substantive planning for and implementation of tech change, and protection against unwarranted electronic surveillance, was pretty much the same as that of the Manitoba Labour Division, quoted earlier. Quite simply, collective bargaining did not appear to be an effective mechanism for dealing with workplace tech change.[47] If it was not an effective mechanism in 1987, when my research study was published, how much less likely it is to be effective today, with labour movements both numerically and politically substantially weaker than they were in the 1980s, and with the far greater potential for abuse of workers from the increasingly powerful surveillance and monitoring technology now available.

To get around the inherent difficulties of collective bargaining in addressing tech change issues, the method I proposed in the conclusion of my Economic Council study was mandatory joint committees for dealing with such issues. In effect, these would have been single-issue works councils, and they would have applied in all workplaces, non-unionized as well as unionized ones.[48] Given the immense health and safety effects of the new technologies, especially those like Zoom, the method I propose in the final chapter will be to have the effects of new technology addressed by health and safety committees, which like the committees I proposed in 1987, would apply in all workplaces, non-unionized as well as unionized ones. I'll be going into more detail on this recommendation in the book's concluding chapters.

However, before discussing in any detail recommendations for dealing with the effects of Zoom and related technologies, technology's so-called second wave, it's necessary to look carefully at those effects and see just what they have been. It's important to bear in mind that, as my Economic Council project team consistently pointed out throughout its work on labour markets and technological change, such change has major organizational as well as physical and emotional impacts.

Technology's Second Wave: Zoom and Its Discontents

While Zoom and related video conferencing technologies have many of the same negative physical effects on workers, causing headaches and neck and eye strain, as did the computer technologies of the first wave, these new technologies have some special effects of their own: users are unable to see body language or make eye contact, and they are often required to interact with many different faces. All of these issues make video conferences particularly challenging and stressful, especially when workers use the new technologies for long periods of time at once.[49] Such long periods of use became far more frequent during the Covid-19 pandemic, which saw Zoom change from a technology many had not even heard of, and that even those already familiar with it typically used only occasionally, to a staple of office life. (Between October 2019 and October 2020, Zoom's number of annual meeting minutes increased by more than thirty-fold, from ninety-seven billion minutes in the former month to 3.3 *trillion* minutes in the latter month.[50])

It would be a mistake to say that Zoom's effects have been entirely negative. By providing a forum for the visual interaction of participants, it has allowed a wide variety of work, ranging from legal trials and hearings to university teaching, and musical and theatrical performances to continue. This has allowed practitioners in these fields to continue working, and it has allowed students to continue taking classes and audiences to continue to take in musical, theatrical, and dance performances. It has also allowed for a broad range of medical procedures to be carried out far more safely than would otherwise have been the case.

Zoom has been a particular boon to older people and those with disabilities, some of whom have found themselves able to do jobs like college teaching better virtually than they had live prior to the pandemic.[51] As for the creative and performing arts, while for many the pandemic did indeed, as music journalist Peter Alexander suggests,[52] strike a dagger in the heart of both lives and livelihoods, Zoom and related technologies would in time provide a means of adapting to what might otherwise have been an utterly hopeless situation. Musicians like Paul Lenarczyk could continue to connect with audiences through forums like Lenarczyk's weekly online "kitchen party,"[53] and community theatre people like Colleen Naomi kept their own theatrical chops honed while providing entertainment and instruction to large numbers of theatre people by offering online workshops.[54] And the invention of what amounts to a new art form, the virtual play, has allowed actors such as Harold Tausch and yours truly to continue to ply our trades,[55] albeit under strange and sometimes trying conditions. (Installing a "set" for a Zoom play is, as I can attest, a major project, requiring great skill and patience on the part of the installer.) I, personally, am glad to have had the opportunity to act in a Zoom play, even if I would far rather act on a stage in front of a live audience.

But while Zoom has enabled the performance of much work that could not have been done without it, it has also taken the joy out of other kinds of work, such as that done by end-of-life physician Bill Newmann. With his end-of-life consulting interviews being done almost entirely over Zoom, Newmann found he "missed the personal directness and the opportunity to get to meet and talk to … family members. It's hard to establish any close relationships with people when everything's being done virtually."[56] Others, such as union representative Denise Giroux, found it much harder to do jobs involving negotiation and conflict resolution in the absence of face-to-face contact with members and management representatives.[57] But beyond that, for those forced to use Zoom for much or even all of the day, like Giroux and psychotherapist Ruth Hawkins,[58] Zoom has brought a special kind of exhaustion — one exceeding that brought by the conventional computer technologies of the 1980s. Seven hours of video sessions with clients would leave Hawkins feeling an exhaustion she didn't remember feeling after a day of in-person sessions. "I feel numb, spent. Can I allow myself to feel *my* feelings while I'm overfull of the feelings of others? I struggle to find bits of empathy for my own family as they rail against the lockdown, new workplace demands, their loneliness, and busy signals on government phone lines."[59]

What is it about Zoom technology that should make it so particularly exhausting? Technology scholar René Riedl has defined Zoom fatigue as "somatic and cognitive exhaustion ... caused by the intensive and/or inappropriate use of videoconferencing tools, frequently accompanied by related symptoms such as tiredness, worry, anxiety, burnout, discomfort, and stress, as well as other bodily symptoms such as headaches."[60] Some of those symptoms (e.g., headaches and fatigue) are the same as those of the technostress caused by the first generation of computers. But Zoom and other video-conferencing technologies have brought with them a whole host of new sources of stress. One such source is asynchronicity. As Riedl notes, if a delay is perceived during video conferencing (even if this perception occurs subconsciously in the range of milliseconds), the human brain works harder and thereby attempts to overcome the issue of asynchronicity, which is accompanied by increased cognitive effort to restore synchrony. Moreover, this effect is likely accompanied by enhanced frustration and stress.

Other problems include lack of body language and of eye contact. Because video conference participants normally see only the interaction partners' faces (but typically not the full body), rapid and accurate emotional perception may be hampered. With regard to eye contact, if there is a lack of eye contact, shared attention is more difficult to establish than with eye contact, and this, in turn, leads to coordination difficulty that comes along with increased cognitive effort.

Still other problems arise from the interaction with multiple faces and prolonged staring characteristic of Zoom sessions. Such unnatural interaction with multiple faces during video conferencing, including the feeling of being stared at, comes along with increased stress. One possible way around this problem might be to turn one's camera off for much or all of the Zoom session. But this could lead to problems of its own, including the possibility of multi-tasking, thereby missing much of the session while making the multi-tasking worker even more exhausted, and co-workers' suspicion that one was not really taking part in the session at all. With an eye to ensuring full participation, Zoom professor Betsy Hoffman has requested that her graduate students keep their cameras on throughout the class.[61]

Technology, Work Intensification, Stress, and Distress

Her undergraduate students, Hoffman admits, are a lost cause, with many claiming they don't even have cameras in their computers.[62]

Was there ever any intention that workers would be using Zoom and other video conferencing technologies through an entire workday? If one were to query the technology's original inventors, I suspect that their answer would be no, that video conferencing was designed as a pleasant sort of add-on, allowing, for example, the participation of workers from other regions and countries in company meetings without the company's having to incur huge travel expenses. But whatever may have been the original intentions, the fact remains that many, many workers now spend much or even all of their day on Zoom, resulting in the same kinds of physical and mental stress incurred by those working on computers during the first wave of the 1980s, plus those peculiar to the video conferencing technologies, such as asynchronicity, the lack of eye and body contact, and prolonged staring at others. And taken together, these stresses have finally, in the wake of the Covid-19 pandemic, made an entire generation of workers sick and tired and unwilling to put up with any more. It is these technology-related stresses, more than anything else, that have driven the Great Resignation.

If shorter hours were needed (even if they were not for the most part achieved) to compensate workers for the effects of first wave computer technology, they are even more badly needed now to compensate workers for the even stronger effects of Zoom and other video conferencing technologies. But while necessary, shorter hours alone will not be enough to address all the problems of a sick, exhausted, burned-out generation of workers. New schedules that take into account workers' absolute physical limits in dealing with Zoom and like technologies will need to be devised. It may, for example, be the case that the split shift, long despised as a waste of travel time and fuel, is actually more appropriate than a consecutive shift for those working primarily with Zoom — particularly those doing much or all of their work from home, and for whom travel time and fuel are thus not much of an issue.

Beyond that, and most important of all, workers must be assured of a solid, lengthy period in which they disconnect from office technologies, restore some sense of equilibrium to their lives, and enjoy being with family and friends, free of the possibility of technological distractions coming from the office. The "right to disconnect" has become a hot-button issue in various European and Latin American countries in recent years. While it's not yet as big an issue in North America, legislation granting the right to disconnect has, as we shall see, been introduced in several North American jurisdictions, and passed in at least one — Ontario. Along with proposals for shorter hours and work scheduling more accurately reflecting the nature of today's workplace technologies, right to disconnect proposals will form a key part of the book's concluding policy section.

In the meantime, it's important to see what has already been accomplished around the right to disconnect. This topic will be discussed in chapter 8, following directly after the chapter on "The Great Resignation," in which I consider (among many other things) how the new technology's health and safety effects — and workers' response to those effects — have played out in the post-pandemic labour market.

CHAPTER 7

The "Great Resignation" and Its Effects on Work Hours

The "Great Resignation," a term that hadn't even been invented at the start of 2020, has been on almost everyone's lips throughout my writing of this book. All around the world, but especially in the United States, frustrated, exhausted workers have been leaving their jobs, sometimes to abandon the paid labour force altogether, but more often in the hope of finding something more to their liking. What people are looking for are jobs that pay better, offer more of a future, and demand less of them physically and mentally, jobs where workers are treated with respect. In this new labour market, companies offering shorter work hours and work weeks are at a distinct competitive advantage and may even find it easier to bring workers used to working from home back into the office, post-pandemic.[1]

There is no single or simple cause for the phenomenon known as the Great Resignation. In the end, it would be the Covid-19 pandemic that would start to break entire economies out of the cycle of overwork and excessive stress into which they seemed to have been locked as recently as three years ago — at the cost, in many cases, of severe inconvenience and sometimes even major disruption to businesses and their customers and clients.

How did all of this come about? To begin with, as noted in previous chapters the pandemic significantly increased both work hours and (due largely to Zoom and related technologies) work intensity for many workers, pushing a fair number to the brink and some beyond it. As the pandemic deepened and many died from Covid, an increasing number of workers began to re-evaluate their overall life priorities, recognizing that there are more important things than work (such as one's own health and safety and that of one's family). These workers began to see that not only would their work not love them back, in the words of Sarah Jaffe;[2] it might well sicken and even kill them, or, if not them, their family and friends. This recognition led some to reduce their work hours and others to leave the labour force altogether;[3] the latter appears particularly to have been the case for older workers already nearing retirement. Others, who resented the mistreatment they felt they'd received from customers and employers during the pandemic but who might not have felt it possible to quit during the pandemic, began to do so and to shift jobs as soon as the economy picked up following the arrival of Covid-19 vaccines.[4] And in the United States, a near-record level of job vacancies — some 7 percent through the first quarter of 2022 as compared to a little over 4 percent through the first quarter of 2020 — led many to quit for more traditional reasons of low pay and lack of advancement opportunities.[5] To a great extent, if not quite to the same degree, the same combination of factors appears to have been at work in Canada.[6]

The biggest change was in workers' attitude. After decades of people putting up with increasingly long hours and stressful working conditions, there seems to have been a collective decision, not just in Canada and the United States but around much of the world, not to put up with the situation anymore. Suddenly, workers who didn't like the work hours or other working conditions they'd felt they had no choice but to accept realized that they could quit in search of better conditions. No doubt the wave of resignations was closely related to the large number of available job vacancies, particularly in fields such as accommodation and food services and retail trade. While a record 4.5 million U.S. workers quit for reasons other than retirement in March of 2022, the number of job openings at the end of March, 11.55 million, was also a record.[7]

The sweeping nature of this quitting phenomenon led Texas A&M University business professor Anthony Klotz to coin the term "The Great

The "Great Resignation" and Its Effects on Work Hours

Resignation."[8] It appears that the wave of resignations is being spearheaded by younger workers, particularly Millennial and Gen Z workers. The Microsoft Work Trend Index survey for 2022 found 58 percent of U.S. Millennial and Gen Z workers were somewhat or extremely likely to consider changing employers in the coming year — some 15 percent higher than the figures for the overall work force. Another survey, conducted in November 2021, found that 23 percent of U.S. workers planned to quit over the next year. The major reasons cited were the desire to improve working conditions (including work hours), burnout, and a search for higher wages.[9]

How widespread has this Great Resignation been? While it has been most widely publicized and very possibly most widespread in the United States, which saw forty-seven million resignations in 2021 and a monthly record 4.5 million in March 2022, according to that country's Bureau of Labor Statistics,[10] its spirit has spread as far as China. There, as was noted earlier, the "lying flat" movement — passive resistance to the extreme workaholism endemic in Chinese society — has been led by former factory worker Luo Huazhong and widely embraced by young people, who have come to realize, in the words of social anthropology professor Xiang Biao, that "material betterment is no longer the single most important source of meaning in life." While Luo's blog post, "Lying Flat Is Justice," was taken down by censors, it would achieve celebrity status in American media outlets. Luo believes that a "slow lifestyle" is his right. With impeccable logic, he has asked, "Do we have to work twelve hours a day in a sweatshop, and is that justice?"[11] Globally, the trend of lying flat, or "quiet quitting," as this form of resistance to overwork has become known in the Anglosphere, has spread to Singapore, Australia, the United Kingdom, and, perhaps most important of all, to the online world, where videos of young people describing horrific job experiences and explaining why they have felt compelled to quit have recently become commonplace.[12]

In the United Kingdom, as in the United States, resignations have reached record levels, with about 400,000 Britons leaving their jobs voluntarily in the third quarter of 2021 alone.[13] While *The Economist* suggests that "some of the churn may be transitory," it notes that there is also reason to believe that "higher rates of churn are here to stay. The prevalence of remote working means that more roles are plausible options for more jobseekers. And the pandemic has driven home the precariousness of life at the bottom of the income ladder."

In the words of professor of management studies Simone Phipps, the Great Resignation is "definitely *not* [just] an American phenomenon. All over the world, the Great Resignation (or some version of it) has disrupted industries and markets, and impacted all stakeholders, including ... the community.... The community ... is ... affected as service in restaurants and retail establishments is often lacking, and supply chain disruptions and hold ups make goods and services scarce resulting in higher prices."[14] Phipps then goes on to describe some of the Great Resignation's global manifestations, including the departure of millions of European workers from the labour market in industries as diverse as meatpacking and hospitality. In China, she notes, younger workers have been leaving manufacturing jobs, while Vietnam has faced labour shortages resulting from migrant workers leaving the cities for their rural homes not returning after pandemic lockdowns were ended, and India has lost large numbers of workers in information technology. South Africa has also faced a significant increase in employee turnover, while Jamaica has seen some people leaving employee status to start up their own businesses.[15]

Given the broad range of evidence Phipps cites, few could dispute her conclusion that the Great Resignation is certainly a global phenomenon that organizations worldwide must innovatively navigate."[16] Phipps's conclusion is supported by evidence offered by Julia Horowitz.[17] According to a LinkedIn survey cited by Horowitz, about 58 percent of European workers said they were considering changing jobs in 2022 while nearly the same percentage (57 percent) of British nurses in a Royal College of Nursing survey said they were either considering quitting or actively planning to leave. Similarly, LinkedIn data for January 2022 showed a significant increase in the number of workers switching industries in Spain, the Netherlands, and Italy compared to early 2021, while in France, the number of resignations during the third quarter of 2021 was the highest since 2007.

Just how serious a phenomenon is the Great Resignation in Canada? Here, the jury is still out. Kristy Carscallen and Doron Melnick warn in

The "Great Resignation" and Its Effects on Work Hours

their article "Where the Great Resignation Might be Headed in Canada" that "while Canada has not seen the Great Resignation wave U.S. companies experienced, the underlying factors leading to an unprecedented number of Americans quitting their jobs are also at play north of the 49th."[18] These factors include especially high quit rates among "frontline service workers," such as healthcare workers, and others deemed essential, and remote workers, whose experience working from home "has reduced the extent to which many put their careers at the centre of their identities," while also proving they can be just as productive working from home. Workers in these groups now have a fundamentally different relationship with their employers than they did prior to the pandemic and are less apt to tolerate what they consider abusive treatment from their employers or conditions involving extreme overwork than they may have been in the past. People who in the past may, reluctantly, have tolerated severe overwork or abusive treatment for fear of being left unemployed and unable to find another job are now more willing to leave situations they find intolerable, confident they will soon be able to find another job as good or better as the one they are leaving. As a result, a Bank of Canada survey in January 2022 found 19.3 percent of workers expecting to quit their jobs within the next twelve months. Carscallen and Melnick conclude that "while likely not at the same level as in the United States, we can expect a significant uptick in the number of Canadians who choose to change jobs in the next year."

Grace McGrenere[19] offers a similar kind of "mixed bag" report, noting that while a 2021 Statistics Canada Labour Force Survey found that two-thirds of the unemployed who returned to work within a year did so within their old industry, all is definitely not well with Canadian workers. For example, the November 2021 edition of Life Work's Mental Health Index reported one in four Canadians feeling that their personal and work lives had worsened since the pandemic. Earlier, the September 2021 edition of that same index found slightly over one-third (35 percent) considering leaving their jobs.

On the question of why the Great Resignation seems to be proceeding more gradually in Canada than in the United States, McGrenere quotes Carleton University professor Paul Mkandwire, who suggests one reason may have been Canada's generally more humane and less polarized response to the pandemic, with greater support for affected workers and businesses. Canadian workers may thus not have reached the same level of desperation about their situation as quickly as did their American counterparts.

Another factor — one seldom noted in any of the comparative discussions about the Great Resignation — is surely Canada's much higher union membership rate compared to that of the United States. As of 2021, 30.9 percent of all Canadian workers were union members, a figure precisely three times that of the United States' 10.3 percent.[20]

There are a number of reasons why a more heavily unionized workforce might expect to see fewer resignations than a less heavily unionized one. In general, leaving aside the special situations of highly paid professionals, entertainers, and business executives, unionized jobs tend to be better jobs than non-unionized ones, being in the main better paid, offering significantly more in the way of benefits, and providing more protection against arbitrary workplace treatment.

In most unionized settings, work hours and overtime are strictly regulated through collective agreements, which make it much more difficult for employers to impose overtime arbitrarily and provide a remedy, in the form of a grievance process, against arbitrary or abusive employer behaviour regarding work hours. Given the existence of the grievance process, those protesting such arbitrary or abusive behaviour don't have to worry about being singled out for protesting, as most collective agreements also contain provisions barring employers from retaliating against employees exercising their collective agreement rights. It is also worth noting that health and safety provisions are generally more strictly enforced in unionized than in non-unionized workplaces.[21] It would thus take more to induce someone to leave such a job than to leave a non-unionized job offering little beyond the hourly wage; those in unionized jobs would typically feel they had more to lose by quitting.

In addition, through collective agreement grievance procedures, consultation mechanisms, and various other mechanisms, unions offer workers a collective say in determining working conditions. Unionized workers who disagree with an employer's actions are not, in effect, forced to quit if the

The "Great Resignation" and Its Effects on Work Hours

disagreement continues, as they generally are in non-unionized workplaces, since they can take the matter to their union, often with at least some hope of achieving redress. This comparatively greater possibility of achieving a collective as opposed to individual solution to problems is undoubtedly a factor that would reduce the rate of resignations in Canada.[22]

But just because Canadian workers aren't quitting at the same rate as their American counterparts doesn't mean Canadian employers can afford to be complacent in the face of the Great Resignation. Stiff competition for workers has become a fact of life here just as it is south of the border. And all the evidence suggests that organizations offering workers shorter hours, and hours better suited to their individual life circumstances, will be better able to attract and, above all, retain good workers. This is a point to which we'll be returning both at the end of this chapter and in later chapters.

For now, it's worth taking a closer look at some of the manifestations of the Great Resignation, both for individual workers and for the community at large. To begin with, it's important to note that for the most part, except for workers at or near retirement age at the start of the pandemic, who may simply have used the pandemic as an excuse to retire earlier than originally planned, it might be that the world of work may, in the words of Australia's treasurer, Josh Frydenberg, be seeing "a 'Great Reshuffle' rather than a 'Great Resignation.'"[23] In other words, people are not leaving the labour force; they're simply moving to a different part of it.

Supporting Frydenberg's notion, at least for Canada, is the fact that Canadian labour force levels are up to what they were before the Covid-19 pandemic.[24] What is observable is a massive shift from an employers' to an employees' labour market, resulting from what Alistair Steele in "Where Have All the Workers Gone? Don't Blame COVID, Economists Say," describes as "virtually unprecedented labour shortages across nearly every employment sector,"[25] but manifesting itself particularly strongly in construction, manufacturing, and accommodation and food services. With workers now having many more choices than they did just two or three years ago, those unhappy with their wages, work hours, or other working conditions are now much more likely than they would have been to quit their jobs in favour of work "in an industry where there's a better career stream and where the wages are higher and the hours are more predictable."[26] And the same basic pattern appears to be true in the United States, where according to Emma Goldberg,[27] "many of last year's job quitters are actually job swappers." Citing Bureau of Labor Statistics and census data, Goldberg notes there's "a nearly one-to-one correlation between the rate of quitting and swapping," with the highest rates of swapping in leisure, hospitality, and retail.

While some career shifts may involve moving to a job quite closely related to one's old job, as in the case of senior British nurse Joan Pons Laplana, who now works as a teacher training people from disadvantaged backgrounds so they can find jobs in the National Health Service,[28] others, like that of former private school history teacher Melissa Villareal, who now works in industrial design for a large beauty company, amount to a full 180-degree turn. Driving Villareal's switch from a job and field she loved were health and safety and workload concerns that began when she was called back into the classroom during the pandemic after only a short break and was made to juggle in-person and remote learners simultaneously, which led to a spike in her workload and stress. While she felt guilty about leaving her students, Villareal decided she could no longer remain on a job where she was "being under-valued and unheard."[29] The current booming economy makes it much easier for workers who feel as Villareal did to make the kind of shift she made than it would have been even two years earlier.

At the societal level, the Great Resignation plays out in a number of different ways, as noted in the Simone Phipps article cited earlier in the chapter. The most dramatic manifestation is staff shortages, of which, as noted earlier, almost all of us have had some experience by now. These shortages have not been confined to the hospitality industry. In Boston, a shortage of drivers has forced the city's transit authority to reduce bus service.[30] (Of note, nearby Lawrence, which increased the pay of its bus drivers, has hired more drivers and brought in more frequent service[31] — a fact that suggests that pay increases may at least help mitigate some of the effects of the Great Resignation.)

The industry perhaps hardest hit by staff shortages is the airlines, which have been unable to hire back enough of the people they were forced to lay off or furlough during the Covid-19 pandemic to meet a suddenly increased

The "Great Resignation" and Its Effects on Work Hours

demand for air travel.[32] During the summer of 2022, U.S. airlines collectively cancelled thousands of flights,[33] nearly 950 of those cancellations having occurred on a single Sunday in early August, along with more than 7,700 delays.[34] The result of all these cancellations and delays, in the words of Stephen Jones, has been "long queues at airports, lost luggage, long layovers, and acute disappointment."[35]

Hampering the airlines' search for ground crew workers, of which thousands more are needed, is their apparent inability or unwillingness to pay wages competitive with those offered by Amazon and other large employers for jobs that are performed under pleasanter working conditions.

Less dramatic, perhaps, but no less frequent have been staffing shortages in retail, accommodation and food services, and personal services. As has been the case with the airlines, pay and working conditions (including work hours) have been key drivers of these new staff shortages. Economist Armine Yalnizyan sums up the situation succinctly when she says, "People are finding other places to work. There just aren't enough people [in an economy marked by severe labour shortages] willing to do poorly paid jobs that are marginal at best."[36] Continuing high demand for workers in fields like accommodation and food services will likely lead to substantial wage increases in those fields, suggests Carleton University business professor Ian Lee.[37]

It's also important to note that outright resignations (or threats to resign) and staff shortages aren't the only manifestations of the Great Resignation. Another, which has become particularly prominent in recent months, is the phenomenon known as "quiet quitting." Instead of leaving outright, the "quiet quitters" have basically stopped doing more than their job absolutely requires, engaging in behaviour that, in a collective unionized setting, might well be described as working to rule. Because most of the quiet quitters evidently don't work in unionized settings, their protests are somewhat more individualized than those one would see in a formal work to rule campaign. But the protests should be no less concerning to managers, as a sign of employee burnout and disengagement, than widespread working to rule would be in a unionized environment. Of late, the term has taken on such resonance that a July 2022 TikTok video describing it as quitting "the idea of going above and beyond at work" collected more than three million views and helped popularize the phrase.[38]

Signs of quiet quitting could include putting up more boundaries around work and saying "no" more. They could also include withdrawing from the work team, limiting communication and interaction to the bare minimum required. In other cases, they could include people letting their attention shift, focusing on projects that "aren't really in the scope of their job," in the words of employee engagement expert Natalie Baumgartner. The danger — and the reason why managers need to intervene quickly at the first signs of quiet quitting, according to workplace transformation director Joe Grasso, is that negative individual attitudes can quickly become collective. "Much like quiet quitting is becoming a trend on social media, it could also become an infectious attitude in the workplace as employees start to compare notes and recognize that they are having similar experiences about work taking more than it is giving."[39]

What can and should employers and managers do to combat the rapidly growing phenomenon of quiet quitting? One approach might be to fight back, moving quickly to terminate those they see as malingerers and troublemakers.[40] But given current labour market dynamics, such a course of action would be ill-advised. Not only would it add staff shortages to the organization's list of human resource problems, it would only serve to worsen existing morale problems and might well also damage the organization's reputation in such a way that it would find it difficult to recruit people for some time to come.

Another, certainly more constructive approach outlined by global HR officer Michelle Hay[41] is to recognize that it's understandable people should be feeling tired and frustrated at the end of the pandemic, and to do detailed surveys (including exit interviews) aimed at helping managers understand "the full picture of engagement" in the organization. In addition, Hay says, managers should encourage their staff to take breaks during the day and should avoid sending non-urgent messages after the end of the working day, setting a good example by taking time off themselves and not responding to emails sent to them outside of working hours. The idea of "disconnecting" from work outside of work is a good one. Indeed, it's an issue of increasing

The "Great Resignation" and Its Effects on Work Hours

importance in today's remote and hybrid workplaces. I'll be taking it up again, in considerably more detail, in the next chapter, devoted exclusively to the right to disconnect.

At the end of the day, the causes of the low morale, cynicism, and reduced productivity that characterize quiet quitting are apt to be pretty much the same as those driving the Great Resignation, namely low or inequitable pay (in many though not all cases), excessive workloads, overly long and inflexible work hours, and lack of respect from managers and clients or customers. Organizations wishing to recruit and retain top quality staff must attend to all of those issues. While pay may be the single most important issue in recruitment, workload and work hours are critical to retention. We no longer live in a world where, for most workers, productivity is simply a linear function of the number of person-hours worked. The right setting (including significantly shorter hours) can greatly increase productivity and improve morale. Conversely, the wrong setting (including longer hours designed simply to prove one has been present at work rather than actually accomplishing something there) is likely to decrease productivity and lower morale. Organizations that recognize this fact and tailor work schedules so as to maximize employee productivity and engagement seem likely to enjoy a significant competitive advantage, not just in the near term but for the foreseeable future.

In the book's first six chapters, I've tried to show how work hours in many countries, including Canada and the United States, have remained stubbornly long despite strong indications that such long hours are bad for workers' health and also have had deleterious effects on health care systems and the environment. In this chapter, I've shown how an increasingly large number of workers have started to respond to highly stressful pandemic and post-pandemic work conditions and labour market shortages, by leaving those jobs where conditions are the worst. Such a "Great Resignation" is a new development in today's workplaces and marks a shift to a fundamentally different kind of workplace. The next two chapters, on the "Right to Disconnect" and "Hybrid Workplaces," will discuss two other new and different aspects of today's workplaces. It is to the former that the discussion now turns, in chapter 8.

CHAPTER 8

The Right to Disconnect

Having shorter regular hours of work doesn't mean much if your employer can still bombard you with emails, texts, requests for Zoom talks, and all other kinds of electronic communication at any hour of the day or night, whether you are on duty or not, and expect a speedy response from you. In extreme cases, such a situation does away with the whole idea of regular work hours. Even in less extreme cases, the expectations generated can be a source of physical and mental stress for the employee and can lead to a significant interruption of normal home and family life, particularly if the employer's demands along these lines are at all frequent.

It wasn't all that long ago that off-hours communication was simply not an issue for most working people. As recently as the mid-1990s, only a very small number of workers — generally emergency medical personnel such as doctors — carried cellular phone equipment that would allow them to respond quickly in the event of an emergency. These old cellphones were large, cumbersome, and extremely conspicuous. Few of us envied the people who carried them. I can personally recall feeling sorry for them. The thought that I might one day carry such a device myself — albeit a far more easily portable device — never crossed my mind. No amount of money would have induced me to allow such a brazen breach of the firewall between home and office into my life.

By the beginning of the new millennium, the situation had begun to change. A sizable number of people had begun to carry much smaller cellular phones in their purses or in their pockets. While some used them only occasionally, as for example to call a cab in the city, others were making them their more or less constant companions. My then boss, the late John Fryer, for whom I worked between 1999 and 2001,[1] was definitely of this latter contingent. About halfway through my time with John, one of his children gave him one of the then-new BlackBerries. John was clearly delighted by this new toy. The thought of being constantly connected with the outside world did not bother him; in fact, he positively welcomed it. Generally, he would make or reply to at least two or three calls as we walked together to a meeting, or to a restaurant for lunch. Though for obvious reasons I never shared my feelings about this with John, inwardly I shuddered every time I saw him playing with his new machine. Why was a man who had for three decades led large public-sector unions, first in British Columbia and then in Ottawa, and who was recognized as an international authority on public sector labour relations, wasting his time with such a silly little device?

Less extreme than many of today's cellphone addicts, John at least had the decency to turn his device off during in-person meetings, of which we had a great many during the course of gathering information for our reports. Never once was a meeting interrupted by an irritating bleep from the machine — a proud record all too rarely achieved today even in situations, such as when watching plays or dance performances, where cellphone ringing is seriously distracting to performers and audiences alike. And he never once suggested that I get a cellphone. As a matter of fact, I suspect that if I had requested one, he'd have turned me down. The Fryer Committee's budget was small, and since we did almost all our information gathering together, there really wasn't any reason for us both to be carrying cellphones.

On reflection, I can now see that John's devotion to and constant use of his BlackBerry made perfect sense. Unlike me, he was an extrovert, and far more of a talker than a writer. The more or less constant interruptions that I would have found a serious distraction were, for him, all a part of the day's work. After several decades of union work, John had a large circle of friends and an even larger circle of acquaintances with whom it was important, for professional reasons, for him to keep in at least some kind of contact. I did not have such a circle. Any friends or relatives I needed to contact I could contact quite easily on my landline.

While by this point I was beginning to see the possible usefulness of cellphones for certain people, I still couldn't see any point in my getting one. My attitude, at the time, was that I really wasn't an important enough person to need to be constantly connected, and I certainly had no desire to be constantly connected. If the government wanted me to be constantly connected, they were going to have to pay me $150,000 or $200,000 a year — then the salary range of assistant deputy ministers — to compensate me for such a serious intrusion on my personal life.

My own introduction to cellphones would come two years after I left John, in 2003. By that time, I was working for the Professional Institute of the Public Service of Canada (PIPSC), where I would spend the rest of my professional career. Having spent my first two years at PIPSC as a researcher, I was given a developmental assignment to become an employment relations officer. Researchers didn't need cellphones at work because they almost always worked in conjunction with negotiators, who had them. But employment relations officers were often on their own, and sometimes worked odd hours. In such a situation, a cellphone was clearly necessary. The one I was issued — an old-fashioned flip phone — suited me perfectly. It had the minimum possible number of bells and whistles, and it would serve me well through the rest of my time in Ottawa. Gradually, I became more reconciled to the device, though I continued to use it almost exclusively on an as-needed basis. It did prove quite useful when I was travelling to the United States, which I did on average two or three times a year to visit family or attend school reunions. And on one occasion, it may have been a lifesaver, enabling me to summon help to get my son Alex to the hospital when he developed food poisoning from eating a past-its-prime pizza just after we'd moved — and before the landline could be installed. (I didn't own a car at the time.)

Following this incident, I vowed never again to be without some kind of cellphone. But the incident did not change my basic view that a cellphone was something to be used solely for business purposes and/or in emergencies.

The idea that such a device could be a toy, a plaything, or possibly even a substitute for human interaction remained, as it has remained to this day, anathema to me. The all-too-numerous TV ads in which technology companies attempt to humanize new technologies by depicting them as cute or even lovable little animals strike me as truly sinister.[2] To me, a serious firewall — the one between human and non-human behaviour — has been breached here. Am I the only person in the world who feels this way, I sometimes wonder?

Whatever the answer to this admittedly rather esoteric question, it was, by the early years of the new millennium, becoming clear that another traditional firewall, that between workers' work lives and their home lives, was beginning to be breached quite frequently, owing to the growing use of technologies such as email and cellphones. As noted in Wikipedia's excellent and compendious review article on the right to disconnect, "The modern working environment has been drastically changed by new communication and information technologies. The boundary between work life and home life has shrunk with the introduction of digital tools into employment. While digital tools bring flexibility and freedom to employees they also can create an absence of limits, leading to excessive interference in the private lives of employees."

Early Developments

FRANCE

The first recognition that workers should have a right to disconnect from the technologies connecting them to the workplace during off-work hours was made in France in the early 2000s. This right was first enunciated in a decision issued by the Labour Chamber of the French Supreme Court. The October 2, 2001, ruling held that "the employee is under no obligation either to accept working at home or to bring there his files and working tools." This decision was affirmed and somewhat extended in a 2004 Supreme Court decision involving an employee who had been terminated for not answering his cellphone outside of working hours. In this decision, the Supreme Court held that "the fact that [the employee] was not reachable on his cellphone outside working hours cannot be considered as misconduct."

Both of these Supreme Court decisions would be used as legal support for later French right to disconnect legislation, such as the "El Khomri" law, which will be discussed in some detail later in the chapter. The El Khomri law, named after the French labour minister at that time, was also a response to a 2015 report on the impact of digital technologies on labour that supported a right to "professional disconnection."[3]

GERMANY

It's important to bear in mind that, unlike French labour law, German labour law contains no statutory right to disconnect.[4] However, laws such as the Implementation of Measures of Occupational Safety and Health to Encourage Improvements in the Safety and Health Protection of Workers at Work (*Arbeitsschutzgesetz*) Act and the Working Hours (*Arbeitszeitgesetz*) Act, plus Directive 2003/88/EC of the European Parliament and of the Council of 4 November 2003 (the Working Time Directive) set certain legal limits with regard to the constant availability of employees.

In 2016, the Ministry of Labour and Social Affairs provided the white paper "Work 4.0" (*Weissbuch Arbeiten 4.0*), which set out a guideline to balance the flexibility needs of companies and workers while at the same time maintaining health and safety at work. In this context the minister of labour and social affairs, companies, social partners, civil society, and academia reached a broad consensus regarding the fact that working time must be organized in a way that better takes into account particular and differing time needs. As a consequence of this consensus, it was agreed that there was no need for further legislative action. According to the parties involved in the project, the best way to address the issue would be to negotiate collective agreements, make flexibility compromises and draft works agreements.

Little progress was made early on with negotiating collective agreement provisions addressing the right to disconnect, though the metal workers' union IG Metall, long a national leader in issues related to work hours,[5] did address the dissolution of boundaries between working time and private life at a conference in October 2017. However, through May of 2018, no collective bargaining agreements addressing this subject had been negotiated.

A considerably more fruitful approach has been the negotiation of works agreements under the auspices of the German Works Council Constitution Act, which provides for a codetermination right of the works council with regard to working hours. A strong tradition of employee representation in many large German companies has facilitated the negotiation of works agreements on the issue of the right to disconnect. BMW, for example, has set out in a works agreement that employees are allowed to insist on their right to inaccessibility during holidays, the weekend, and after the end of work. Volkswagen went further, in 2011 implementing a policy of stopping email servers from sending emails to employees' mobile phones between 6 p.m. and 7 a.m.[6] A similar policy has been in place at the automaker Daimler since 2014, when the company introduced software called Mail on Holiday that automatically deletes all incoming messages received while the out-of-office message is enabled, forcing senders to resend their posts during regular working hours.[7]

Less stringent though still significant policies were put in place by various other German companies. For example, in 2010 Deutsche Telekom established a policy that employees were not obligated to check their emails after working hours but did not provide any enforcement mechanism. Similarly, Bayer, BASF, and E.ON declared explicitly that their employees would not have to check their smartphones or emails after work. However, unlike the situation applying in other companies, there was no concrete works agreement in place to undergird the policy. For its part, Henkel established that nobody, including senior management, would need to check their emails after official working hours. The company's CEO declared that on one day of the week — Saturday — he himself would not check his emails. Furthermore, he prohibited all executive board members from contacting him between Christmas and New Year's Day. Meanwhile, Puma and Deutsche Bank have stated explicitly they do not expect that employees can be contacted by email during their holidays. In the latter company, it is possible for employees to set an out-of-office reply in their email accounts.

A somewhat different approach was taken by the electronics firm Siemens, which was more flexible and did not have any fixed agreements. There, it was up to employees to decide on their own whether or not they wanted to be available after working hours. That said, in general, Siemens did not require employees to check their emails after working hours or during holidays.[8] For its part, Evonik used an "email brake" set out in a works agreement that applies to all employees of the company. The employees, together with their supervisors, defined a period of availability. Beyond that period, employees did not have to answer emails, but unlike the situation at Volkswagen and Daimler, email servers were not turned off and emails were not blocked.

While most German right to disconnect policies applied to the private sector, one German ministry, the employment ministry, has established such a policy. In 2013, seeking to protect the mental health of its workers, Germany's employment ministry banned its managers from contacting staff after hours as part of a wider agreement on remote working.[9]

More Recent Legislative Provisions

FRANCE

Having already laid the groundwork for right to disconnect legislation through the court cases discussed earlier in this chapter, the French government wrote the right to disconnect into its Labour Code, in the form of legislation (the El Khomri law) that was a response to a 2015 report on the impact of digital technologies on workers supporting a right to "professional disconnection."[10] The report, presented to Labour Minister Myriam El Khomri, had recommended a right to disconnect law, noting that for the new digital technology to have a positive effect on workers' quality of life, a proper balance between work and private life was essential, and that for this balance to be maintained, workers needed to be able to disconnect, given that constant connectivity was likely to lead to cognitive and emotional overload, which in turn could lead to a sense of fatigue. Further impetus for right to disconnect legislation came from a 2016 study that found that 37 percent of workers were using such professional digital tools as work mobile phones outside of work hours, and that 62 percent of workers wanted more controls and rules to regulate off-hours use of digital technology.

The El Khomri law took the form of an amendment to Article 55, Chapter II of the Labour Code (Adapting the Labour Law to the Digital Age). The following paragraph was added to the Labour Code:

> The procedures for the full exercise by the employee of his right to disconnect and the establishment by the company of mechanisms for regulating the use of digital tools, with a view to ensuring respect for rest period and leaves as well as personal and family life. Failing agreement, the employer shall draw up a charter, after consultation with the works council or, failing that, with the staff delegates. This charter defines these procedures for the exercise of the right to disconnect and furthermore provides for the implementation, for employees and management and management personnel, of training and awareness-raising activities on the reasonable use of digital tools.

This right to disconnect provision came into force January 1, 2017.

The El Khomri regime is marked by a high degree of voluntarism. It's important to note that the law doesn't prescribe any particular right-to-disconnect provisions, instead allowing companies, in collaboration with their employees and, where they are present, their works councils, to develop policies suited to their particular circumstances.[11] In companies with more than fifty employees, the right to disconnect must be included in the Mandatory Annual Negotiation (MAN) on gender equality and the nature of quality of life at work. But while there is an obligation to negotiate, there is no obligation to reach an agreement; thus, if no agreement is reached, the right to disconnect can't be applied and enforced. Companies with fewer than fifty employees are expected to provide a charter to their employees outlining rules on disconnection for their company. There is, however, no penalty for companies failing to draw up such a charter, although large employers who fail to include the right to disconnect in their MAN are deemed to have obstructed the exercise of union rights and are liable to criminal prosecution possibly resulting in a fine and imprisonment.

Despite the legislation's lack of compulsion, it has clearly had an effect on the right to disconnect policies in place in French companies. For instance, Natixis, a large financial enterprise, has developed a policy titled "For a proper use of emails," inviting its employees to disconnect, in particular during the weekends and vacation periods, and recommending that they be selective as to the recipients of emails and that messages sent be clear and concise. For its part, the French bank Société Générale has undertaken to draft and ensure the distribution of an electronic messaging policy and to provide training aimed at raising employees' awareness with regard to the use of technological devices. Such training is indeed a mandatory part of the legislation. It stipulates that companies must ensure that their personnel, blue-collar workers and executives alike, are effectively trained to make a reasonable use of digital devices made available to them.[12]

The French law has become a kind of model for similar laws proposed or actually adopted both in other European countries and in Canada, as well as in various Latin American countries and the Philippines.

Other European Legislative Provisions

BELGIUM

A Belgian law that came into effect on February 1, 2022, allows that country's civil servants to switch off work emails, texts, and phone calls received out of hours, without fear of reprisals. The law was a response to the blurring of the line between home and work life resulting from the pandemic-induced shift to remote working, which had left many answering calls, texts, and emails at all hours.

The purpose of the legislation is to protect the country's sixty-five thousand public-sector employees from exposure to being permanently on-call, although out-of-hours contact is permissible in exceptional circumstances. Plans are being discussed to extend the new laws to employees in the private sector. As Belgium's public administration minister Petra De Sutter told the BBC, the hope is that the new law will "help prevent burnout and reinforce the importance of establishing a work-life balance."

ITALY

The right to disconnect became law in Italy in 2017 through Article 19(1) of Senate Act 2233-B, "Measures to safeguard non-entrepreneurial self-employment and measures to facilitate flexible articulation in times and places of subordinate employment." Article 19(1) states, "The Agreement on Aggregate Work shall be stipulated in writing for the purpose of administrative and probative regularity and shall govern the performance of work performed outside the premises of the company.... The agreement also identifies the worker's rest periods as well as the technical and organizational measures necessary to ensure that the worker is disconnected from the technological equipment."[13]

LUXEMBOURG

In September 2021, a bill to amend Luxembourg's Labour Code by including a right to disconnect was introduced into the country's Chamber of Deputies (Parliament). The bill distinguishes itself from the French bill on which it is otherwise largely modelled, and from most other right to disconnect legislation, by providing sanctions against violators. After a lengthy delay, the bill was finally passed by Luxembourg's Parliament on June 13, 2023. The legislation states that when employees use digital devices for their work, a scheme ensuring that the right to disconnect outside working hours is respected must be introduced for the company or sector in question. Such schemes should be adapted to the specific situation of the organization or sector, and should set out, where applicable, any necessary practical arrangements and technical measures for disconnecting from digital devices, appropriate awareness-raising and training measures, and compensation arrangements in the event of one-off exceptions to the right to disconnect. As for implementation, the legislation provides that schemes can be defined in collective bargaining agreements or subordinate agreements. Failing that, they should be established at the organization level.

PORTUGAL

Portugal, long a trailblazer in the European Union on remote work issues, recently enacted some of Europe's strongest right to disconnect legislation. As of November 2021, the Portuguese Labour Code stipulates that "employers have the duty to refrain from contacting workers during their rest period, except in situations of force majeure" (i.e., dire emergencies). Breaches of this provision of the law, which was passed following the growth of the home office during the Covid-19 pandemic, are a serious offense, punishable by fines of up to 9,690 euros. Such sanctions put Portugal a step beyond France, Spain, and most other European countries that have passed right to disconnect legislation.

SLOVAKIA

In February 2021, the National Council of the Slovak Republic passed an amendment to the country's labour code (Act No. 311/2001 Coll.) that introduced a right to disconnect for remote-working employees. Under Sec. 52(10) of the amended Slovak Labour Code, effective March 1, 2021, employees working remotely were given the right to abstain from using work equipment during their designated rest periods, including vacations and public holidays. The provision further stated that if employees exercised their right to disconnect, the employer could not consider such an act a breach of professional duty.[14]

SPAIN

In Spain, a law approved in 2019 establishes employees' right to disconnect from digital devices during off-work hours to ensure respect for their rest time, holidays, and privacy. The law calls on employers, after hearing from workers' representatives, to set up internal policies defining for employees how to exercise the right to disconnect, including training for staff on reasonable use of technology to help avoid computer fatigue. Spain's law emphasizes that employees working remotely are guaranteed the right to disconnect.

Madrid-based employment lawyer Raquel Flórez noted that the new Spanish law, like the French law on which it was modelled, doesn't impose penalties on employers that fail to comply. "At least this is bringing the discussion to the table," she said.[15] It appears that like a number of other right to disconnect laws, the Spanish one has adopted a position midway between doing nothing and backing up its provisions with strict sanctions against violators.

THE EUROPEAN UNION (EU)

In early 2021, the European Parliament, made up of representatives from the EU's twenty-seven member countries, voted by an overwhelming 476–126 margin (with eighty-three abstentions) to support a right to disconnect law. While the EU's executive branch, the European Commission, must take action before the bill can take effect — a process likely to take several years — the large approval margin and the fact that a fair number of European countries have already enacted or at least introduced similar legislation suggests that full EU enactment will be just a matter of time.

· · · · · ·

Right to disconnect legislation hasn't been confined to Europe. Such legislation has been passed in three Latin American countries and introduced (though not yet enacted into law) in the Philippines. In the United States, a right to disconnect bill was introduced into New York's City Council but stalled there. Most recently, such legislation was introduced in Kenya, the first African country to do so.

Latin America

ARGENTINA

Following on the heels of Chile but moving far beyond the Chilean law (see below) on which it was originally modelled, Argentina's Senate adopted new legislation, Law 27.555, on telework on July 30, 2020. Article 5 of the new law introduces a right to disconnect, noting that remote workers have the right to disconnect from electronic technology outside of their regular working day and on holidays. The law further stipulates that employers can't communicate with or ask their employees to perform tasks outside of normal working hours. It was the first law, globally, with specific language protecting workers from employer reprisal for exercising their right to disconnect.

A draft law was introduced in the Senate earlier in 2020 to establish a right to disconnect for all Argentinean workers. The draft contained several important elements of a comprehensive right to disconnect policy, including the aforementioned prohibition on employer reprisal and a statement to the effect that the right to disconnect can be suspended only in the event of emergencies.

CHILE

In Chile, where there is a teleworking agreement, teleworkers are subject to working hours restrictions, unless the parties agree that the employee is exempt from the working hour limit under the Labor Code, in which case they cannot generate overtime.[16] However, it's presumed that teleworkers are subject to working hours restrictions if the employer exerts functional control over the way in which their work is performed and its timing, in which case they are entitled to overtime.

The law establishes a right to disconnect for at least twelve continuous hours in any twenty-four-hour period for distance employees free to establish their own working hours, and for teleworkers not subject to working hours restrictions. In that period of disconnection, the employer is not allowed to expect the employee to respond to communications, orders, or other requests. In addition, employers are not allowed to communicate or make orders or other requests on days falling within employees' rest, leave, or annual vacation periods.

PERU

Peru has established a fairly comprehensive right to disconnect policy regime. The Peruvian legislation begins with a framework statement: "It is the right of workers to disconnect from the computer, telecommunications and similar means (internet, cellular phones and computers, among others) used for the provision of services." The right to digital disconnection applies to management, those not subject to immediate supervision of working hours, and those who provide "intermittent services," as well as ordinary workers.

The digital disconnect time starts at the end of the working day and ends at the beginning of the next day. During the period of disconnection, employers may not require their workers to perform any type of work, respond to communications, or establish coordination that may be considered labour, unless it has been agreed that work performed will be considered overtime. However, the company may assign tasks or send communications to workers during their digital disconnection period, provided that workers are not required to attend to those tasks outside of their regular workday. Should the worker and employer agree that the former will perform any work or coordination during the disconnect period, such work will be considered overtime work and paid or compensated with substitute rest.

As for workers not subject to a regular working day, they are not to carry out work by means of any computer, digital, or analog means for at least twelve continuous hours in any twenty-four-hour period.

Companies are specifically warned not to intimidate workers into performing tasks, responding to communications, or coordinating during their time of digital disconnection. Failure to abide by this prohibition is a serious administrative offense punishable by a fine, the amount of which is based on the number of workers affected.

The legislation also contains three specific recommendations to companies: they must implement concrete measures on digital disconnection in their internal work regulations; they must develop a remote work policy that establishes rights and obligations; and they must limit access to the company's computer systems during rest periods.

Other Countries

KENYA

Kenya recently became the latest country (and the first African country) to introduce right to disconnect legislation. Its proposed Employment (Amendment) Bill seeks to prevent employers from expecting their employees to answer phone calls, texts, or emails outside of regular working hours, or on weekends or public holidays. The bill would require firms with more than ten employees to consult staff or trade unions about their out-of-work policies. Violators of the rules would face fines of $4,000.

THE PHILIPPINES

If a bill introduced in early 2022 into the Philippines' House of Representatives by Representative Joaquin Chipeco is passed, the Philippines could soon be joining the growing list of countries with right to disconnect legislation in place.[17] The right to disconnect was included in a broader "Workers' Rest Law," Bill 10717, with the primary objective of defining employees' rest hours so as to ensure their welfare.

In explaining the rationale for his bill, Chipeco noted that the growth of digital technology, triggered in large measure by the Covid-19 pandemic, has all but completely blurred the "delicate line between the home and the workplace so much … that many employees have been reduced to an 'on call' status at practically any time of the day." This, combined with the excessive work hours expected of those working from home, is not good for workers' mental health and also has adverse effects on their family life, Chipeco said.

One of the bill's most notable features is its right to disconnect provision, which bars employers from contacting employees for work and work-related purposes using telephones, emails, messages, or any other form of communication, unless such communication is related to a specific emergency as established in various articles of the Labor Code. Employers are further barred from punishing employees exercising their right to disconnect. The bill also prohibits employers from requiring employees to work outside of work hours, and from requiring employees to be on duty, to travel, or to be assigned to a place in connection with work outside of work hours.

At this writing, the fate of Chipeco's bill is not yet known. A similar bill was introduced into the Senate at about the same time by Senator Francis Tolentino.[18] Tolentino's bill goes even further than Chipeco's, including fines, prison sentences, and heavy payments to employees as penalties for employers violating the law, though it excludes several classes of workers (including domestics) from the law's operation. It should be noted that these are not the first attempts to establish a right to disconnect in the Philippines. Then representative Winnie Castelo put forward such legislation in 2017, though the bill would eventually die in a House committee.[19]

The Right to Disconnect in Canada and the United States

CANADIAN GOVERNMENT

In 2019 the Canadian federal government established the Right to Disconnect Advisory Committee. Its overall mandate, as laid out by the labour minister, was to improve labour protections in the Canada Labour Code. More specifically, the committee was mandated to "co-develop new provisions with employers and labour groups that give federally regulated workers the right to disconnect." The committee's functions were to share information on issues relevant to the right to disconnect, hear from experts, workers, other witnesses, and sectoral representatives, and to develop recommendations and provide a report outlining the committee's advice on how best to implement the right to disconnect. To this end, the committee held over ten meetings, starting in October 2020, and heard from various parties including former members of the Expert Panel on Modern Federal Labour Standards, French and German representatives of the International Labour Organization, and representatives from a number of different federally regulated sectors. Its report, initially presented to the labour minister in June of 2021, was released to the general public in February 2022.

Given that the committee's goals included providing employees with boundaries on the use of workplace communications devices outside of standard working hours, providing clarity on what is working time and what is not, providing details on workplace procedures for emergency situations where there may be need to use workplace communication devices outside of employees' normal working hours, and outlining situations where operational requirements dictate that employees (or groups of employees) must regularly be available to receive workplace communications, one would have expected something in the way of substantive policy recommendations on the right to disconnect. But there was substantial divergence between unions and NGOs on the one hand, and employers on the other, particularly with regard to whether the right to disconnect should be legislated. Unions and NGOs argued that a legislated right to disconnect is needed to protect employees from employer reprisal when they refuse to receive workplace communications during their "right to rest periods." For their part, employers said existing Canada Labour Code provisions on rest periods were sufficient, and that the parties should be encouraged to work together to develop their own work-life balance policies. A further concern for employers was that legislation might not sufficiently recognize the need for employer flexibility to enable employers to do business with provincially regulated companies or with international firms not subject to the same laws.

Despite its lofty initial aims, in the end the committee wound up issuing nine recommendations that can be best described as being of a "motherhood" nature. The recommendations are as follows:

- Employees should be paid for work performed.
- Establishing a positive work-life balance is a key goal of both employers and workers.

- There is a need for flexibility for both workers and employers.
- There is a need to protect health and safety, and there are some situations where communication with employees is critical.
- There is a need to recognize existing arrangements, such as collective bargaining relationships.
- Absolute limits (such as shutting down email servers or network access) may not be realistic in some situations.
- There is a need to recognize the varied nature of the federal jurisdiction.
- There is a need for clarity in whatever is implemented.
- There is a need to protect the privacy and security of workers.

In "Federal Advisory Committee Offers Insight into Disconnect from Work Policies for Employees," an analysis written for law firm Weirfoulds, Daniel Wong, writing with Megan Mah and Alfred Pepushaj, notes, rather dryly, in a comment immediately following the list of recommendations, that it "remains to be seen whether the Government of Canada will implement any legislative measures for federally regulated employees as a result of the Report." I would only suggest that I would not hold my breath waiting for such a development to occur. Looking at the nine recommendations above in light of the committee's original mandate, the number of witnesses it called, and the amount of work it did, a phrase from classic Greek literature comes to mind: The mountain laboured and brought forth a mouse. It's truly a sad commentary that so much effort was expended with such paltry results. Even Ontario's right to disconnect law (see below), toothless though it is, at least recognizes the existence of the problem, and is thus of more practical benefit than the advisory committee's report. Given the federal government's apparent lack of political will to take serious action on the right to disconnect, one can only hope that in the near future the provinces will fill in the void, taking the matter into their own hands to emerge with legislation that offers embattled and exhausted workers some real protection of their right to rest and privacy in their off-work hours.

The Right to Disconnect

ONTARIO

To date, only one Canadian jurisdiction — Ontario — has enacted right to disconnect legislation. Québec solidaire members of that province's National Assembly have made several attempts to get right to disconnect legislation passed in Quebec. Thus far, however, their attempts have not resulted in anything. As mentioned, at the federal level, a Right to Disconnect Advisory Committee was established to consider appropriate legislation for federally regulated workers. But employee and employer representatives on the bipartite committee could find little common ground, and in the end, the committee's final report[20] stopped short of recommending any specific legislation on the subject.

In Ontario, the right to disconnect was covered under the Working for Workers Act, which was passed by the Ontario legislature in November 2021 and took effect on June 3, 2022. It took the form of an amendment to the province's Employment Standards Act.[21] Under the new law, companies with twenty-five or more employees had until June 2, 2022, to have in place a written policy on disconnecting from work. As well, beginning in 2023, companies with twenty-five or more employees on January 1 of any year must have a written policy on disconnecting from work in place by March 1 of that year. "Disconnecting from work," according to the Ontario government, means not engaging in work-related communications, including (but not restricted to) emails, telephone calls, or video calls.

Any employer required to have a written policy in place must provide a copy of that policy to its employees within thirty calendar days of the policy's being prepared or changed. Similarly, all new employees must be given a copy of the policy within thirty calendar days of their being hired. Of note, the written policy may be either a stand-alone document or part of another, larger document (e.g., a comprehensive workplace human resources policies and procedures manual).

The legislation's coverage is broad. It applies to all employees and employers covered by the Employment Standards Act, except the Crown, Crown agencies, or authorities, board commissions, or corporations whose members are appointed by the Crown, and their employees.[22] This includes executives and managers, as the written policy must apply to all the employer's employees in Ontario. But the policy need not be the same for all groups. "For example, a retail employer may decide to have one policy [for] its office staff and a different policy [for] its in-store sales staff." The policy may also lay out different expectations for different situations, such as the time of day or subject matter of the communication in question or the sender of that communication (e.g., client, supervisor, or colleague).

On the content of right to disconnect policies, the legislation is virtually silent, specifying only that any policy must include the date on which it was prepared and the date(s) on which any changes were made. Beyond that, there are no further specifications as to content, and none at all as to length. The legislation likewise has little to say about enforcement, setting out no specific sanctions or penalties for violation. All it says about enforcement is that if the employer's written policy on disconnecting from work creates a greater right or benefit than an employment standard under the (provincial) Employment Standards Act, that greater right or benefit may be enforceable under the ESA. If, on the other hand, it does not create a greater right or benefit than that provided by the ESA, then the policy is not enforceable under the ESA. This rather vague statement seems likely to cause more problems than it will solve. It also seems likely that the overall lack of enforcement even in the case of gross violations of the employer's policy will result in employee representatives tearing their hair out trying to determine whether a particular policy does or doesn't represent an improvement on the ESA.

Substantively, the legislation seems distinctly underwhelming; it is perhaps more noteworthy for what it doesn't contain than for what it does contain. One major concern with respect to the bill is the limitation of its coverage to larger companies (those with twenty-five or more employees). This limitation means there is still potential for many abuses in Canadian workplaces. As has been pointed out by Erin Bury, CEO of Willful, "startups [many of which have fewer than twenty-five employees] are often the worst offenders for toxic work culture."[23] Also of concern is the lack of any specific requirements for the content of right to disconnect policies, and of specific sanctions or penalties for violation and of any meaningful enforcement mechanisms. Still, the fact that such a law has been passed at all does mean something. Through the Western world as a whole, such provisions remain the exception rather than the rule. Hopefully, the law will serve as a basis for meaningful discussions between employers and employees and their representatives on the right to disconnect. Hopefully, as well, the law may serve as a minimum standard on which other jurisdictions can improve through their own right to disconnect legislation.

QUEBEC

The left-oriented Québec solidaire party has over the past several years been active in attempting to get right to disconnect legislation passed in Quebec. Since 2018, QS members have introduced three bills on the subject into the National Assembly.

The most recent of these bills, Bill 799, was introduced in December 2021 by QS member of the National Assembly Alexandre Leduc.[24] The bill would require all employers to develop a clear disconnection policy, which must set out "the periods during that an employee is entitled to be disconnected from all job-related communications" on a weekly basis. In firms with one hundred or more employees, the policy must be developed by a joint employer-employee committee, half of whose members are employees. Companies with fewer than one hundred employees would be required to develop right to disconnect policies themselves but would need to get them approved by the Commission des normes, de l'équité, de la santé et de la sécurité du travail (CNESST).

Notably, the bill provides a sliding scale of fines for employers violating its provisions. The fines range from $2,000 to $50,000, depending on the size of the organization and whether the offense is a first offense or a repeat violation. In the case of repeat violations, fines are doubled.

Bill 799 represents QS members' third attempt to get right to disconnect legislation passed. A party bill on the same subject and with similar objectives was introduced in 2020 but did not pass. Two years before that, QS member Gabriel Nadeau-Dubois introduced a private member's bill on the same subject. It did not pass either.[25] At this writing, the prospects for right to disconnect legislation in Quebec do not appear good. While

Labour Minister Jean Boulet has acknowledged the existence of the problem addressed by the legislation, he has declared that "at this stage, it is not appropriate to legislate to force the adoption of a policy on the right to disconnect."[26]

It should be noted that Bill 799 is significantly more ambitious than the Ontario legislation described above. It applies to all employers — not just those of a certain size, as is the case of Ontario. It lays out specific content that must be included in all employer policies — again unlike the Ontario legislation. And it requires government approval (through the CNESST) of all right to disconnect policies jointly developed by the employer and employees. Perhaps most important of all, it provides specific sanctions for violation of the law's provisions. This is critical. Anyone who knows anything about employment law knows that a law without enforcement provisions is utterly worthless, as employers will feel free to violate such a toothless law with impunity. Though the battle to get this legislation passed won't be an easy one, it is one worth fighting. Unlike the Ontario legislation, the proposed Quebec legislation offers workers real, substantive protection against employer intrusion on their off-work time.

BRITISH COLUMBIA

British Columbia is currently the only Canadian province with an NDP provincial government.[27] One might, therefore, reasonably have expected it to be among the first in the country to introduce legislation on a subject of such importance to workers as the right to disconnect. But this has not been the case. Shortly after Ontario's right to disconnect bill took effect, a journalist asked the B.C. Ministry of Labour if there were any plans to put such legislation into effect in that province. The ministry replied that there were not, at least not at that time, although the ministry was looking at the matter "with great interest." Even though the province now has a new premier, David Eby, it would appear that there are still no plans for British Columbia to introduce right to disconnect legislation.

UNITED STATES

New York City

The United States, whose union membership rates have plummeted to some of the lowest levels seen in any industrialized country, has not in recent years been known as a bastion of workers' rights, to put it mildly. Yet even it has not been immune from attempts to pass right to disconnect legislation, though thus far, none of those attempts have come to fruition.

Most notably, New York city councillor Rafael L. Espinal Jr. in 2017 introduced a bill called the "Right to Disconnect" in the New York City Council. Espinal's bill would have made it illegal for private employers of ten or more workers in New York to require employees to check and respond to electronic communications during off-work hours. There were some exceptions, such as jobs clearly requiring workers to be on-call. Violators were to be subject to small civil fines.

The bill, which appears to have been the first of its kind in the United States, provoked strong debate. Supporters, like San Diego State University psychology professor Larissa Barber, who studies the effects of technology on work-life balance, note that people who experience "telepressure" — the perceived pressure to respond instantly to texts and emails whether within working hours or outside of them — are more likely to experience work burnout and report sleep quality issues. In Barber's view, right to disconnect laws are overdue. "Many labor laws haven't kept up with the changing nature of work. Now, we have 'boundary-less' work that spills over into remote workspaces, like our homes."

For their part, critics, like New York City Department of Consumer Affairs official Casey Adams, regard the bill as virtually unenforceable. Eventually, due to opposition like Adams's, and opposition from business groups who described the bill as "an impediment to firms with global offices and an unnecessary burdensome regulation on small businesses," the bill was defeated. It seems that no attempts to enact similar legislation have been made elsewhere in the United States. In 2021, Patrick Thibodeau noted in his article "The Right to Disconnect vs. America's Always-On Culture" that "there's little interest by state and federal lawmakers in setting limits on America's always-on electronic culture. But Espinal's warning of 'endless work hours spurred by the digitization of work' is getting more attention as work-from-home increases post-pandemic." (It's worth noting that Espinal's bill was introduced in 2017, three years before the pandemic.)

As noted already, with the increase in working from home comes an increase in health and safety concerns around technology, as well as long working hours. One observer, Lehigh University management professor Liuba Belkin, has noted that after-work communications raise precisely such health and safety concerns. "It can increase stress and anxiety and even lead to marital discord," Belkin said. Given this fact and given workers' increasing power in a time of the Great Resignation, it seems likely that even in the United States there will be continued agitation for right to disconnect legislation on the part of government or company policies aimed at achieving the same end. At least one commentator has suggested that California would be the likeliest candidate to adopt such policies at the state level, given the generally progressive nature of its social and employment policies.

......

In a post-pandemic world in which large numbers of workers will continue to work from home or some other remote location all or at least part of the time, right to disconnect legislation is of great importance. It's an essential component of the hybrid workplaces that will be part of working life for most workers for the foreseeable future. With the barriers between home and work life increasingly fragile, and with the new electronic technology putting increasingly great stress on workers' physical and mental health, protection of workers' private time is of increasing importance. Laws and policies to reduce work hours won't be of much help if employers feel free to unilaterally increase work hours by expecting employees to be on call and available to respond to texts, emails, and other electronic communications during their off-hours, when they should be resting, pursuing other interests, or enjoying family life. Nor will workers get the most out of their free time if they are forced to spend it in fear of reprisal from their employers if they don't respond instantly to phone calls, emails, or texts from the factory or office. Such a situation benefits no one. Not just workers but at least the more far-sighted employers must surely recognize that such a stressful situation is likely to decrease, rather than increase their employees' productivity. The question, at this point, is how many far-sighted employers there are, employers willing and able to take the long view on such an important issue.

Just as shorter work hours would seem to be a competitive advantage in today's tight labour market, so, one would think, would be a right to disconnect. One would hope that such a recognition would induce employers to introduce right to disconnect policies for their companies even in the absence of government legislation on the subject. Beyond that, one can only hope that in the months ahead pressure from workers prepared to quit their jobs rather than continue to put up with working conditions they find intolerable will spread from workplaces into the political arena, leading progressive lawmakers to introduce new, effective legislation on the subject.

No genuinely shorter working hours can be achieved without serious consideration of the right to disconnect. Here is a policy area on which much more work remains to be done. The concluding chapter contains a number of specific recommendations on the right to disconnect. The fact that this issue has not yet achieved the same degree of public prominence as the four-day week or other forms of reduced hours doesn't make it any less important. Far from being a separate issue from reduced hours, it is merely the opposite side of the same coin.

The right to disconnect becomes a particularly important — and tricky — issue in hybrid workplaces. The dividing line between home life and work life, which has already become somewhat blurred due to the introduction of new technologies, becomes even more blurred when employees are spending a good deal of their time working from home, which makes it doubly important to ensure that employees' private time is protected. It is to these hybrid workplaces that the discussion now turns.

CHAPTER 9

Hybrid Workplaces and Their Implications for Work Hours

One of the most distinctive features of work, post-pandemic, and recently one of the more contentious, is the so-called hybrid workplace, in which people work on site for part of the week and off-site — usually though not always at home — for the remainder of the week. The issue of hybrid workplaces has taken on particular importance in Ottawa because of a much-publicized battle between the Treasury Department, the official employer of Canadian federal government employees, and the unions representing those employees over how many hours a week federal government employees should be expected to spend in their offices.

(All too readily forgotten, in the heat of this debate, was that Canadian federal government employees, like workers all across the country and indeed around much of the world, had initially worked from home out of necessity, because the Covid-19 pandemic made it unsafe for large numbers of workers to gather together under the same roof. The Treasury Board president's protestations that choice of work location is a management right rang more than a little hollow after a period of more than two years in which government employees had voluntarily provided their own homes, furniture, and in many cases office equipment, not to mention electricity, so that they could do their jobs.)

There has also been a debate — slightly lower-key — over the merits of the hybrid model under which Canada's House of Commons has been operating for the past two years. This issue — how much in-person time should be required of hybrid workplace employees — has also arisen in the United States. In both countries, the right to work shorter hours and the right to work a sizeable share of the week from home or some other remote site are manifestations of the tendency to grant workers more freedom in how they do their jobs — manifestations resulting in large measure from the Great Resignation phenomenon discussed in chapter 7, which in turn resulted from the first significant labour shortages North America had seen in several decades. While work hours have to do with the *time* spent working, hybrid workplaces are primarily concerned with the places and spaces in which work is done. But there is, as will be noted in more detail later in the chapter, no hard-and-fast line between these two dimensions of work. In particular, the *place* in which one works may be critically important in determining the *schedule* by which one should work.

Many of the issues around hybrid and off-site workplaces are not new. Back in 2007, for example, Amherst College alum Sarah Rubenstein was trying to balance raising two small children with part-time work as a litigator, an added complication being that she was also riding horses competitively at least three or four times a week. Rubenstein writes in her "Class Notes" for the alumni magazine:

> The net result is not pretty — my life is a delicate balance. For example, when the contractors redoing our master bedroom failed to properly hook up the new pipes, and water came cascading down into our kitchen, I had to drop everything and deal. Or when my kids have two separate activities in two separate locations thirty minutes apart. And god forbid a kid gets sick. Or vacation? Date night? Ha!! I often find myself working late at night, or while waiting for dinner to cook (although unfortunately not much cooks itself other

than takeout). [But] I'm not sure I'd change anything, or even how.[1]

Much of what Rubenstein was saying over fifteen years ago will resonate with people (particularly women) who have recently been through the Covid-19 pandemic working from home all or part of the time, and who were thus facing the challenge of balancing work responsibilities with family responsibilities such as child care. There is, however, one important difference. In 2007 work situations like Rubenstein's weren't all that common. Typically, they would have been one-off arrangements negotiated by people like high-level professionals to meet special needs, such as Rubenstein's need for time to pursue her riding career. In 2020 and 2021, such a situation was almost the norm for working women, with the Canadian federal government and many other large employers shifting immediately to off-site work at the onset of the pandemic.[2] It continues to be something close to the norm even today, with the gradual ongoing return to offices and other worksites. With hundreds of thousands of workers, many represented by unions, still spending at least part of their work week working from home, there is a need for collective solutions to such problems as how to make work schedules appropriate to hybrid workplace settings, how to coordinate the schedules of those working from home and those working at the office, and how to ensure that those working from home are doing so under safe conditions.

Hybrid workplaces are as yet new and untried enough that it would be foolhardy to attempt any evaluation of how well they have worked thus far, let alone any prediction of how they might operate in the future. In this connection, a caveat written in 2021 by Charlie Warzel and Anne Helen Petersen at the end of their book about out-of-office work, *Out of Office: The Big Problem and Bigger Promise of Working from Home*, bears repeating. Say Warzel and Petersen, "There's a fair amount of hubris involved in writing a book about the future of anything. This is doubly true for work, which is a vague term that doesn't begin to adequately describe the universe of industries, jobs, expectations, injustices, and strategies that make up our collective laboring. We are attempting to peer around a corner and offer potential visions of what's to come. It's not lost on us that this is treacherous territory."[3]

If writing about the future of work is doubly hazardous, writing about the future of hybrid workplaces qualifies as triply hazardous. Those writing more generally about the future of work at least have some kind of history to guide them, even if, as Warzel and Petersen also note, that history has often been wrong.[4] Here there are no guidelines, or precious few of them. Employers and employees alike have been flying (and continue to fly) by the seat of their pants. The best that I'll be able to do, in writing about this brave new reality of hybrid workplaces, is to identify some of the major trends I've observed and briefly discuss some of the most significant issues I see as arising from hybrid workplaces. It must inevitably be left to others to fill in the details of the very broad-brush sketch I'm providing here.

It follows that there really is no hard-and-fast answer to the question of whether hybrid workplaces are good for workers or for society as a whole. On the one hand, a reduction in the number of work-related commutes is good for the environment. On the other hand, entire days spent on Zoom and using other modern technologies — the all-but-inevitable result when working from home replaces in-person work — are potentially hazardous to employees' physical and mental health.[5] The flexibility gained from being able to fit medical appointments or child care responsibilities into a daily schedule is a plus, particularly for working mothers, but the loss (whether full or partial) of the workplace as a place outside the home where it's possible to gain validation as an adult and find camaraderie and support is a clear minus, even — perhaps especially — for those same working mothers. And while the potential cost savings to government and other large employers from reducing the amount of office space they must own or rent to accommodate their employees may be significant, these savings often come at a cost — a cost employers may not have been fully aware of when they first undertook the changes in office space. A major reduction in office space is likely to require significant redesign of the remaining space, often with the result that those requiring privacy to do all or part of their jobs will find it difficult to get that privacy. From an economic and political perspective, a large-scale shift to off-site work can seriously depress markets for office buildings and leave large downtown areas looking almost like ghost towns. Detailed socioeconomic research, which we are years away from having

Hybrid Workplaces and Their Implications for Work Hours

anything like enough to data to conduct, will be necessary to determine whether the pluses of hybrid working outweigh the minuses. Even then, the answers will likely be different depending on the perspective one brings to the issue.

Perhaps we can start by considering what exactly is the difference in work schedules and work hours between those working from home, all or part of the time, and those whose entire week is spent working on site. The one thing that can be said with any certainty is that work hours and work schedules will not be the same when one works from home as they would be if one were working from the office, even if the employee's job description has remained the same.[6] The precise nature of the differences depends on a whole host of factors, beginning with, most obviously, the type of work being done in the two situations. Someone whose job entails providing direct assistance to clients or other employees will need a different — and almost certainly more structured — schedule than someone whose job involves mainly writing, editing, or the provision of policy advice. Such work could, at least in theory, be done at almost any hour of the day or night. In the former instance, it's necessary to arrange work schedules to meet periods of client demand. In the latter instance, the employee can be given considerable latitude as to when the work gets done, so long as it does in fact get done.

Nor is this by any means the only difference between the two types of schedule. Logistical considerations dictate that in most settings, leaving aside factories, hospitals, and certain types of retail, most workers be present during roughly the same hours each day. Even where a four-day week has been adopted, management will usually want to have workers present during the same hours, so they can meet at least on the days when all are in the office together. This matters a lot less in hybrid settings — most of the time. When time comes for all-staff meetings involving both on-site and off-site workers, the difficulties of coordination can be formidable.

One issue for which the two types of work setting differ greatly is that of the split shift. For those working on site, whether that site is a factory, office, or store, split shifts are anathema; they entail extra travel time, gas money, and in some cases additional child care costs. The split shift has been met with particular disfavour in retail, where workers will struggle mightily to obtain enough seniority so they can work one, regular shift. For those working from home, at least on the days when they are working at home, it's quite a different matter. (Note that the aforementioned Sarah Rubenstein was working a type of split shift, even if she wouldn't have used the term to describe her work schedule.) The three hours "between shifts" that would likely be next to useless if one were working some distance from home can become the perfect amount of time for a walk, lunch with a friend, or a quick shopping trip. Far from being a drain on one's energy, as such a break would generally be if one had to drive to and from a work site, the three-hour pause can leave one feeling refreshed and more productive on returning to work. More generally, even if a worker doesn't go so far as to work a full split shift, a hybrid work schedule allows for more breaks during the workday — breaks that are apt to benefit people who work intensely but find it difficult to work straight through six or eight or even four hours without some kind of break.

At the same time, the challenges posed by the new workplace arrangements are numerous and at times serious. Workers with young children, generally though not invariably women, have frequently found their time and attention divided between job responsibilities and child care or even home-schooling responsibilities. Not infrequently, it has been necessary for these employees to work on their job at night just to get caught up.

Working from home has also entailed sharing workspace, computer time, and internet access with other family members. The last of these, in particular, can be problematic, especially in rural areas where internet service had never been all that good to begin with, and where the increased demand resulting from large numbers of people working from home led to frequent service failures, which in turn were a significant disruption from the job or jobs at hand.[7] Also making "the job at hand" more difficult were the increased difficulties of communicating with other workers or managers through Zoom or other new technologies. Bringing people together, never an easy thing to do in government even at the best of times, became increasingly difficult — and increasingly unproductive when it did occur. It's entirely possible that bringing people together will become even more challenging as those attempting it must blend on-site workers with those still working from home.

Hybrid Workplaces and Their Implications for Work Hours

Perhaps the one thing that can be said with some degree of certainty is that to achieve the complicated transition to a part in-person, part-remote workplace requires and will require much tolerance, understanding, and goodwill, as well as effective communication between the workplace parties. The key to organizational success post-pandemic, says Carleton University business professor Linda Duxbury, who researched remote work during the pandemic, is flexibility and a willingness to listen to employees and hear what their needs are. "You've got to ... actually start talking to your people [and] stop pretending ... that there is some magical plan you can implement and it'll be a miracle."[8] In particular, Duxbury says, there is no one ideal schedule that can be applied to all or even most workers in hybrid workplaces post-pandemic. At least in the near future, she suggests, work schedules are likely to become highly individualized, to the degree that there may not even be any single "normal" work hours arrangement comparable to the 8x5 week that held sway for so long. "I'd like to be able to give you one answer [to the question of what a 'normal' working arrangement would look like] ... but it's much more nuanced than that," Duxbury says.[9]

Initially, the Covid-19 pandemic was the primary reason for people to work from home or some other remote location. It remains an important reason. At the same time, having tried out remote work — a fair number for the first time — a good many have found that they like it, for at least a part of their work week. There appears to be considerable resistance, on the part of employees, to returning to the office full time. An Angus Reid survey conducted in early March of 2022 reported that nearly one-quarter (23 percent) of respondents would quit immediately if ordered to return to the office full time, while a third (33 percent) would return grudgingly but would also start looking for another job. Slightly less than one-third (29 percent) said they would be fine with a full-time return to work, while the remainder were unsure.[10] While I don't know whether the degree of resistance to a return to full-time on-site work would be the same today as it was a year ago (this chapter is being written in early March 2023), the bitterness of the battle between the federal government and its unions over the Treasury Board's attempt to impose a uniform hybrid work schedule suggests that significant resistance continues to exist. (It did little to help matters that the pay raise the federal government had offered its unionized employees at the bargaining table was far below the inflation rate.[11])

The possible variations in hybrid workplace work schedules are nearly infinite, with some employers asking only that employees come into the work site one day a week, or even one or two days a month, while others want their staff on site as much as three or four days a week.[12] Only about a year into the post-pandemic return to work, it's still too early to speculate as to which particular patterns have become most popular, and in which industries.

One trend that *has* been observed in certain Canadian cities is an apparent modest preference for those working part of the week at home to take their at-home days on Mondays and Fridays.[13] Foot traffic in urban centres such as Toronto, Montreal, Vancouver, Calgary, Edmonton, and Ottawa was found to be lightest on Mondays and Fridays, heaviest on Tuesdays through Thursdays. Similarly, public transit use in Toronto was found to be heavier on the midweekdays, and lighter on Mondays and Fridays, although the differences were relatively modest — an average of about 12 percent more subway traffic on Thursdays than on Mondays.

A second trend, one that has become especially noticeable during the past few months,[14] is a hardening of employer attitudes around work schedules, a growing insistence that employees spend a significant part of their work week on site. This new tough approach to hybrid scheduling has appeared in both public and private sectors, and in both Canada and the United States.[15]

Initially (in early 2022), employers were cautious, almost hesitant about attempting to impose any particular hybrid work arrangement. Indeed, so cautious were many Canadian employers on this point that *Financial Post* writer Victoria Wells, quoting the results of a worker survey on hybrid work schedules, found many employees wishing their employers would impose *more* structure; it appeared that many workers simply didn't know where they stood under the new regime.[16] For its part, the Canadian federal government adopted a "local option" model under which departments made their own decisions about remote and hybrid work, with several departments opting for a full remote work model.[17] At the time, the government's rationale, as stated by Treasury Board president Mona Fortier, was that any return-to-office policy should "consider the nature of each department's work and the services they provide to Canadians."[18] South of the border, the social media giant Twitter (now renamed "X" but discussed hereafter using "Twitter") adopted an indefinite work-from-home policy in October, 2020 — among the first of many American corporations to do so.[19]

By the end of 2022, both the Canadian federal government and Twitter had made significant changes to their remote work policies. Citing the "need for consistency in how hybrid work is applied," Fortier imposed an across-the-board model that would require Canadian federal government employees to go to work in their offices at least two to three days a week, or 40–60 percent of their working time. The transition to the new model would begin by January 16, 2023, with full implementation by March 31 of that same year. In justifying the imposition of an across-the-board model, Fortier insisted that the location of work in the federal public service is an exclusive management right.[20] At the same time, she insisted that the government had no intention of bringing its employees back into the office full time. "The Government of Canada has chosen a hybrid model," Fortier said. "Hybrid work is the future of the public service.... A common hybrid work model will ensure coherence and equity across the federal government, providing public servants with regular opportunities to work with colleagues and partners in service to Canadians, while still having flexibility to work off site."[21]

The initial announcement of the new hybrid work policy suggested that there might be a few, very limited exceptions to the new policy, including Indigenous public servants "whose location is critical to their [ability] to work from their communities," and those working remotely more than 125 kilometres from their designated worksites. But in late January, the government announced much broader exemptions to be applied to a sizable share (20 percent) of its IT workforce. According to a memo from Canada's chief information officer, Catherine Luelo, "high-priority IT" staff comprising around 20 percent of federal government IT workers will not be expected to work from the office. These include non-managerial roles in IT software solutions, IT security, and IT cloud solutions. Luelo said such exemptions "make sense for recruitment and retention," which is proving a challenge — particularly in the digital and tech space — for both the private and public sector in Canada and beyond.

The exemption of IT staff from the new hybrid model makes sense operationally. Even before the pandemic, IT workers were one group that tended to do a lot of their work from home. Beyond that, Luelo's memo reveals (perhaps inadvertently) an important aspect of the relationship between hybrid work schedules and the Great Resignation. How far an employer is willing to go in pushing in-office work requirements — in this case not far at all — on a particular group of employees may well depend on the position that group occupies on the Great Resignation spectrum. At the end of the day, labour market considerations may well trump the "need for consistency" that Mona Fortier made so much of in her announcement of the new hybrid policy.[22]

Otherwise, while the new hybrid model seems in many ways a quintessentially Canadian sort of compromise, seeking to have federal government workers in their offices about half the time, and although the new model offers some scope for reasonable exemptions, it nonetheless led to fierce conflict between the government and its biggest unions. Within a few days of the announcement of the new model, the Public Service Alliance of Canada (PSAC), Canada's largest federal public service union, announced it would be filing a labour board complaint over the new plan, on the basis that the location of work was currently being bargained, which meant that a statutory "freeze" must be imposed on existing terms and conditions of employment.[23] At the end of January, the PSAC announced it would be filing policy grievances over the government's unilateral imposition of the policy. In its announcement, it said it would be demanding, among other things, that the government immediately rescind the new hybrid workplace policy and that it immediately engage in joint consultation with the union on the return to workplace issue.[24]

For their part, the presidents of the Professional Institute of the Public Service of Canada (PIPSC)[25] and the Canadian Association of Professional Employees (CAPE), respectively the second and third largest federal public service unions in Canada, took to the press, writing a joint open letter published as an op-ed in the *Ottawa Citizen* on January 16. PIPSC president Jennifer Carr and CAPE president Greg Phillips criticized the new policy as having been driven not by operational requirements but by political motivations.[26] A premature forced return to work, said Carr and Phillips, would put federal government employees' health and safety at risk, since some would be forced back into government office buildings still dealing with such pre-pandemic issues as bats, bed bugs, and asbestos.[27] Others forced back into buildings under renovation would be obliged to work from the floor or from lunchrooms or washrooms ill-equipped for office work. In their view, it made no sense to return employees to offices when many of those offices had been closed or downsized or were undergoing renovations. The two presidents closed their op-ed by urging the federal government "to reconsider its position and engage in a constructive dialogue with employees and their unions, to devise a better, safer, and sensible return-to-office plan."

Meanwhile, the debate over Canada's hybrid model for Parliament, in effect since 2020, continues. Thus far, this debate has not attracted as much attention as has been the case for federal government department employees. Nonetheless, it illustrates the extent to which debate over hybrid workplaces has become politicized, with Liberals and New Democrats generally supportive of a hybrid Parliament and Conservatives generally opposed. Praising the new arrangement are B.C. Liberal MP Parm Bains and B.C. NDP MP Laurel Collins.[28] In Bains's case, the hybrid arrangement has allowed him to deal with such health issues as dialysis and a kidney transplant while continuing to represent his constituents. For Collins, a new mother, the new arrangement has made it easier for her to balance her work responsibilities with those of her job. "If you want more young women to enter politics, if you want more women to stay in politics, make Parliament more family friendly. Hybrid Parliament is a tangible way to do that," Collins says. Another NDP MP from British Columbia, Taylor Bachrach, says Parliament should consider making the hybrid format permanent. While conceding the value of informal personal contacts from in-person sessions, Bachrach cites the flexibility the hybrid model provides for young parents, those with accessibility issues, and members from remote ridings (like his) who "might have to be on the other side of the country at a certain time."[29]

On the other side of the debate is Alberta Conservative MP Blaine Calkins. Stressing the value of informal personal contacts, Calkins says, "This is supposed to be a place where people get together and the good ideas bubble to the top for the benefit of all. My concern is that if we're not here, or at least not enough of us are here on an ongoing basis, then we're not going to get the best decision."

Falling somewhere between the two poles is House Speaker Anthony Rota.[30] While noting that the hybrid format has been generally successful in allowing Parliament to function securely and reliably through the Covid-19 pandemic, he also suggests that the format has faced a number of challenges, including co-ordinating across multiple time zones and (perhaps most serious of all) the health and well-being of parliamentary interpreters. Like Calkins, Rota thinks it advantageous for MPs to be in Ottawa in person so they can meet informally. On the other hand, he admits that parliamentary decorum has improved with the presence of fewer people in the House.

How to maintain personal contact virtually strikes me as a real but far from insurmountable problem. If publishers can hold virtual launch parties[31] and colleges can host virtual reunions, there seems no reason why, with ingenuity and a bit of good will, Parliament could not be broken into small multi-party groups for informal discussion of issues. Such meetings could be preceded or followed by a social hour. The interpreters' work situation is a much more serious matter. Well before the end of the first year of hybrid sittings, it was becoming clear that the virtual proceedings were putting interpreters' health and safety at serious risk. A survey administered less than ten months after the launch of the hybrid Parliament in April of 2020 found over 60 percent of respondents reporting they had been forced to go on sick leave to recover from a wide variety of auditory issues.[32]

As has been discussed, heavy Zoom users experience numerous physical problems, including headaches, back and neck strain, chronic fatigue, and more. As workers forced to spend their entire day on Zoom — a platform never intended for interpretation — interpreters would have experienced all of those problems. In addition, because of the nature of their work, they were experiencing tinnitus (a constant ringing of the ears), nausea, hearing loss, and "acoustic shock" resulting from their being forced to interpret MPs online with fuzzy laptop mikes and poor internet connections. The added strain of Zoom-based parliamentary proceedings has led to shorter shifts and an increased number of requests to transfer to non-virtual assignments, which in turn has led to a severe shortage of interpreters available for virtual work.

Despite these serious issues, there appears to be growing parliamentary consensus in favour of making a hybrid parliament permanent. In a report released in late January, a majority of MPs on the Procedure and House Affairs Committee said they wanted to see hybrid sittings and electronic voting become permanent. But the recommendation came with a number of caveats, four of them having to do specifically with the interpreters' work situation; clearly, the health and safety issues experienced by the interpreters were of great concern to MPs. Among other things, the House administration was directed to investigate the use of simultaneous interpretation in other parliaments that have a low injury rate among interpreters to see how the House system can be improved. The House administration was also directed to ensure that adequate audiovisual equipment be provided to both virtual participants and interpreters. In addition, the House was instructed to roll out a series of mandatory policies meant to protect interpreters, including requiring virtually appearing witnesses at committees to use high-quality headsets and to have strong internet connections or face rescheduling of their appearance.

If the Canadian federal government's new hybrid work policy raised hackles in Ottawa, Twitter owner Elon Musk's complete reversal of his company's previous work-from-home policy sent shock waves, not just through Twitter but through the entire IT community. On taking over control of the company in the fall of 2022, Musk wasted no time ending the earlier, permissive work-from-home policy. "The road ahead is arduous," he wrote in a memo to staff soon after taking over, "and will require intense work to succeed." Under the new regime, remote work would no longer be allowed except for those with specific exemptions. Musk also stated that Twitter employees were expected to be in the office for forty hours per week, which he pointed out is less than he expects of his factory workers at his other companies.[33]

But this was only the warm-up act to an ultimatum Musk emailed to all Twitter employees on November 15: Commit to a new "hardcore" Twitter or leave the company with severance pay. Employees were told they had to sign a pledge to stay on with the company. Anyone not signing the pledge by 5 p.m. Eastern time on November 16 was told they would receive three months of severance pay, the email message said.

If Musk's aim was to reduce the size of his workforce — it's difficult to find any other rationale for sending such a message to one's entire staff — he succeeded, perhaps beyond his wildest dreams. Taking him at his word and disgusted by his ultimatum and his statement that staffers need to sign up for "long hours at high intensity" or leave, disgruntled Twitter employees left by the hundreds.

Technology writer Cindy Davis[34] suggests that Musk's recent actions at Twitter may be a sign that the hybrid workplace experiment is entering a new phase, with full-time or at least greatly increased return to on-site work becoming the norm as the economy becomes more uncertain and the job market tightens. Davis wonders whether Musk's complete "return to work" decree opens the door for a similar wave of announcements, or whether there is rather a common middle ground to be reached serving both the corporate entity and the health and well-being of its workers.

In the volatile economy and job market seen today, only a fool would attempt any firm predictions as to what most hybrid work schedules will look like a year or even six months from now. If, for example, the economy should enter a deep recession, all bets would be off. But there are some preliminary indications of how Musk's move has played out. Few of them look good for the company.

To say the company hasn't thrived under its new regime would be to put things very mildly. On March 6, Twitter experienced its sixth outage of the still very young year.[35] The repeated outages have done little to inspire confidence in a company already seriously embattled on several other fronts. Advertising revenue, Twitter's single biggest source of income, has by Musk's own admission taken a "massive" hit since his takeover in October. One source reported that Twitter's daily revenue in January was down 40 percent from the previous year. The company has also become involved in disputes with its suppliers of office space, janitorial supplies, and even web-hosting services, resulting from its failure to pay the bills owed for those services, and with Amazon Web Services over the cost of cloud computing service.

Most recently, Musk became personally involved in a nasty dispute with a Twitter employee with a disability whom he mocked, engaging in a lengthy online exchange, characterized by some as a "public exit interview," with the employee who had asked if he still had a job with Twitter after being locked out of his computer.[36] While Musk has since apologized to the employee, who has had muscular dystrophy for twenty years, it may be too late to repair the damage to his and Twitter's reputation resulting from the needless brouhaha.

One can't blame all of these problems on Musk's new work schedule policy, with its attendant staff shortages resulting from employees' inability or unwillingness to work under such a policy. But it certainly hasn't helped. Some observers, such as Steven Murdoch, professor of security engineering at University College, London, have suggested that staff reductions, particularly in the engineering team, have resulted in reduced monitoring and oversight, which in turn has meant that problems that in the past might have been caught while they were still small have turned into big problems for lack of sufficient monitoring and oversight. And the hit to the company's reputation resulting both from the outages and from incidents like Musk's set-to with his disabled employee may take years to overcome, putting Twitter at a severe disadvantage in what is still a highly competitive job market for engineers and other IT staff.

What Twitter has gone through in recent months would not appear to augur well for the future of hardline back-to-the-office policies. Also instructive, in this connection, is the experience of people like New York City mayor Eric Adams, an early back-to-the-office "hawk," who, by February of 2022, was saying that New York workers needed to return to the office, mocking people who, he said, were afraid of Covid on Monday but were out at clubs on Sunday,[37] and who in June of 2022 imposed a full-time back-to-the-office policy on city employees.[38] Recently, Adams has begun backpedaling on the issue of his back-to-office requirement. The reason? Serious staff shortages in several key departments resulting from large numbers of unfilled positions. With the city already lagging behind the private sector with regard to employee compensation, the rigid back-to-the-office requirement has put it at a severe competitive disadvantage vis-à-vis more flexible employers willing to consider a hybrid model. In effect conceding defeat on the location of work issue, Adams has admitted, "There's a pulse shift that you have to go out now and compete." If this means allowing city employees to work from home at least part of the time, then so be it.

Taken together, the survey results discussed at the beginning of this chapter, together with the experiences at Twitter, with Canada's hybrid Parliament, and in New York City, would appear to suggest that hybrid work schedules are likely to be with us for some time to come. It is, I think, particularly significant that serious consideration is being given to making Canada's hybrid Parliament permanent, and that the president of Canada's Treasury Board has declared that hybrid work is here to stay. The fact that hybrid work is no longer just a temporary sort of arrangement suggests that it's time to take a closer look at some of the issues raised by "normalizing" such work. These include issues around the use of space both in offices redesigned for part-time work and in private dwellings now also serving as workplace offices, health and safety considerations, the possible need for different schedules for those working on a hybrid basis, the effects (whether positive or negative) of such schedules on the environment, and the blurring of the line between work time and private time, an already ongoing phenomenon that has significantly increased since the beginning of the pandemic with the attendant growth in working from home.

Issues Arising from Hybrid Work Scheduling

As noted above, hybrid work arrangements are likely to entail, and in many cases have already led to, significant redesign of the space in which work is carried out, including most notably the conversion of much (sometimes all) of what used to be private office space into large, open-concept spaces suitable for people working collectively on projects.[39] To the extent that workers continue to need private space to discuss confidential matters with customers or clients, whether in-person or over the phone, the matter of arranging hybrid work schedules may be complicated still further by such redesigns. Speaking from my personal experience as a union labour relations officer who conducted many confidential conversations with members,

Hybrid Workplaces and Their Implications for Work Hours

generally but not always by appointment, I can attest that one doesn't always know just when one will need to have a confidential conversation. Often the need for such a conversation will arise suddenly and urgently, resulting from a traumatic incident such as a dismissal or suspension or major health or family crisis. If office spaces don't contain at least a certain number of private conference rooms equipped, at a minimum, with phones and computers, workers who may need privacy at a certain point but aren't sure they can find it in their redesigned office spaces may decide to err on the side of caution and continue to work at home even when it would otherwise not be necessary, or when they might prefer to be among colleagues. Such a situation does not serve anyone well.

Even leaving aside the privacy issue, it also needs to be pointed out that not everyone thrives in an open-concept workplace. Some positively enjoy working in such a setting. Others can tolerate it but may not always do their best work there. Still others (including some perfectly good workers) are intimidated by being constantly surrounded by other people and find it difficult or even impossible to work in such a setting. In extreme cases, such workers' difficulties in adjusting to the new setting may prompt them to take long-term stress leave, to seek a transfer to another department or branch, or even to quit. Again, no one is well served by a situation in which good, capable workers are marginalized, if not forced out altogether, due to difficulties in adjusting to the redesigned space that could and should have been anticipated and taken into account as part of the overall redesign process.

A different but equally significant set of issues is raised by the use of private dwelling space as workplace office space, as inevitably occurs under hybrid workplace schedules. Had I still been working during the pandemic, I'd have been well equipped for the transition to work from home. As a freelance writer, I've always made sure I had a room set aside as a dedicated office. But many workers did not (and do not) have that luxury. Even those living alone often didn't have an extra room they could use as an office. Some, like my daughter, who first made me aware of this issue, live in open-concept lofts or apartments, in which the only doors they have are those to the bathroom, or perhaps to the bedroom.

While my daughter's apartment is extremely attractively designed, it's easy to see how unsuitable it would be for use as a full-time or even half-time office. There really isn't room to bring in a computer or proper office furniture without seriously detracting from the available floor space. For those living with a family or a roommate, and who must therefore share space with those other people, the problems can be even more serious. In such a situation, it may be hard to find even a private corner in which to set up shop, let alone an entire room. Finding one's work competing for one's attention with one's kids or an elderly parent may be an everyday fact of life. It may be necessary, in such a case, for the employee to work outside what would be considered normal working hours (see below for more details).

Hybrid work schedules also raise a number of health and safety issues. As noted, the heavy use of Zoom results in significant physical problems. While these issues may not be as serious when employees are working from home only part of the time, they will still exist. A sensible employer will try to arrange things so that as many meetings as possible can be held in-person on in-office days, with a virtual option available for those who can't, for whatever reason, make an in-person session. Nor is Zoom the only potential health and safety issue. Those who needed ergonomically designed desks, chairs, and computers at the office will still need them at home. It's imperative that logistical difficulties not get in the way of seeing to it that those working from home have the equipment they need to do so productively and safely. On-site inspections of furnishing and wiring may be necessary to ensure that employees' premises are safe for the work they are doing there.

A perhaps inevitable consequence of hybrid work schedules is an even further blurring of the line between work time and personal time. In a situation in which it may be difficult even to know what constitutes work time and what personal time, it may be emotionally and even logistically difficult for employees to "just say no" to responding to communications arriving outside what they believe are their work hours. As difficult as making the distinction may be, employees must nonetheless do so in order to preserve their sanity. In this regard, a well-defined right to disconnect, whether one enshrined in legislation, as in Ontario and several European countries, or one contained in a company policy is of huge advantage to employees.

Hybrid Workplaces and Their Implications for Work Hours

On a more positive note, hybrid work schedules are definitely good for the environment, though determining just how much the environment will benefit will require research extending far beyond the scope of this book. Most notably, the air will be cleaner with the major reduction in commuting trips that a hybrid work schedule inevitably entails, as opposed to an on-site schedule. Such schedules will also mean reduced consumption of a host of other things, ranging from prepackaged foods to dry cleaning fluid. This will benefit the environment as well, albeit not to the same extent as the reduction in commuting. And the time and money saved by not commuting several days a week can be used to get out into nature and appreciate its wonders — an appreciation that in turn could help the environment down the road.[40]

One final issue around hybrid work schedules, particularly schedules that aren't the same for all workers, is their potential for inadvertently creating a status divide based on the amount of time a worker spends at the office. As Charlie Warzel and Anne Helen Petersen have noted in *Out of Office*, hybrid work schedules threaten to deepen already existing divides between those currently in favour with the boss and those less so. Say Warzel and Petersen, "Single parents, workers with elderly family members, disabled employees, and those who simply don't want to live in proximity to the office risk being overshadowed by those who come in every day. And even if a manager is careful, a recency and proximity bias might emerge." The result, again, is good for nobody. "Ambitious, competitive employees will sacrifice remote flexibility and work relentlessly in person, while remote employees, motivated by the anxiety of not seeming productive, will live in fear of managers and compensate with overwork. Both sides end up driving the other to misery."[41] The solution, paradoxical as it seems, to this admittedly knotty problem is to make the office seem *less* appealing, so people will, if anything, prefer to work from home.[42] Just how this is to be done, Warzel and Petersen don't make entirely clear. Still, such a job shouldn't, one would think, be beyond the ability of any enterprising and well-trained manager. Companies could even have some fun with the idea, running contests that offered managers prizes for the best ways to keep employees away from the office more hours than they needed to be there.

For all of the problems associated with hybrid work schedules — and as noted, there are a good many — their potential to help organizations recruit and retain staff suggests that they will be with us for some time to come. This brief overview does little more than scratch the surface of an extremely complex subject. By the time this book is released (early in 2024), the bigger picture regarding hybrid work may be quite different than it is today (in March 2023) as I complete this chapter. In closing, I can do no better than repeat Linda Duxbury's advice, cited earlier, on the need for flexibility, good employer-employee communication, and understanding. Organizations following that advice are likely to fare much better in the years to come than those taking the "My way or the highway!" approach promulgated by Elon Musk and his ilk.

As I've been at pains to say throughout this chapter, it's much too early to predict the future of hybrid workplaces. The one thing that can be said is that there is no firewall between work sites and work hours. Where one works and with what technology and equipment will definitely have an effect on the hours one works, even if it is still too soon to predict with any precision just what that effect will be. For example, I doubt that anyone would have predicted a four-day week being offered as a trade-off to induce employees to return to the office after the Covid-19 pandemic. Yet, according to work hours guru Joe O'Connor, more than one employer has offered just that. Will other "hours for location" offers be made as the pressure to bring employees back into workplaces increases? All that can be said, at this point, is "Stay tuned."

CHAPTER 10

What's Been Happening Lately on the Shorter Hours Scene?
(Spoiler Alert: A Lot)

When I first returned to the work hours issue early in 2022, after more than two decades away from it, I half-expected to find it the same sort of mildly exotic boutiquey issue it had been during the late 1990s, when I'd done most of my previous work on the subject. At that time, there were a handful of dedicated crusaders, like author Bruce O'Hara, whose work I cited at the beginning of this book, and Anders Hayden, founder of the Toronto-based organization 32 Hours, that as much as any organization kept alive, during those dark days of globalization, trade liberalization, and all but universal overwork the more humane notion of working to live rather than living to work traditionally advocated by the labour movement. There were also a number of supportive progressives such as political economist and development consultant Ted Jackson, who was willing to commission my research piece on shorter hours for the Carleton University think tank of which he was the director.[1] But even within the labour movement, support for shorter hours was at best lukewarm, and the issue had no traction at all within government, or in society at large. What were people like O'Hara, Hayden, and me seeing that more than half the Canadian labour movement and 90 percent of the Canadian population apparently weren't seeing?

I recounted my experiences with the shorter hours issue during that period in a 1997 article for the *Christian Science Monitor*.[2] What I found both illuminating and discouraging — exceptionally discouraging — was attending a shorter hours conference put on by 32 Hours during the fall of that year and not hearing a single concrete proposal for reducing work hours or even for making it harder for employers to make their employees work overtime (such as increasing overtime pay rates under employment standards legislation, a measure that would also have led to the creation of more jobs). Yes, there was all manner of good talk about kids needing more time with adults and society valuing money too much and people too little. But there was not even one suggestion for specific ways to make those good things happen — this despite the fact that many German, Dutch, and other European workers were already reaping the benefits of shorter hours. Was society moving backwards, I wondered, as I noted that even the most progressive labour speakers at the conference had stopped well short of measures fairly routinely advocated and occasionally even actually adopted by American *Republican* politicians and members of that country's business community during the 1920s and 1930s? The irony of a situation in which no concrete proposals for hours reduction were made at a conference hosted by an organization whose very name was inspired by just such a proposal was not lost on me.

Sometimes it's good to be proven wrong. It didn't take me long to discover that work hours were no longer a boutique issue in the radically changed political and economic environment of 2022. The issue was clearly one attracting interest across both the political and socio-economic spectrums, and among Canadians of all stripes. The first indication I had of this came when, following my internet publication of the CBC Opinion piece that launched me on to the present venture, I immediately received requests for both TV and radio interviews. I don't recall the media showing such interest in any of the presentations at the 1997 shorter hours conference, even though most of the presenters were far better known than I was. The second indication came when CBC closed off new comments for my piece when

What's Been Happening Lately on the Shorter Hours Scene?

the number of existing ones reached one thousand. I found the idea that one thousand people cared enough to write comments on work hours really quite mind-boggling.

I might have taken more time reading the many comments and perhaps harvesting some of them as raw material for the book, but by then I was already launched on my own preliminary research, of a different sort. Half an hour on the internet showed there was a lot already happening on the issue of work hours, both in Canada and around the world. In addition to the Toronto company whose work in this area had first piqued my interest when I read about it on a CBC News page, a number of other Canadian companies were clearly working along similar lines. Provincial legislation on the subject had been introduced in Ontario, and federal legislation in the United States. And a New Zealander named Andrew Barnes had written a book titled *The 4 Day Week*, a book whose eminently worthy premise turned out to be backed up by a lot of good, solid research.

In short, I was on to something big. Something hot. What had turned this former fringe issue into something hot was, quite clearly, the Covid-19 pandemic, which changed the way a great many people thought about a great many things, but nothing, perhaps, more than work and its meaning in their lives. People came to engage in some fundamental questioning of their values around work, in a way that hadn't been seen since the hippie movement of the 1960s. As they saw friends, family, and co-workers sickening and in many cases dying all around them, many began to wonder why they'd put work at the centre of their worlds for so long. From this group, many, if not all, came to the conclusion that it was past time they reoriented their priorities around work. Many swore to themselves (or in some cases out loud, to family, friends, and co-workers) that they weren't going to kill themselves at work anymore. It was from this newfound spirit of questioning and a determination to make better and healthier lives for themselves that the phenomenon known as the Great Resignation arose.

One of the most thoughtful yet succinct statements of today's changed values around work appears near the end of the recently published research report on the U.K. trials of the four-day week, a report that will be discussed at some length shortly. Commenting on the overall meaning of the four-day week, the CEO of a non-profit in the United Kingdom said, "We want to give people the gift of time." The CEO went on to say, "I hated the pandemic, but it's made us all see each other much more in the round, and it's made us realise the importance of having a healthy head and that family matters."[3] In short, a resounding "No" to the question of whether work is or should be all there is in a person's life.

From both employers' and employees' perspectives, a significantly reduced work week is a logical, eminently reasonable response to the moral challenges posed by the Covid-19 pandemic. If work isn't in fact all there is to life, why not free up as much time as possible (subject to maintaining productivity) for workers to do other things with their lives? From a more practical perspective, in labour markets that have suddenly become far more competitive than they were due to the pandemic and subsequent Great Resignation, a four-day or some other form of significantly shortened week is, as more than one manager quoted in the 4 Day Week Global research report recognizes, a competitive advantage. Indeed, in industries where workers already enjoy the freedom to work off-site, much if not all of the time, as is the case in many high-tech companies, a four-day week may be a competitive necessity. In such sectors, firms wishing to recruit and retain the best talent need to go beyond offering a hybrid workplace since that is already the norm. A four-day week may be their best option for doing just that.[4]

Given all the advantages offered by the four-day week, it shouldn't be surprising that the U.K. trial, the largest trial of a shorter work week ever conducted, found overwhelming support among both employees and managers/executives.

Trial Results

UNITED KINGDOM

The trial was conducted in the United Kingdom over a six-month period, from June through December of 2022, by a partnership of 4 Day Week Global, the 4 Day Week UK Campaign, and the British think tank

What's Been Happening Lately on the Shorter Hours Scene?

Autonomy. Trial design involved two months of preparation, with workshops, coaching, mentoring, and peer support; the experience of companies that had already moved to a shorter week was drawn on. Participating firms were drawn from a broad range of industries, and no single shorter week model was imposed, so long as employees' pay remained at 100 percent of its previous level and employees received a "meaningful" reduction in work hours.[5] While the study used generally similar research methods to an earlier 4 Day Week Global international trial, whose results are discussed later in the chapter, it supplemented quantitative results with staff interviews, including a number of interviews of CEOs.[6]

The trial involved sixty-one different companies and, initially, about 2,900 workers, of whom 1,967 completed a baseline survey and about 1,400 also completed an end-point survey.[7] The largest group of firms was drawn from the marketing/advertising sector, followed by professional services and charities/non-profits. Beyond that, participating companies were distributed over a range of industries, including health care, arts and entertainment, retail, construction, and manufacturing.[8] The vast majority of companies were quite small. While the sample did include one large company of about one thousand employees, about two-thirds of the firms had twenty-five or fewer employees and only 12 percent had over one hundred.[9]

Respondents (those completing both surveys mentioned above) were heavily white and female and tended to be well-educated and employed in a professional or managerial capacity, and to live in the United Kingdom. Specifically, 62 percent of respondents identified as women, 37 percent as men, and 1 percent as "other." Almost 90 percent lived in the United Kingdom when surveyed, with a smattering hailing from the United States, Australia, Canada, or some other country. And 90 percent of the respondents were white, with a smattering of people of Asian, Black, and mixed-race descent. Age, on the other hand, was fairly evenly distributed across the spectrum, with 37 percent below age thirty-five, 30 percent between thirty-five and forty-four, and 33 percent age forty-five or older.[10]

As for education, slightly over two-thirds of the sample (68 percent) held at least a bachelor's degree, with about the same proportion working either as executives or managers or in some professional capacity. Of note, about

70 percent of surveyed employees were either married or living common law with a partner, and slightly over half (52 percent) had at least one child. Clearly, this was a group to whom issues of work-family balance would be important.

As noted earlier, no single model of shorter week was imposed on trial participants. In the end, participating firms wound up trying five different models: 1) fifth-day stoppage, where the entire organization shuts down one day per week; 2) staggered stoppage, where staff take alternate days off (e.g., half take Monday while the other half take Friday); 3) decentralized stoppage, where each department chooses its own form of four-day week, perhaps even including other types of work week such as five shorter days; 4) annualized work weeks, where staff work an average of thirty-two hours per week throughout the entire year, but may work more during periods of high demand and less during periods of lower demand;[11] and 5) conditional hours reduction, where staff entitlement to the four-day week is tied to ongoing performance monitoring.[12] The most common choice among the forty-four firms responding to questions on this issue was a fifth-day stoppage with Fridays off for all (used by 32 percent of respondents). Close behind, at 25 percent, was a staggered pattern with Monday or Friday off. Another 25 percent of responding firms did not have a common day off for all staff, or changed the day from week to week, or offered a combination of full and half days off.[13]

The length of the work week dropped by an average of four hours per employee during the trial, from thirty-eight to thirty-four hours. Nearly three-quarters (71 percent) of sampled employees reported a decline in their working hours during the trial. Of note, slightly over one-third (34 percent) of employees reported reductions in overtime hours worked, and there was also a reduction, albeit not a large one, in the average number of days spent remote working.[14]

Firms' and employees' response to the shorter week was as uniform — uniformly positive — as the types of shorter week tried out were varied. Asked if they would continue with the four-day week after the trial, fifty-six of the sixty-one participating companies (92 percent of the sample) said they would, with nearly one-third (eighteen) of the companies going so far as to

What's Been Happening Lately on the Shorter Hours Scene?

say they would make the policy permanent.[15] Of the five companies not definitely planning to continue with the shorter week, three said they were extending their trials and two more said they were pausing them. There was not a single outright rejection of the idea in the entire sample.[16]

Companies rated their overall experience of the trial as 8.3/10. Revenues rose an average of 1.4 percent over the trials. But compared to a similar period from previous years, participating organizations reported average revenue increases of 35 percent.[17] There was a 65 percent drop in absenteeism (sick and personal days used per month) and a 37 percent decline in new hiring. The latter finding is hardly surprising given that there was a 57 percent drop in quit rates during the trial period, a result that lends strong credence to the use of the four-day week as a means of employee retention.[18]

Employee results were just as positive. A full 90 percent said they definitely wanted to continue with the four-day week; not one said they definitely did not want to.[19] Over half (55 percent) reported an increase in their ability at work. Job satisfaction increased over the trial period from 7.12 to 7.69 on a 10-point scale, with about half of respondents reporting an increase in job satisfaction.[20] With regard to health and well-being issues, 71 percent reported reduced levels of burnout by the end of the trial, 39 percent said they were less stressed, 43 percent felt their mental health had improved, and 54 percent felt a reduction in negative emotions. And physical health seemed to improve as well as mental health. About three-eighths (37 percent) saw improvement in their physical health, 46 percent experienced a reduction in fatigue, and 40 percent saw a reduction in sleep difficulties.

Finally, employees were also more satisfied with the way in which they were spending their time, with 73 percent saying they had greater satisfaction with their time, 60 percent finding an increased ability to combine work with care responsibilities, and 62 percent finding it easier to combine work with social life. Interestingly, the time men spent with children increased by more than double the rate found among women (27 percent to 13 percent).

How did employees use the additional time afforded them by their shorter working hours? While not many appear to have taken up completely new activities, most reported using their extra time off to spend more time on activities they already enjoyed. Such activities included everything from playing music to spending time with friends, engaging in sports, exercising, watching TV, visiting out-of-town family members, and volunteering at an animal shelter. A small number used their extra day to undertake professional qualifications.[21]

Employees clearly attach a high value to their extra day off. Asked for their preference between a four-day and a five-day week, 96 percent opted for the former.[22] Even more remarkably, 15 percent declared that no amount of money would induce them to go back to a five-day week on their next job. A further 8 percent said they would require at least a 50 percent pay increase to do so, while another 29 percent said they would require a raise of 25 to 50 percent. The data shows that over half the participants (52 percent) either would not be willing to go back to the longer week at any salary or would require a massive pay increase to induce them to do so. Employers, please take note.

In all likelihood, it wouldn't have been possible for participating firms to have substantially reduced their employees' work hours without losing productivity had they not, at the same time, made some significant changes to the way they worked. Such changes included, among other things, the following:

- Reforming the norms around meetings, making them shorter and less frequent and with clearer agendas and objectives
- Reforming email etiquette, encouraging staff to be more attentive to the purpose of their messages and to who needs to be involved
- Asking staff to analyze and time each step of the manufacturing process, to identify ways to save time and develop a new set of production targets
- Introducing a "heads-down" or "focus" period — a designated time of day for staff to conduct independent work uninterrupted
- Automating certain aspects of work (for example, introducing auto-filling reports, email templates, or automating certain aspects of customer service)

What's Been Happening Lately on the Shorter Hours Scene?

- Adopting new project management software, or consolidating internal communications and documents into a single piece of software
- Reorganizing calendars to promote "monotasking," eliminating the time wasted switching between tasks
- Creating a task list for the following day before leaving work, in order to hand over to colleagues or to be able to hit the ground running on the following day[23]
- Reducing the number of staff involved in any given process[24]

As pointed out to me by shorter work hours specialist Joe O'Connor during a recent interview,[25] such trimming away of the "fat" not only allows firms to achieve their shorter hours objectives; it is likely to create a better and richer work experience in and of itself, with employees wasting less time on peripheral or trivial matters and spending more time on what matters most to them and to their organization. Some of the innovations, such as asking employees to analyze and time each step of the manufacturing process, also seem likely to promote employee empowerment over the longer term, particularly if adopted systematically.

At the end of their research report, the U.K. research team conclude that the U.K. trial added "a wealth of 'on-the-ground' knowledge for the next wave of adopters to make the four-day week a reality."[26] After seeing such overwhelmingly positive results over a broad range of companies and employees, one can't help but agree.

UNITED STATES AND IRELAND

While quite remarkable, the U.K. results just discussed are in no sense unique. They are, indeed, surprisingly similar to results obtained early in 2022 in a six-month, multinational trial of the four-day week by thirty-three firms, twenty-seven of whom responded to the final survey.[27] The firms, the great bulk of which are located in the United States and Ireland, are predominantly from three sectors: administrative, IT, and telecom;

professional services; and non-profits. The firms employed, at the time of the trial, 903 people, of whom 495 completed surveys at both the beginning and end of the trial. The respondents were almost equally distributed between women and men, with about two-fifths living in the United States and smaller numbers coming from Australia, Ireland, the United Kingdom, New Zealand, and Canada. On the whole, respondents tended to be quite young, with nearly half under age thirty-five, and well-educated, with about three-quarters of the sample holding at least a bachelor's degree.

Response to the trial was uniformly positive for both participating firms and participating employees. Of the twenty-seven firms that filled out the final survey, eighteen said they would definitely continue, while another seven were planning to continue but hadn't yet made a final decision. One more firm was leaning toward continuing and the remaining firm wasn't yet sure. Not a single firm said it definitely wouldn't be continuing with the four-day week.

When asked specifically about productivity, the responding firms reported an average score of 7.7 on a scale of 1 to 10. When asked how their overall company performance had been affected by the trial, they reported an average score of 7.6.

From an employee perspective, the experience was equally successful if not more so. On a scale of 1 to 10, employees' average experience of the trial was 9.1, with virtually all (96.9 percent) wanting to continue the trial. When asked to rate their current work performance compared to their lifetime best, the average score rose from 7.17 at the beginning of the trial to 7.83 at its end. Stress, burnout, fatigue, and work-family conflict all declined, while physical and mental health, positive affect, family and work-life balance, and satisfaction "across multiple divisions of life" all increased. Employees used their days off for hobbies, household work, and personal grooming — a result not dissimilar to that obtained nearly a century ago at Kellogg Company.

What's Been Happening Lately on the Shorter Hours Scene?

ICELAND

Some of the first large-scale trials of a shorter work week took place in Iceland between 2015 and 2019. The trials, in which workers were paid their previous wage for working shorter hours, were an "overwhelming success," with productivity remaining the same or improving in the majority of workplaces, and led to many workers moving to shorter hours, researchers have said.[28]

The trials, run by Reykjavík City Council and the national government, eventually included more than 2,500 workers, which amounts to about 1 percent of Iceland's working population. A range of workplaces took part, including preschools, offices, social service providers, and hospitals. Many of them moved from a forty-hour week to a thirty-five- or thirty-six-hour week, researchers from U.K. think tank Autonomy and the Association for Sustainable Democracy (Alda) in Iceland said.

The trials led unions to renegotiate working patterns, and now 86 percent of Iceland's workforce have either moved to shorter hours for the same pay, or will gain the right to, the researchers said.

Workers reported feeling less stressed and at risk of burnout and said their health and work-life balance had improved. They also reported having more time to spend with their families, engage in hobbies, and complete household chores.

Commenting on the results of the Icelandic trial, Autonomy's research director Will Stronge said, "This study shows that the world's largest ever trial of a shorter working week in the public sector was by all measures an overwhelming success. It shows that the public sector is ripe for being a pioneer of shorter working weeks — and lessons can be learned for other governments." In this connection, it may not have been coincidental that Spain (listed below) announced it would be starting its own shorter-week trials soon after the release of the Icelandic study results.

PORTUGAL

In Portugal, while some companies had already been experimenting with a four-day week, a major pilot was scheduled to start in 2023 and last for about six months.[29] The only stipulation was that total weekly hours would have to be reduced. Various forms of shorter work would be tried out. Some of the sixty-three companies expressing interest in participating said they would be "going all in," cutting their work week from forty to thirty-two hours, while others would be making a more cautious reduction to thirty-six hours. The pilot is being financed by the Portuguese Institute of Employment and Professional Formation.

SOUTH AFRICA

South Africa, which has been looking at the new U.K. trial results with interest, started its own four-day work week trial on March 1, 2023.[30] The trial involves twenty-seven firms, specializing in such areas as IT, events planning, tax, marketing, and property development, and about five hundred workers. The model used is the same "100-80-100" model used by 4 Day Week Global in its earlier trials; this means that pay will remain at 100 percent for employees working 80 percent of their previous time in return for a commitment to deliver at least 100 percent of their normal output. As in the case of Japan, discussed below, South Africa's shorter week trial is noteworthy in that the country has hitherto been "distinguished" for its long work hours, by world standards.[31]

BRAZIL

While not yet in general use throughout Brazil, the four-day week has recently been attracting some support, particularly among advertising companies.[32] The largest Brazilian four-day-week company to date is Zee.Dog, which has about two hundred employees.

The head of a small advertising agency, Shoot, located in the city of Porto Alegre, has already made innovative use of the four-day week, even though it is still a novelty in the Brazilian business world. He has put his staff on a staggered four-day week, with customer service people working Monday to Thursday and creative staff, Tuesday to Friday. The staggered schedule allows the customer service folk to line up business on Monday, which gets the creative staff off to a good head start when they arrive on Tuesday morning. Each week there is a staff meeting on Tuesday, the first day all staff are in the office together. This is just one of many possible examples of how innovative work scheduling can lead to business advantages even beyond the usual health, hygiene, and recruitment and retention impacts normally attributable to a shorter week.

GERMANY: A LAW UNTO ITSELF

In the work hours world, Germany can only be described as *sui generis*. It was here that at the end of the 1960s the concept of flexible working hours — flextime as it is more familiarly known — was invented by an entrepreneur named Wilhelm Haller, whose numerous contributions included the development of time-recording equipment to measure the time spent on work by employees, as opposed to the number of hours they were on site.[33] Without such measuring equipment, flexible hours as such would not have been possible.

An evangelist for making work fun, Haller did a great deal during his too-short life to disseminate the concept of flexible hours, going to the extent of creating the slogan *"I laik Gleitzeit"* (I like flextime) that appeared on many cars as bumper stickers and that came to be discussed across West Germany. He even appeared on TV shows, in addition to writing books and both popular and professional articles on the subject of work hours. It is probably thanks to Haller that concepts such as the four-day week, flexible working hours, and annualized hours are not novelties in Germany as they are in much of the rest of the world but an ordinary part of everyday discussion around work.[34]

Space doesn't permit anything like a proper discussion of how far ahead of most other countries Germany is on work hours, with regard both to theoretical understanding of the issue (including its relationship to productivity) and practical measures for reducing and modifying "normal" work hours. The German contributions to these areas deserve, and will I hope before long receive, book-length treatment. Although Germany now has among the shortest average weekly work hours in the world (at thirty-four), there are many in the country, including the powerful German metalworkers' union IG Metall, who would like to see that number reduced to thirty-two. Given IG Metall's longstanding partnership with the German Social Democratic Party, which is now in power, a thirty-two-hour week seems achievable within the foreseeable future.

Evidence of just how far the ideas of shorter and more flexible hours have penetrated the business world can be found from a quick scan of a list of some of the 300+ companies that have adopted a four-day or some other form of shorter week and are hiring remotely.[35] One of the companies appearing on the list's first page is Hivemind Technologies, which describes itself as a "software engineering consultancy with a conscience. Functional. No bullshit." With respect to hours, Hivemind is extremely flexible, with arrangements that can range from twenty to thirty-eight hours per week, although its most common arrangement entails five six-hour days — the same week used by Kellogg ninety-odd years ago. (Given the extreme intensity sometimes entailed in work around new technology, such a week may make more sense than one composed of four "normal" days.) In its company manifesto, Hivemind declares, "We don't work more than 38 hours per week — and don't do overtime." Overtime, the company believes, is mainly caused by inadequate staffing, bad planning, and poor work practices. While this may be just a bit extreme — I have certainly experienced in my own working life some one-off crises for which the only way out was to work overtime — it's definitely the case that if a company is regularly asking its staff to work overtime, it needs to be hiring more people.

To a progressive, this company sounds almost too good to be true. Its "conscience" is demonstrated through, among other things, its refusal to do business with defense or fossil fuel companies or organizations involved in surveillance. Even leaving this last point aside, the company seems to have an extraordinarily firm handle on the relationship between shorter work hours and overall productivity.

The United States may have been the world leader in shorter hours during the 1920s and 1930s. Now, with the United States ranking among the world's laggards, not leaders, it is unquestionably Germany to whom the world should look for leadership, on both the theory and the practice around the shorter hours issue.

CANADA

Although Canadian developments around the four-day week haven't been as widely publicized as developments in other countries, such as the United Kingdom and the United States, the concept is definitely gaining traction here as well as in those other countries. A survey published in January 2023 found 91 percent of senior managers in corporate Canada in support of a four-day week for their teams.[36] Most would evidently agree with Work Time Reduction Center of Excellence director Joe O'Connor's statement to the effect that there has been a sea change in attitudes toward work hours since the Covid-19 pandemic. Says O'Connor, "The world of work is not going back to the way it was in 2019. The genie is out of the bottle and I think the future of work will absolutely be shorter and it will be smarter."[37]

Since early 2022, 4 Day Week Global has been running a trial of the four-day week in Canada.[38] One group of companies began the trial early in 2022, while another group began in October of that same year. In all, ten companies have participated, most of them high-tech firms such as the "open publisher" Pressbooks, the mobile retail platform Tulip, and the e-commerce delivery platform Mavtek. Nine of the ten firms moved to a work week of four eight-hour days, while the tenth moved to a week of four nine-hour days. Results to date suggest that the trial has been a success, with eight of the ten firms having implemented the shorter week permanently (six of the eight give their staff every Friday off), and a ninth having given its staff a choice between a four-day and a five-day week. (The tenth firm is still in trial mode.) Hopefully, in the coming months, more firms, including some from outside the high-tech sector, will be added to the trial.

There isn't space here to give even brief mention to all the shorter hours developments that have been occurring in Canada of late. One, however, is unusual enough to be worth noting. In late March, the Ottawa-Carleton French Catholic School Board announced it would be piloting a four-day week in two of its schools, one in Orleans, east of Ottawa, and the other in

Kanata, west of Ottawa. This was the first such announcement I had seen from any school board, anywhere.

In a news release on March 23, the Ottawa-Carleton French Catholic School Board said, pending approval from the education ministry, families who opted in would start the school year a week early, spend thirty-eight minutes more learning per day and end the school year three days later than students on the traditional five-day week. That would have added up to the same amount of teaching hours, said the board, which believes it would be the first in Ontario — and one of the first in North America — to try this kind of schedule, citing school-life balance and well-being.[39]

"It will enable [students and staff] to spend quality time with family, focus on their passions, participate in recreational activities, go to appointments, pursue their studies, engage in personal projects or simply rest," the news release said.

The board said it would be gauging interest from its families until April 10 and then would open the program up to any family in the city who can get to one of the schools, a situation similar to what exists in other specialty programs.

While the type of schedule proposed did not, itself, represent any kind of radical departure — the proposed school year contained elements of both a compressed work week and annualized work hours, neither in anyway new — the extension of such concepts to the public education sector was definitely noteworthy. Regrettably, the Ontario Ministry of Education, in its infinite wisdom, saw fit to kill the proposal before it had even had a chance to be fairly launched.[40] One can only hope that a more far-sighted jurisdiction will take up the idea in the near future. It's an idea that strikes me as offering potential benefits to students and teachers alike.

Ontario

A bill designed to move Ontario toward a four-day week has now passed first reading and awaits further legislative action. The private member's motion, Bill 55, which was introduced in 2022 by NDP MPP Bhutila Karpoche, would establish a Four-Day Work Week Commission that would develop recommendations on how to implement a pilot project designed to determine the effectiveness of a four-day work week in Ontario.[41] The pilot project would last one year and would be implemented by the minister of labour, immigration, training and skills. After that, the minister would be required to prepare a report, in consultation with the commission, setting out recommendations for a four-day week in the province. While the bill's having passed first reading is a positive step, its eventual fate remains unclear. As Alex Treiber and Irene Xie suggest in their McCarthy Tétrault article on the legislation, "It remains to be seen whether Bill 55 will ultimately become law, with second reading and corresponding debate yet to be scheduled."

UNITED STATES

Federal

Similar uncertainty attaches to a thirty-two-hour work week bill initially introduced in the U.S. House of Representatives by Representative Mark Takano (D-CA) in December 2021 and then reintroduced in early March 2023 after dying in committee in 2022, despite having almost immediately earned the support of the Congressional Progressive Caucus.[42] Takano's bill would not ban overtime work beyond thirty-two hours in a week, but it would require that overtime be paid after that point.

The bill's reintroduction follows its endorsement by 4 Day Week Global, the AFL-CIO, and two large private sector unions, the Service Employees International Union and the United Food and Commercial Workers.[43] Perhaps creating a more favourable environment for the bill's passage are the highly successful results of the U.K. pilot program on the four-day week. But a complicating factor is the shift of control over the U.S. House from the Democrats to the Republicans following the 2022 midterm elections, a shift that will make it harder to get any progressive measures onto the legislative docket, let alone passed. It remains to be seen whether the U.K. study and others involving U.S. firms such as the multinational trial also discussed earlier in the chapter have created enough momentum for a shorter work week to overcome the deep partisan divide in the U.S. House.

California

It should come as no surprise that California is one of three U.S. states to have introduced or proposed shorter hours legislation to date. Not only is California the country's largest state, but it's also arguably the country's most progressive state, with a tradition of support for a broad range of social measures. It should be remembered that the state is home to the lion's share of the country's high-tech firms. Not only are such firms noted for their technical innovation, they have also been leaders in social progress. While it must be admitted that a significant number of tech companies do require their workers to put in long hours, this is by no means the norm. In fact, many tech firms have been at the forefront of the shorter hour movement. The single most comprehensive source of information I have yet found on the shorter work week is the website run by high-tech entrepreneur Henry O'Loughlin from his company headquarters in San Diego.

As it happens, the selfsame O'Loughlin has quite succinctly chronicled the fate of California's shorter hours bill, AB 2932.[44] The bill was introduced into the California Assembly in early 2022 by members Christina Garcia and Evan Low. It would have amended Sec. 510 of the state's labour code by reducing the standard forty-hour work week to thirty-two hours, but only for a select group of workers, namely those employed in firms of five hundred or more employees. In those firms, overtime would have kicked in at thirty-two hours; otherwise, the old standard of forty hours would have remained in force. In addition — and quite inexplicably — the bill would not have applied to unionized workers.

At present, the bill is stalled, although O'Loughlin has hazarded the guess that it might be "picked up again" sometime in 2023 (this is being written at the end of March 2023).

As many readers will already be aware, it is not unusual for shorter hours bills to be stalled in some legislative committee or another. Indeed, through the course of my research for this book, I've found that this sort of thing happens frequently enough that it can almost be considered the norm for shorter hours bills, and the successful passage of such a bill an exception.

Almost all such bills deserved to be passed into law. The same, alas, cannot be said of AB 2932. While the bill was introduced with the best of intentions — in the words of co-sponsor Garcia, it was drafted with an eye to creating "a better work-life balance" for California workers, an intention one can't help but applaud — the measure is fatally flawed from an equity perspective. The size threshold and exclusion of unionized workers from the bill's operation seem destined to breed conflict, both among firms and among workers. Indeed, the bill's design goes against the very intention of employment standards legislation, which is meant to be applied to all workers, whether or not they're represented by a union.

Granted, it is conceivable that a blanket shorter hours bill might work serious, even undue hardship on certain public sector organizations providing emergency services, such as hospitals and fire departments. A better idea than blanket exclusions of the sort contemplated by the original California legislation would be a provision allowing organizations providing essential services to make the case why they should be excluded from the hours bill's overtime provisions. A better idea yet might have been to phase in the introduction of the shorter week over a two-year or even three-year period, to allow organizations, public and private sector alike, time to plan and budget for the new work hours regime.

While the right-wing rhetoric of business groups, such as the Chamber of Commerce's description of the bill as a job-killer,[45] can be dismissed out of hand as uninformed propaganda that flies in the face of all recent evidence about the shorter work week, the bill's design flaws seem to me to be fatal ones. Unless the bill is redrafted so that no particular group of workers or firms is at an advantage over any other group, the bill will not and should not pass. In its present form, the measure does little more than breed conflict where none existed before.

Maryland

The Four-Day Work Week bill was introduced into the State House of Representatives on January 18, 2023. The bill, also known as House Bill 0181 the Four-Day Workweek Pilot Program and Income Tax Credit, proposes to "give the Maryland Department of Labor the ability to promote, offer incentives, and support the experimentation and study of a four-day work week by both private and public employees."

Pennsylvania

Three state representatives, Dave Madsen, Chris Pielli, and Joshua Siegel, have announced plans to provide firms in the state with tax incentives for moving to a four-day work week.[46] In announcing their plan, the three representatives specifically referenced the successful results of the U.K. pilot program.

Under their proposed plan, if an eligible employer participates in a four-day work week pilot program through the Department of Labor and Industry, that employer may be eligible for a state income tax credit. To receive the tax credit, a qualifying company would have to comply with certain program requirements.

In a memo announcing their legislative proposal, the three representatives said, "Studies have shown that a four-day work week reduces employee stress, burnout, and fatigue.... Moreover, a four-day work week would provide workers with flexibility, allowing them to be more present parents and more active community members." Their hope is that a legislated four-day work week would provide Pennsylvania workers with the same benefits received by U.K. workers in the 4 Day Week Global trials, such as improved physical and mental well-being and a better work-life balance, without negatively affecting their employers' productivity and revenue.

INTERNATIONAL LEGISLATION

Outside of North America, a fair number of jurisdictions have recently begun experimenting with shorter hours or flexible-hours legislation. What's interesting is that these experiments haven't been confined to the British Isles or continental Europe, but have also been occurring in Asian, African, and Middle Eastern countries, suggesting that the move to shorter hours is in the process of becoming a worldwide phenomenon.

Australia

In Australia, the Senate's Select Committee on Work and Care has recommended that the country trial a four-day week, at 100 percent pay, in exchange for a commitment to delivering 100 percent of the normal work outputs.

What's Been Happening Lately on the Shorter Hours Scene?

Belgium
In 2022 Belgium became the first country in the European Union and just the third in the world, after Iceland and New Zealand, to formally allow its workers to put in a four-day week with no loss of compensation. The Belgian legislation, which was passed in February of that year and took effect in November, would allow Belgian workers the choice of working four 9.5-hour days or five 8-hour days.[47] Under the new legislation, Belgian workers will be able to work more during one week and less during the next, which will allow them to better manage their work–private life balance.[48] Also included in the new legislation is a right to disconnect after regular working hours, though this provision applies only to companies with twenty or more employees.[49]

While the new Belgian legislation was announced with some fanfare, there is perhaps less to it than meets the eye, since it doesn't actually reduce working hours but merely allows for their redistribution; in effect, it is a form of compressed work week. The announcement of the new legislation wasn't greeted with great enthusiasm by either employers or unions, with the former fearing that the new compressed week could lead to organizational issues and the latter concerned that the shorter week might simply mean a bigger workload for employees during the rest of the week.[50]

India
Legislation similar to the Belgian law has recently been proposed in India. There, revisions to the country's labour code would allow workers to put in their weekly quota of forty-eight hours over four days instead of five. But as in Belgium, the change would not result in any actual reduction in work hours.

Japan
The country's annual economic guidelines, released in June 2021, revealed plans to push Japanese employers to adopt a four-day, thirty-two-hour work week. The measure is noteworthy in that Japan has long been notorious for its workaholic culture.

Lithuania
Federal legislation passed April 21, 2022, and coming into force in 2023 allows public sector employees with children under the age of three to work thirty-two hours per week with no loss of pay. The legislation doesn't apply to private sector employees.

Malta
Under legislation passed February 25, 2022, businesses are to be given incentives to participate in a national four-day, thirty-two-hour work week trial. The proposal is part of a new "social pact" that also includes the introduction of a living wage.

Scotland
Under a proposal announced September 3, 2021, Scotland announced plans to launch a four-day, thirty-two-hour work week with no loss of pay. The program was to be funded by the ruling Scottish National Party government to the tune of £10 million. The program has since been launched, and while Scotland hasn't brought in a legislated four-day week, the idea appears to be gaining traction. More than one-third of Scottish businesses have said they plan to move to a four-day week in the near future, and the Scottish government has announced plans to begin its own trial later this year.

Spain
Legislation passed February 17, 2022, stipulates that the country will engage in a formal trial of a four-day, thirty-two-hour work week without any reduction in pay.

United Arab Emirates
A bill passed December 7, 2021, moves federal employees to a four-and-a-half-day, thirty-six-hour week on a trial basis. The purpose of the measure is "to boost productivity and improve work-life balance."

United Kingdom

A bill initially proposed by Labour MP Peter Dowd would reduce maximum weekly work hours from forty-eight to thirty-two. The bill was introduced into the House of Commons on October 18, 2022. It has yet to be passed and the bill's fate remains unclear. What is clear is that from its initial introduction, the bill was controversial, with at least one Conservative MP comparing it to a "hand grenade" thrown into the economy.[51]

OTHER COUNTRIES

Henry O'Loughlin has identified eight other jurisdictions that have not yet passed or proposed four-day week legislation but where "notable politicians" have recommended serious consideration of such legislation. These jurisdictions include New Zealand, Finland, Wales, Sri Lanka, and Thailand. In the first two countries in this group, New Zealand and Finland, a current or former prime minister was the politician making the recommendation.[52] Also of note, New Zealand is the home country of Andrew Barnes, one of the founders of the 4 Day Week Global organization active in conducting four-day week pilots around much of the world of late.

· · · · · ·

The above provides only a sample of the huge amount of activity around the shorter work week in recent years, particularly since the Covid-19 pandemic. Much more could have been included, but space simply would not have permitted that.

What's most striking to me, particularly in the results of the company trials, is the uniformly positive attitude toward shorter hours displayed by both employers/managers and employees/unions. Such a degree of near consensus is something one rarely finds in today's workplaces, as I can attest from my eleven years working for a union.

The following chapter contains proposals, in the form of recommendations, for action on shorter hours. These recommendations are directed to companies, unions, governments, and (in one case) an international body, the International Labour Organization. While some of the recommendations may seem very bold, I believe the time for tinkering is long past. The near unanimity found in the company trials suggests the likelihood of strong support for bold government action, should the evidence from those trials be effectively deployed. At the same time, the climate crisis and the crises in most country's healthcare systems, both of which are to a significant degree connected to our collective overwork and overproduction, demand strong and immediate action from all parties. Our survival as well as that of our planet requires nothing less.

CHAPTER 11

Recommendations

The previous chapter discussed what various individuals and organizations are already doing to help achieve shorter work hours. Drawing on that discussion, and moving beyond it, it's time to consider what needs to be done, by companies, governments, unions, and individuals. In developing this package of recommendations, I've tried to be comprehensive, addressing the full gamut of issues related to shorter hours, including the right to disconnect and electronic monitoring of employees by employers. I've also tried to be flexible, aware that there is often more than one way of achieving the same objective (e.g., shorter hours) and that it is often best to allow parties to work out their own solution, specific to the firm or industry, while still achieving the overall objective. The first recommendation is a prime example of such flexibility.

1. The maximum standard work week should be thirty-two hours. Employees should have a minimum rest period of forty-eight consecutive hours every week. The shorter work week should be written into employment standards legislation.

While many people and organizations have been working specifically for a four-day week, and while such a week offers many advantages, including most notably a one-fifth reduction in the number of work-related commutes, a four-day week is not the only way to reduce work hours. As noted earlier, the Kellogg Company achieved great success both for itself and for its employees with its work week of five six-hour days. In cases involving work that's extremely intense or extremely monotonous, such a week might be more suitable than one of four eight-hour days. And there could be other possibilities, as well; two that come to mind are a four-and-a-half-day week, with the week ending at noon every Friday, or a four-and-a-half-day week with a full day off every other Friday. So long as the overall standards of thirty-two weekly hours and forty-eight consecutive hours of rest are not breached, there seems to me no reason to impose any particular pattern on the structure of the work week.

2. Employers should be required to pay the same salary for a thirty-two-hour work week as they now pay for a forty-hour week.

An hours reduction achieved at the cost of a salary reduction isn't really an hours reduction. All it is is a switch from full- to part-time work. Such a switch benefits nobody.

3. The maximum allowable amount of overtime should be eight hours in a week, sixteen hours in a month, and one hundred hours in a year. Overtime beyond the weekly and monthly maxima would require government approval and should be allowed only in cases of genuine emergency.

It is imperative that overtime be strictly limited, both in order to preserve workers' health and as a way of preserving jobs. Organizations that regularly require large amounts of overtime should be hiring more people rather than putting additional strain on their existing workers.

4. Overtime premiums for work beyond the maxima listed above should be 100 percent for work on weekdays, 150 percent for night work, and 200 percent for work on weekends and holidays.

Recommendations

Having such stiff premiums in place for excessive overtime would force companies to plan their work more carefully and would undoubtedly serve to keep the amount of overtime worked to a minimum. For overtime work within the above maxima, premiums could remain the same as they are now.

5. The details of how shorter hours are to be achieved should be worked out within each workplace by a joint consultation committee.

Modelled after North American health and safety committees and European works councils, these bodies, composed of equal numbers of employee and management representatives, would be in place in all organizations above a certain size threshold (e.g., twenty-five employees). Their most important function would be working out specific work schedules to enable the company to meet the overall objectives listed in Recommendation 1 above. Other duties might include working out special (shorter) schedules for those engaged in particularly hazardous work, collecting "before and after" data on the health effects of shorter work hours, and first-step enforcement of hours maxima and right to disconnect provisions. To prevent conflict with unions currently representing workers, in unionized establishments committee members would be drawn from among active union members. To allow for some kind of representation of employees in firms not meeting the size threshold, there could be industry-wide or regional committees created to serve the same purposes as the firm-level committees discussed above.

6. Companies should be given grants to study ways of increasing productivity while reducing work hours. Governments should also conduct such studies on their own.

The scientific management experiments conducted during the First World War helped provide a solid basis for the major hours reductions achieved during the 1920s. Again, there seems to be no good reason why this might not happen again.

7. Employers should have up to two years from the coming into force of the legislation to adopt a thirty-two-hour week.

The change proposed in my first recommendation is undeniably a major one and may take some time for certain organizations to achieve. A two-year phase-in period allows plenty of time for the necessary financial and logistical adjustments, and for employees to adjust their lives to the shorter week.

8. Governments at all levels — federal, provincial/state, and municipal — should set good examples for other employers by reducing their own staff's work hours.

In the past, a reduction in the hours of government workers often proved an impetus to more general hours reductions. There seems no reason to believe that this could not happen again.

9. Canadian jurisdictions should increase their statutory minimum vacation entitlements to three weeks after one year of service, and four weeks after five years.

Canadian vacation entitlements are very low by international standards. Most European countries require a minimum of four weeks' vacation. There seems no good reason why this situation should be allowed to continue. In addition to being a way of improving workers' health, such a move could reduce turnover by giving workers an incentive to stay with their existing employers.

10. Labour ministries should hire significant numbers of new staff specifically charged with enforcing work hours and overtime legislation.

Through the years, enforcement of most employment standards legislation has been slack.[1] Almost everyone knows that laws that aren't enforced are at the end of the day, worthless, as employers will feel free to violate such laws with impunity. In this case, however, additional staff charged with enforcement should be looked on not as an expense but an investment, since by effectively policing work hours they will be helping to reduce the demand on our severely overstressed healthcare system. The hiring of the new staff should be accompanied by a publicity campaign pointing out the negative effects of overwork and excessive overtime and emphasizing the connection between reduced working hours and reduced sickness and accident levels.

> 11. Educational institutions should include courses on work hours in their human resources and industrial relations curricula, and perhaps in their labour history curricula as well. The issue should also be addressed in adult education curricula.

Educating more people about the effects of work hours is a good way to increase public awareness of the issue, and to help build the political momentum needed to bring about lasting change through legislation. A strong adult education movement, especially among labour activists, was a major factor in building such momentum prior to the First World War.[2] Again, it seems likely that a renewal of this kind of adult education effort could have a similar effect today.

> 12. As in the case of work hours, leisure studies need to be included in university and adult education curricula.

There are far too many people today who really don't know what to do with their non-work hours, beyond turning on some kind of electronic device. An understanding of leisure studies could help provide a greater knowledge base, which would enable workers to make healthier and more informed choices in this area.

> 13. The labour movement should re-engage with the work hours issue, both internationally and nationally. In particular, the experience of IG Metall, the big German metalworkers' union, should be drawn upon.

At the time of the Great Resignation, it seems the time is ripe for a renewed assault on excessive working hours. This needs to happen at the bargaining table, as well as in company boardrooms and legislative forums. With work hours again a priority at the bargaining table, as well as in the labour movement's agenda for political action, momentum for lasting country-wide change can be built.

> 14. The International Labour Organization should hold an international conference on work hours at the earliest possible opportunity.

The ILO was perhaps the single most important player in the achievement of the eight-hour day through most of the industrialized world in the 1920s. It continues to command global respect today, and it seems entirely possible that another ILO conference could bring about major and lasting reductions in work hours worldwide.

> 15. The right to disconnect from the workplace is a critical aspect of any broader work hours reduction. This right should be enshrined in employment standards legislation or health and safety legislation, or perhaps even both.

If shorter hours legislation is going to mean anything at all, it must be accompanied by a strong right to disconnect, one that includes clear standards and stiff penalties for violation. Such legislation is especially important in an era of hybrid workplaces, when the line between work and private life has already become increasingly blurred. It's particularly important that workers be protected from employer reprisal for exercising their right to disconnect, a protection granted in the Argentinian legislation discussed earlier. Within Canada, although Ontario's legislation is a start, the proposed Quebec legislation would afford far more meaningful protection to workers and should be considered a more appropriate model.

Recommendations

16. Specific legislation must be developed to address the issue of electronic monitoring of those working from home (as in the case of hybrid workplaces) and to prevent abuses of such workers.

With the type of electronic technology now available, it is possible for employers to find out, electronically, far more about their workers' private lives than is necessary for any legitimate business purpose. Such legislation must clearly outline the scope of permissible monitoring, and the reason for it. Electronic monitoring would also be an appropriate subject for consideration by the joint work hours committees proposed in Recommendation 6.

17. The thirty-two-hour maximum proposed in Recommendation 1 should be considered a starting point, not an end point. Detailed experiments measuring workers' productivity and the health effects of new forms of technology must continue, with an eye to working out an optimal workday and/or workweek — very possibly a workweek shorter than thirty-two hours.

In this connection, experiments should be conducted to determine whether hybrid workplaces, where travel time to and from work is no longer an issue, warrant different schedules than completely on-site workplaces.

Conclusion

As I've tried to show throughout this book, the Covid-19 pandemic and its aftermath have led to great, almost certainly irreversible changes in how we work and how we think about work. Working less will be just one of those changes, but in all likelihood it will be the single most important one. As noted in the "Hybrid Workplaces" chapter, work is now being done in many different places — often but not always workers' homes — and it now involves the use of more demanding technology than was in general use prior to the pandemic.

Perhaps most significantly, the nature of post-pandemic work is already leading, and will likely continue to lead, to a fundamental change in the way we think about time, and to our values around time.[1] This in turn has already led, and will continue to lead, to major changes in the relationship between employers and their employees. Prior to the pandemic, there was an unspoken assumption that employers could demand as much of their employees' time as they wanted, and employees generally had little choice other than to go along, no matter how great the disruption to their personal lives or even the effects on their physical and mental health. In a perpetually slack labour market marked by high unemployment, quitting was simply not an option for most workers.

For many, if not all, workers today, this is no longer the case. With the labour shortages that led to the Great Resignation, a growing number of workers have felt free to leave work settings marked by chronic overwork or other kinds of abuse, confident that they will be able to find new jobs with less abusive working conditions within a reasonable period of time. And there is also growing recognition, as the line between work time and personal time becomes increasingly blurred in an era in which much work is done off site, that workers need to be able to set limits to their employers' ability to make demands of them outside of regularly scheduled work hours. While the right to disconnect (discussed in chapter 8) has not yet been firmly established in Canada, as it has through legislation passed in a number of European and Latin American countries, the passage of such legislation in Canada's largest province and its introduction in the federal jurisdiction suggests that this is a topic we shall be hearing a lot more of in the future.

While the pandemic was teaching us all about the extreme fragility of life, it was also teaching all those prepared to listen that there's more to life — a lot more — than work. Hopefully, this newfound wisdom will guide everyone — workers, employers, unions, and policy-makers alike — in establishing new work schedules and practices that, while assuring that society's essential work continues to get done, also preserve the lives and health of the people doing that work, and of the planet.

Acknowledgements

Had it not been for Dundurn publisher Kwame Scott Fraser, this book would not exist. It was he who took an idea expressed in embryonic form in a CBC Opinion piece and offered me the opportunity to make a book out of it. My gratitude to him is immense.

My editor, Dominic Farrell, has done a lot to strengthen the manuscript, mainly by pointing out new areas for inquiry and implications that I might otherwise have missed. And he has done all this while allowing me to be myself as a writer — a truly Herculean achievement. Managing editor Elena Radic has patiently and knowledgeably guided me through the publishing process, in particular making the business of getting a contract far less painful than I had previously been led to believe it would be.

My frequent literary partner in crime, Ann McMillan, has been immensely supportive throughout, providing encouragement and on occasion tasty home-cooked meals at moments when I was just about prepared to give up. And my dear friend and former colleague Denise Giroux has been a source of inspiration, holding to "the faith" about the kind of workplace and society we both want in the face of numerous temptations to give up on the battle.

Many — more than I could possibly acknowledge here — came forward with suggestions and ideas during the book's composition. Fellow writers Sharon Hamilton and Ingrid McCarthy were particularly generous in this regard. My thanks to them. I'd also like to acknowledge the contribution of work hours specialists Joe O'Connor and Henry O'Loughlin, who generously gave their time for interviews used as the book's appendices.

Most of all, I'd like to acknowledge the contribution of my life partner, Elizabeth Zimmer, who has been there for me in bad times and good and has been consistently encouraging to me in my work on this project. Without her loving support over the past year and a half, I'm not sure I would ever have completed the book.

Gatineau, Quebec
July 2023

APPENDIX A

Profile of Joe O'Connor: He Works so You Can Work Less

Joe O'Connor is a guy who works hard so you can work less hard — or at least less.

For the past five years, O'Connor has devoted himself to working for shorter hours — first in his native Ireland, then in the United States, and most recently in Toronto, where he's now Director of the Work Time Reduction Center of Excellence, an organization he co-founded. Before moving to Toronto last fall, he was CEO at 4 Day Week Global, the organization responsible, as much as any other, for launching and carrying out the recent highly successful and much-publicized trials of a shorter work week in the United Kingdom.[1]

Though he's no longer directly connected to 4 Day Week Global, O'Connor is delighted with the results of the company trials he had a big hand in designing while there. These results showed 92 percent of participating companies and 90 percent of participating employees in favour of continuing with a shorter week.

"These results will be a game-changer, at least for companies," O'Connor says. "The trials have pushed the issue of a shorter work week front and centre at places like shareholders' meetings, where it is now at the head of the agenda. There's been a big change in momentum around the issue. Companies we were reaching out to six months ago (several months before the release of the trial results) that were sort of non-committal are now coming to us and saying, yes, let's do it."

More often than not, the switch that companies want to make is from a five-day to a four-day work week. While O'Connor insists that there's no "one size fits all model" for a shorter week — what will work best for any given firm depends on the type of industry, the size of the company, and several other variables — there are reasons why the four-day week is far and away the most popular choice.

First off, it's the best-known choice. In recent years, a sizable literature has been amassed around the four-day week. The same isn't true for other types of shorter week, such as one involving five six-hour days. The four-day week thus starts off with the advantage of being familiar to employees and managers alike; in O'Connor's experience, some 80 to 90 percent of employees interested in a shorter week are interested in that particular type of shorter week.

Second, while this might not be true for all workers in all industries, for the vast majority of people an extra day off is seen as a much greater benefit than two extra hours off each day. It thus has a greater ability to motivate workers to work smarter and more efficiently than do other forms of shorter work week. "Why wouldn't you choose a model that generates motivation?" O'Connor asks.

It's also worth noting that in a world in which the boundaries between work time and private time have become increasingly porous owing to e-mail and other applications of computer technology, employees, particularly those working from home, can "hang on" to a complete extra day more easily than they could to a couple of extra hours at the end of each day, when the "blending" of work and personal time would be more likely.

Finally, although this would not be the primary reason for choosing a four-day week over other models, the four-day week offers greater environmental benefits, since it would mean a reduction in work-related commuting, at least for those still working on-site a good part of the time.

Appendix A: Profile of Joe O'Connor

This doesn't mean that O'Connor favours *all* types of four-day work week. One he has no interest in promoting is the *compressed week*, in which employees work the same number of hours as before but do so over fewer days. For example, instead of working five eight-hour days, employees would work four ten-hour days.

For knowledge workers, in particular, longer days might defeat the whole purpose of a four-day week, which is to make workers more productive. "I'm not persuaded that four longer days leads to more productive employees (in the case of knowledge work). It might well have the reverse effect."[2] Granted, for governments and other public sector organizations, a compressed week may be the best they can do toward providing their staff with more flexible work arrangements, given legislative, political, and operational constraints. But in O'Connor's view, schedule changes like compressed work weeks that don't result in an actual reduction in work hours are mere tinkering. "You don't need us to do that," he concludes.

What is O'Connor's take on the shorter-hours legislation introduced over the past two or three years in various Canadian and American jurisdictions? While he has met with people like Ontario MPP Bhutila Karpoche, author of a four-day week bill (discussed earlier in this book), and would like to work with legislative bodies on crafting shorter-hours legislation, he is not generally in favour of the mandatory approach found in some shorter-hours bills.

His preference is for laws like one recently introduced in Maryland (and also discussed earlier in the book) that would provide tax incentives for companies offering their workers shorter hours. In his view, the appropriate shorter-hours role for government is to invest in research, to make sure a strong infrastructure is in place, and to try out various innovations with its own employees, thereby serving as a sort of model employer. Commenting on a mandatory legislative approach such as that contained in recent California and U.S. federal legislation, O'Connor says, "It's too early in the cycle for that."

What about the right to disconnect? Has O'Connor's new organization been doing anything with that? It turns out that the answer to this question is yes, indeed they have. In his view, the "right to disconnect" is all about boundaries. "You have to address questions around boundaries," he says. To that end, "We train organizations how to set appropriate boundaries."

At the same time, he insists that in order for the four-day work week to succeed, companies must retain an element of discretion, in order to be able to respond to crises. This requires learning as well. "You need to learn to differentiate between things that require an immediate response and those that don't."

Overall, O'Connor is optimistic about the prospect of wide-scale work week reduction. "It's quite possible that within the next five years, *not* offering such a week could become a competitive disadvantage." Not only is a shorter week good for employee morale and for recruitment and retention; it helps make companies more efficient and more productive. "The shorter work week acts as a forcing function to compel firms to work more efficiently. It requires making time a scarce resource, to force change."

Given all of this, what's not to like about it?

APPENDIX B

An Interview with Henry O'Loughlin

Henry O'Loughlin is a San Diego–based consultant specializing in remote work and work hours. He maintains a comprehensive listing of companies from all around the world that have adopted a four-day week — a listing that I have come to know as "Henry's List." I recently interviewed him via email.

......

Jon Peirce: You got involved in work hours, you've said, through your earlier involvement in remote work. What's the connection between the two, and are there particular issues around work hours in remote workplaces?

Henry O'Loughlin: Remote work and alternative work weeks (like the four-day week) are both major steps in questioning the status quo of how white-collar work has been done over the past century – five workdays, forty hours, full-time employees, management structure, and a centralized office.

Once your company chooses to question one (like the office with remote work or the standard work week with a four-day, thirty-two-hour week), you inevitably question the others. You disconnect time and physical presence from work output. Therefore, once your company is fully remote and you can no longer "see" every employee, you focus on output and value rather than presence. Once that happens, you start to question set work hours.

JP: If I understood correctly from our earlier talk, you're now working full-time on work hours. How is that working out for you? Was the transition from remote work to work hours a difficult one?

HOL: I discuss remote work and work hours on my site to help business owners and managers think about preparing their companies for the future. I haven't transitioned away from remote work.

With my consulting work, I help clients operate a business remotely, which includes figuring out how to build a policy on work hours, asynchronous work, and expectations for being online.

JP: I don't suppose that when you were growing up, you said, "I'm going to work with people on remote work and work hours." How did you happen to become interested in those subjects?

HOL: Funny enough, my father worked from home starting in the late '70s through to his retirement a few years ago (2019). So, you're right — I didn't hope to grow up to help people run remote or four-day businesses, but there is a childhood tie seeing my father work this way.

My interest in remote work really grew when I started working for a fully remote company in 2013. We grew that business remotely for six years on a thirty-six-hour work week (or, "Half-day Fridays"). I knew a business could grow with alternative locations and hours, so in late 2019, we decided to implement the four-day (thirty-two-hour) work week. We were early to remote work and early to the four-day work week. Running a successful business with alternative thinking got me interested in working on these topics full time.

JP: Have you noticed any changes in the key issues since you started working on work hours?

HOL: The four-day work week has graduated from a niche, generally unaccepted idea to a popular, trendy, press-worthy idea since 2020. That has been the biggest change I've noticed. It is now "cool."

JP: What effect do you think the Covid-19 pandemic has had on work hours? Is that effect still ongoing, in your view?

Appendix B: An Interview with Henry O'Loughlin

HOL: Like I said in my answer to question #1, there are generally accepted principles of how work is done: set hours, set days, full-time employees, centralized work location.

When Covid-19 started, everyone who could work from home did just that (most of them for the first time). Many businesses realized that could work for them and their employees might be happier. By being forced to question a standing principle of how work is done (the office), it naturally opens up more questions, like how often work should be done.

In 2020, everyone went remote and liked it. By 2021–2022, people started trying the four-day work week. This is still playing out and will likely for the next decade.

JP: How and when did you hit on the idea for "Henry's List"?

HOL: I'm assuming you are talking about these two posts, just so we're on the same page — *buildremote.co/four-day-week/4-day-work-week-companies* — since I don't have anything formally called "Henry's List."

A few months into Covid, I read over and over how companies were deciding to go remote permanently (regardless of the pandemic). I thought people might find it useful to track which companies are doing this and why, so I started this list.

When I noticed the same trend happening for the four-day work week, I started those lists for the same purpose. People might want to know who is doing the four-day work week, why, and how it's going.

JP: What are your sources for "Henry's List"?

HOL: The sources are all linked to from within the articles. I have Google News and Twitter alerts set up to scan new stories that mention four-day work weeks. Then I add every new company or country or bill to the list weekly.

JP: Tell me about any companies you've found that seem to you to be doing particularly innovative stuff around work hours.

HOL: Buffer: Buffer is fully remote, has a four-day work week, works asynchronously, offers unlimited PTO [paid time off], and paid sabbaticals for employees with 5+ years at the company. This company questions everything about how and when work is done.

Shopify: Shopify has 15,000+ employees and implemented a seasonal four-day work week for summertime. They also offer unlimited PTO and claim to work asynchronously. All three of those concepts challenge the standard work week.

Nectafy (my former employer): This is a small business, about ten people, but they are fully remote, they started with a thirty-six-hour work week, then a four-day/thirty-two-hour work week, and they offer "essential PTO" (which gives a minimum amount of days off that you'd get paid out for if you were to leave and you can take as much as you want on top of that).

JP: Which countries, in your experience, are doing the most around this issue? What is it about these countries that has them taking a leadership role on the issue?

HOL: Iceland: Iceland was the first country to take the step toward a four-day work week with a big trial of reduced working hours from 2014–2021.

U.S.: Many companies in the U.S. have trialed a four-day work week with the help of 4 Day Week Global and multiple states have proposed thirty-two-hour work week laws (nothing has passed yet).

Belgium: In 2022, Belgium passed a law that gives workers the right to choose a four-day work week (but with the same number of hours, thirty-eight per week).

The common threads for all of these countries seem to be: 1) a higher standard of living; 2) more share of knowledge workers/white-collar workers as part of the working population; and 3) a culture for innovation in business.

JP: Which countries are lagging behind on work hours, and why, in your opinion?

HOL: The countries with the longest average work weeks are poorer countries: Mexico, Nigeria, Malaysia, Myanmar. Presumably, the sheer amount of work is required to grow incomes personally and the economy as a whole.

JP: Where does the U.S. stand on this issue?

HOL: Well, it's a big country with fifty states so there isn't one unified approach to work hours. However, the U.S. has been a leader in trialing and proposing fewer work hours:

Appendix B: An Interview with Henry O'Loughlin

From my research, it has the first or second most four-day work week companies. The U.K. is the other country that switches from the first to second spot. The U.S. has had trials of the four-day work week with 4 Day Week Global. There have been multiple bills proposed [in] California, Pennsylvania, Maryland.

JP: What measures should American companies, unions, and governments be taking on work hours at this point?

HOL: I think individual companies should choose to question work hours, and then offer fewer work hours as a benefit to attract talent. That has the most potential to grow the trend since it has an aspect of competition which would force other companies to adjust to keep up.

Personally, I do not think it works well having shorter work weeks mandated by governments. If states mandated that companies start to pay overtime at thirty-two hours instead of forty, the companies are more likely to leave or go out of business and remove those jobs altogether.

JP: What does your own weekly work schedule look like?

HOL: My wife and I both work for ourselves and we have two toddlers. We each work in the mornings while our kids are in preschool until around lunch, then we trade off working in the afternoons. We're all together on Friday afternoons and the weekends.

All in all, it probably puts me around twenty-five hours of work per week, alternating days that end around lunch time.

JP: I'd have thought that particularly in remote firms, the right to disconnect would be a huge issue. Do you do any work on that issue, and, if so, what kind of work?

HOL: That was the single biggest issue I noticed at the beginning of Covid when everyone started working remotely. Most of the advice I read from people who just started with remote work was to have more meetings, connect more frequently for check ins, be more available on the company chat tool.

All of this is wrong. Companies that work with Buildremote (using what I call "The Remote Operating System") do the opposite of that. Come on and say hello, then log off so you aren't distracted. Check your email in blocks, then close it. Question each meeting and cancel the recurring ones that don't provide value. Discourage people that reply on weekends or nights. Schedule emails to go out to your team in the morning.

Give your people autonomy, give them time for meaningful work, and then make sure you have the right people on the team.

JP: How is your work on work hours evolving? What do you see that work looking like in one year? In five years?

HOL: I lay out my theory on this best in an article I published last year — on January 6, 2022, to be precise — on the Buildremote website. The article is entitled "The Future of Work Lies 12,000 Years Ago." Basically, I think we are in a turning period where all of the ways of work we built over the last century will fall. They are no longer needed and they no longer provide an advantage because of the internet.

An office was a place to collaborate, which is no longer needed with the internet. It's now a disadvantage to have an office (it restricts your talent pool).

Shift work and set hours drove the assembly line. That's not applicable to knowledge work.

Employees and salaries gave structure and consistent results when hours were much more linked to output.

We're in a period where all of these old principles will fall and work will look very different in a decade or two. Most people will work for themselves. Most people will work unset hours. Most people will work remotely.

APPENDIX C

People and Organizations Working for Shorter Hours

People

Abildgaard, Pernille. Danish management consultant and efficiency expert, and a member of Work Time Reduction Center of Excellence's Expert Advisory Board. She is founder and CEO of the Danish organization Take Back Time, which seeks to create "happier employees and healthier companies," and is also the author of *The Secret of the Four Day Week: How to Make Your Business Grow by Working Less*, published by Amazon in 2020.

Barnes, Andrew. New Zealand businessman, co-founder of 4 Day Week Global, and author of the 2020 book *The 4 Day Week*.

Hunnicutt, Benjamin. Historian and leisure studies scholar, professor at University of Iowa. Author of several books about various aspects of work hours.

Karpoche, Bhutila. Ontario NDP legislative member, author of a four-day week bill currently under study by the Ontario legislature.

Lockhart, Charlotte. Co-founder of 4 Day Week Global.

O'Connor, Joe. Co-founder and director of Work Time Reduction Center of Excellence, previously CEO of 4 Day Week Global.

O'Laughlin, Henry. Author of "Henry's List," a listing of every company doing a four-day work week, and of the jobs offered, at buildremote.co. Updated weekly.

Petersen, Anne Helen. Journalist who often writes about work-related issues. Co-author (with Charlie Warzel) of *Out of Office*.

Schor, Juliet. Economist and sociologist, professor at Boston University, author of books on overwork in the United States, research director of recent four day week trials.

Takano, Mark. Democratic U.S. Representative from California, author of a federal work hours bill introduced into the U.S. House of Representatives.

Thompson, Derek. Journalist who writes regularly about work for *The Atlantic*, author of a recent (2023) book of essays on various aspects of work.

Warzel, Charlie. Journalist who often writes about work and work hours issues. Co-author (with Anne Helen Petersen) of *Out of Office*.

Organizations

Autonomy

A progressive U.K. think tank that focuses on (among other things) the future of work and shorter work hours. It was heavily involved, along with 4 Day Week Global, in the recent four-day week trials in the United Kingdom.

Curium Solutions

A U.S.-based transformation company that helps "organizations of all sizes realize more of their potential by implementing interventions that change them for the better. And stick." To this end, Curium has partnered with Work Time Reduction Center of Excellence to use reduced work hours as a means of bringing about improved organizational efficiency and productivity.

Flex Jobs – flexjobs.com

A job site devoted entirely to non-traditional work arrangements, from remote and off-site work to part-time jobs, jobs with flexible work hours, and jobs offering shorter work weeks.

Appendix C: People and Organizations Working for Shorter Hours

4-Day Week Campaign
Provides advice and consultation to U.K. firms considering a shorter week and maintains an accreditation scheme for "4 Day Week Employers."

Four Day Week Ireland
Four Day Week Ireland is a campaign advocating for a gradual, steady, managed transition to a shorter working week for all workers, in the private and public sectors.

4 Day Week Global
4 Day Week Global is a not-for-profit New Zealand–based organization established by Andrew Barnes and Charlotte Lockhart to provide a platform for like-minded people who are interested in supporting the idea of the four day work week as a part of the future of work. Among other things, the organization was heavily involved in planning and carrying out the recent four-day week trials in the United Kingdom. It publishes a monthly newsletter.

IG Metall
German metalworkers' union — and the biggest union in Germany — which has long pushed for shorter hours. IG Metall is now calling for a thirty-two-hour week at no reduction in pay in order to, among other things, make work in the steel industry more attractive to young people.

Work Time Reduction Center of Excellence
Joe O'Connor, co-founder and director. hello@worktimereduction.com. A Toronto-based organization that, working mainly with firms, seeks to "change the world of work through shorter hours, smarter working, improved performance, and enjoying a greater quality of life." To further its mission of organizational excellence, it has partnered with the U.S.-based Curium Solutions (see above).

Notes

Introduction: Suddenly, the Time Is Now (Once Again)
1 "Introduction: Suddenly the Time Is Now (Once Again)," Jon Peirce, *The Case for a Shorter Work Week* (Ottawa: Carleton University Centre for the Study of Training, Investment, and Economic Restructuring, 2000).
2 The two measures, by California Democratic Representative Mark Takano and Ontario NDP MPP Bhutila, are discussed in some detail in Chapter 10.
3 See, among others, Jon Peirce, *Canadian Industrial Relations*, 2nd ed. (Toronto: Pearson, 2003), 85; Craig Heron, *The Canadian Labour Movement: A Short History* (Toronto: Lorimer, 1989), 14–15. Except as otherwise noted, all subsequent references to Peirce's *Canadian Industrial Relations* will be to this edition.
4 Peirce, *Canadian Industrial Relations*, 87.

Chapter 1: Working Ourselves Sick
1 Bruce O'Hara, *Working Harder Isn't Working* (Vancouver: New Star Press, 1993), 17–18.
2 Andrew Barnes with Stephanie Jones, *The 4 Day Week: How the Flexible Work Revolution Can Increase Productivity, Profitability, and Wellbeing, and Help Create a Sustainable Future* (London: Piatkus, 2020), 21.
3 Ibid., 41.
4 Juliet B. Schor, *The Overspent American: Why We Want What We Don't Need* (New York: Harper, 1998).
5 Quoted in O'Hara, *Working Harder Isn't Working*, 28–29.

6. Barnes and Jones, *The 4 Day Week*, 24.
7. In fairness, some on-call provisions remain in force today. For example, Logistics in Motion, a third-party logistics provider, has in its collective agreement with maintenance employees a provision stipulating that employees be paid a minimum of two hours' straight time for each day they are required to be on call. If actually called into work, they receive the greater of two hours' overtime pay or overtime rates for all hours worked. See Jeffrey R. Smith, "Mandatory On-Call Shifts Reasonable under Collective Agreement: Arbitrator," *Human Resources Director*, June 7, 2023, hcamag.com/ca/specialization/employment-law/mandatory-on-call-shifts-reasonable-under-collective-agreement-arbitrator/448546.
8. Barnes and Jones, *The 4 Day Week*, 10, 12–13.
9. Ibid., 12–13; O'Hara, *Working Harder Isn't Working*, 17.
10. Barnes and Jones, *The 4 Day Week*, 24.
11. Ibid., 40–41.
12. Ibid., 41.
13. Microsoft Work Trend Index, "The Next Great Disruption is Hybrid Work: Are You Ready?" Microsoft, 2021, microsoft.com/en-us/worklab/work-trend-index/hybrid-work/.
14. Ibid.
15. See among others René Riedl, "On the Stress Potential of Videoconferencing: Definition and Causes of Zoom Fatigue," *Electronic Markets* 32 (December 6, 2021), doi.org/10.1007/s12525-021-00501-3. On professional workers' personal experience of the stress caused by Zoom, see Ruth Hawkins, "It's OK if I'm Not OK," in *Plague Take It: A COVID Almanac by and About Elders*, ed. Jon Peirce and Ann McMillan (Ottawa: Loose Cannon Press, 2021), 298–99; and Denise Giroux, "Zooming Our Way into Oblivion," in *Plague Take It*, 322–33.
16. A.J. Veal, *Whatever Happened to the Leisure Society?* (np: Routledge, 2019), 195, 285.
17. Cited in Barnes and Jones, *The 4 Day Week*, 18.
18. Barnes and Jones, *The 4 Day Week*, 17.
19. Ibid., 16.
20. John Paul Tasker, "Chief Nursing Officer Appointed to Help Deal with Health Care 'Crisis': Minister." *CBC News*, August 23, 2022, cbc.ca/news/politics/chief-nursing-office-appointed-1.6559588.
21. Ibid.
22. Teresa Wright, "Code Blue: A Global News Series Delving into Canada's Health-Care Crisis," *Global News*, August 23, 2022, globalnews.ca/news/9071575/code-blue-canada-health-care-crisis-series.
23. Irelyne Lavery, "Canada's Health-Care System Is in 'Crisis.' Are Employers, Leaders Up for the Task?" *Global News*, July 10, 2022, globalnews.ca/news/8980038/canadas-health-care-political-leaders.

Notes

24 Wright, "Code Blue."
25 Ibid.
26 I confess to having done so myself on one occasion in 2021, in Quebec.
27 Wright, "Code Blue."
28 Most notably by University of Toronto's David Foot, whose numerous books were making this point as early as the 1980s and 1990s. For a more recent discussion, see Peter Zimonjic, "Canada's Working-Age Population Is Older than Ever, StatsCan Says," *CBC News*, April 27, 2022, ici.radio-canada.ca/rci/en/news/1879202/canadas-working-age-population-is-older-than-ever-statscan-says.
29 Canadian Medical Association, "Health Care Groups Call on Premiers to Make Canada's Collapsing Health System Their Top Priority," *Canadian Medical Association*, July 7, 2022, cma.ca/about-us/what-we-do/press-room/health-care-groups-call-premiers-make-canadas-collapsing-health-system-their-top-priority.
30 Matt Gurney, "Health Care in Crisis: Part I: Ontario's Hospital-Association President on a System 'Under Massive Pressure,'" TVO, July 18, 2022, tvo.org/article/health-care-in-crisis-part-1-ontarios-hospital-association-president-on-a-system-under-massive.
31 SBSNews, "Australia Experiencing an 'Impending and Significant' Health Crisis, Survey Finds," *SBSNews*, June 21, 2022, sbs.com.au/news/article/australia-experiencing-an-impending-and-significant-health-crisis-survey-finds.
32 Sachin Ravikumar, "Britain's Health Service Facing Worst Staffing Crisis, Say Lawmakers," Reuters, July 25, 2022, reuters.com/world/uk/britains-health-service-facing-worst-staffing-crisis-say-lawmakers-2022-07-25.
33 Richard Lofgren, Michael Karpf, Jay Perman, and Courtney Higdon, "The U.S. Health Care System Is in Crisis: Implications for Academic Medical Centers and Their Missions," *Academic Medicine* 81, no. 8 (August 2006), 713–20.
34 See Katya Ridderbusch, "Can America's Healthcare Crisis Be Solved?" *Georgia State University Research Magazine*, November 12, 2021, news.gsu.edu/research-magazine/can-americas-healthcare-crisis-be-solved. See also Adriana Belmonte, "America's Health Care Affordability Crisis Is Growing Larger and Deeper," Yahoo! finance, December 22, 2021, ca.news.yahoo.com/americas-dysfunctional-health-care-system-burying-vulnerable-households-130318913.html. Belmonte's article notes that data from July 2021 showed that 18 percent of Americans owed medical debt that had been sent to collection agencies, while 30 percent reported having deferred medical care at some point in the three previous months due to cost.
35 Monica Pinna, "On Life Support: Can France's Struggling Healthcare System be Saved?" *euronews Witness*, August 7, 2022, euronews.com/2022/07/08/on-life-support-can-frances-struggling-healthcare-system-be-saved.

36 Alessandro Bramucci, Franz Prante, and Achim Treger, "Decades of Tight Fiscal Policy Have Left the Health Care System in Italy Ill-Prepared to Fight the COVID-19 Outbreak" *Intereconomics* 25, no. 3 (2020), 147–52.
37 Sofia Bettiza, "How Italy's Healthcare Staff Survived the Pandemic," *BBC News*, May 12, 2021, bbc.com/news/world-europe-57071604.
38 Donald Reid, *Work and Leisure in the 21st Century* (Toronto & Dayton: Wall & Emerson, 1995), 18.
39 Ibid.
40 Leyland Cecco, "Canadian Province Declares Emergency amid Worst Wildfires in over 50 Years," *Guardian*, August 9, 2022, theguardian.com/world/2022/aug/08/newfoundland-labrador-wildfires-canada-state-of-emergency.
41 Sabo Aziz, "Here's a Look at Some of the Wildfires Burning Across Canada," *Global News*, August 8, 2022, globalnews.ca/news/9044577/canada-wildfires-august-2022.
42 Canadian Press Staff, "Canada's Western Provinces Battling Multiple Wildfires amid Warm, Dry Weather," *Global News*, July 19, 2022, globalnews.ca/news/9000124/canada-wildfires-western-provinces-july-19-2022.
43 Fireweatheravalanche.org, FWAC Map of Fires, downloaded August 29, 2022.
44 Akshay Kulkarni, "Donnie Creek Wildfire in Northeast B.C. now the Largest Recorded in Province's History," *CBC News*, June 18, 2023, cbc.ca/news/canada/british-columbia/donnie-creek-bc-wildfire-jun-18-1.6880715.
45 M.A. Jacquemain, "Climate Change is Worsening Youth Mental Health, Research Shows," *Weather Network*, August 29, 2022, theweathernetwork.com/en/news/climate/impacts/climate-change-is-worsening-youth-mental-health-research-shows. All the material in this paragraph has been drawn from Jacquemain's article.
46 Allyson Chiu, "How a Four-Day Work Week Could be Better for the Climate," *Washington Post*, August 8, 2022. Except as otherwise noted, all material in this paragraph and the next one has been drawn from Chiu's article.
47 For the purposes of this discussion, I'm assuming that workers are still working five days a week at their workplaces. Extension of the discussion into hybrid workplaces, in which many are and will be working, gets us into a different and more complex kind of mathematics.
48 See the statements by Joe O'Connor and Juliet Schor cited in Chiu, "How a Four-Day Work Week …" See also Schor, *The Overspent American*, 162–163. Note as well that these kinds of environmentally friendly lifestyle choices were made by the Kellogg workers who benefitted from that company's thirty-hour work, with many taking up or spending more time on gardening, hunting, and fishing, and craft work of various kinds.
49 Veal, *Whatever Happened to the Leisure Society*, 284.
50 Chiu, "How a Four-Day Work Week …"

51 O'Connor is now director of Work Time Reduction Center of Excellence, in Toronto.
52 Quoted in Chiu, "How a Four-Day Work Week …"
53 Ibid.

Chapter 2: Historical Development of Work Hours I: The United States

1 R.C. Feenstra, R. Inklaar and M.D. Timma, "The Next Generation of the Penn World Table," *American Economic Review* 105, no. 10 (October 2015), 3150-82. Cited in Charlie Giattino, Esteban Ortiz-Ospana, and Max Roser, "Working Hours," *OurWorldinData*, 2013, revised December 2020, ourworldindata.org/working-hours.
2 David R. Roediger and Philip S. Foner, *Our Own Time: A History of American Labor and the Working Day* (New York; London: Verso, 1989), 1.
3 Along similar lines, economist Robert Whaples has suggested that "estimates of the length of the typical work week before the mid-1800s are very imprecise." See his *Hours of Work in U.S. History* at *EH.net*, eh.net/encyclopedia/hours-of-work-in-u-s-history.
4 Roediger and Foner, *Our Own Time*, 1, 51.
5 See Jon Peirce, *Canadian Industrial Relations*, 2nd ed. (Toronto: Pearson, 2003), 56. See also Dale Yoder, *Personnel Management and Industrial Relations*, 5th ed. (Englewood Cliffs, N.J.: Prentice-Hall, 1962).
6 My earlier work hours paper, *The Case for a Shorter Work Week* (Ottawa: Carleton University Centre for the Study of Training, Investment, and Economic Restructuring, 2000), found virtually no national differences in work hours through the first two-thirds of the nineteenth century.
7 See, for instance, Roediger and Foner, *Our Own Time*, 68, 69.
8 Ibid., 67.
9 Giattino, Ortiz-Ospana, and Roser, "Working Hours." This compendious study is an invaluable source of information for all serious students of historical work hours. I have drawn on it liberally throughout my historical chapters.
10 While far more research is needed to prove this point, the Hubermann-Minns hours data (Michael Huberman and Chris Minns, "The Times They Are Not Changin': Days and Hours of Work in Old and New Worlds, 1870–2000, *Explorations in Economic History* 44 (2007), 538–67) would appear to belie the contention, expressed by some of Roediger and Foner's sources — see, for example, *Our Own Time*, 125 — that the working day in the United States was substantially longer than that in European countries such as Germany and the United Kingdom.
11 Susan Christopherson, "Trading Time for Consumption: The Failure of Working-Hours Reduction in the United States," in *Working Time in*

Transition, ed. Hinrich, Roche, and Sirianni (Philadelphia: Temple UP, 1991), 177.
12 Ibid., 178.
13 Ibid., 179.
14 Roediger and Foner, *Our Own Time*, 146, 178.
15 See Whaples, *Hours of Work*, 2.
16 Roediger and Foner, *Our Own Time*, 51.
17 Ibid., 51–52.
18 Whaples, *Hours of Work*, 2–3.
19 Ibid., 3.
20 Ibid., 7.
21 The first such strike took place in Philadelphia in 1835; it would result in a legislated ten-hour day. See Roediger and Foner, *Our Own Time*, 33.
22 Ibid., vii.
23 Ibid.
24 For a more complete consideration of the "coercive drive" system of management characteristic of the nineteenth century, see Peirce, *Canadian Industrial Relations*, 56–57. See also Claude George, *The History of Management Thought* (Englewood Cliffs, N.J.: Prentice-Hall, 1968).
25 Roediger and Foner, *Our Own Time*, vii.
26 Ibid., 66.
27 Except as previously noted, material for this paragraph has been drawn from Whaples, *Hours of Work*, 7–8.
28 Roediger and Foner, *Our Own Time*, 66, 70.
29 Ibid., 72–73.
30 Ibid., 83.
31 Ibid., 86.
32 Ibid., 85.
33 Ibid.
34 Whaples, *Hours of Work*, 8; Roediger and Foner, *Our Own Time*, 87.
35 Roediger and Foner, *Our Own Time*, 88.
36 Whaples, *Hours of Work*, 8; Roediger and Foner, *Our Own Time*, 90, 101.
37 Roediger and Foner, *Our Own Time*, esp. 106, 109–110.
38 Whaples, *Hours of Work*, 8; Roediger and Foner, *Our Own Time*, 114.
39 Roediger and Foner, *Our Own Time*, 114.
40 Whaples, *Hours of Work*, 8.
41 Roediger and Foner, *Our Own Time*, 116.
42 Peirce, *Canadian Industrial Relations*, 86. See also Gregory Kealey and Bryan Palmer, "Bonds of Unity: The Knights of Labor In Ontario, 1880–1900," *Histoire Sociale/Social History* XIV, no. 28 (November 1981), reprinted in *Canadian Working-Class History: Selected Readings*, 3rd ed. (Toronto: Canadian Scholars, 2006), 240–41.

Notes

43 Roediger and Foner, *Our Own Time*, 123, 132. Not until 1886, after a series of boycotts and strikes, would the brewers win a ten-hour day and six-day week.
44 Roediger and Foner, *Our Own Time*, 124.
45 Peirce, *Canadian Industrial Relations*, 86. The Knights' first Canadian chapter was launched in Hamilton in 1875.
46 Ibid. See also John Godard, *Industrial Relations: The Economy and Society* (Toronto: McGraw-Hill Ryerson, 1994), and Gregory Kealey and Bryan Palmer, *Dreaming of What Might Be: The Knights of Labor in Ontario, 1880–1900* (Cambridge: Cambridge UP, 1982).
47 Peirce, *Canadian Industrial Relations*, 86.
48 Whaples, *Hours of Work*, 8; Roediger and Foner, *Our Own Time*, 124–29. At p. 126, the latter authors note that "from the beginning, the Knights of Labor propagandized in favor of a shorter working day."
49 Whaples, *Hours of Work*, 8.
50 The lower figure is cited by Roediger and Foner at p. 139 as having come from the Commons group; the higher figure is their own.
51 Roediger and Foner, *Our Own Time*, 139.
52 Ibid.
53 Ibid.
54 Ibid.
55 Ibid.
56 Ibid., 140–41.
57 As Roediger and Foner note at p. 141, the threat of a spring storm may have kept the crowd size down.
58 This attribution is made by, among others, Whaples, *Hours of Work*, at p. 9. And this, indeed, is the standard explanation for Haymarket; nonetheless, one can't help wondering if an alternative explanation might be possible.
59 Roediger and Foner, *Our Own Time*, 141.
60 Whaples, *Hours of Work*, 9; Roediger and Foner, *Our Own Time*, 142.
61 Roediger and Foner, *Our Own Time*, 142.
62 Ibid., 141.
63 Ibid., 141.
64 Ibid., 142.
65 Ibid., 143.
66 Ibid., 141, 144.
67 Ibid., 143.
68 Ibid., 141.
69 Ibid.
70 Ibid., 142.
71 Ibid.
72 Whaples, *Hours of Work*, 9; Roediger and Foner, *Our Own Time*, 142.
73 Quoted in Whaples, *Hours of Work*, 9.

74 Whaples, *Hours of Work*, 8; Roediger and Foner, Our Own Time, 136.
75 Roediger and Foner, *Our Own Time*, 136.
76 Whaples, *Hours of Work*, 9; Roediger and Foner, *Our Own Time*, 144.
77 Roediger and Foner, *Our Own Time*, 145.
78 Ibid., 146.
79 Ibid.
80 Ibid., 146–147.
81 Peirce, *Canadian Industrial Relations*, 57–58.
82 Vadim I. Marshev, *History of Management Thought: Genesis and Development from Ancient Origins to the Present Day* (np: Springer, 2021), 141–42.
83 Peirce, *Canadian Industrial Relations*, 58–59.
84 Roediger and Foner, *Our Own Time*, 147.
85 Whaples, *Hours of Work*, 10.
86 Huberman and Minns, "The Times They Are Not Changin'."
87 See Whaples, *Hours of Work*, 3–4, for examples of some of those variations.
88 This assumes no vacation or paid holiday time. While American workers generally did not yet enjoy paid vacations, they did by 1900 get a small number of paid holidays — perhaps four or five on average. Correcting for those paid holidays would add a small amount of time — probably just under one hour per week — to the average work week. Such a correction would not be big enough to change the overall narrative.
89 Except as otherwise noted, information for this paragraph has been drawn from Giattino et al., ("Working Hours") using the Huberman-Minns ("The Times They Are Not Changin'") data referred to in earlier notes.
90 See Whaples, *Hours of Work*, Tables 2 and 3, 3 and 4.
91 Roediger and Foner, *Our Own Time*, 213.
92 Giattino et al., "Working Hours."
93 Cited by Whaples, *Hours of Work*, in Table 2, 4.
94 Ibid., Table 3, 4.
95 Once again, weather factors would have to be taken into account to evaluate the significance of this finding.
96 Here, again, one must take into account days lost due to strikes, overproduction, seasonal unemployment, and simple mismanagement to evaluate the significance of this seemingly counterintuitive finding.
97 Whaples, *Hours of Work*, Table 3, 4.
98 Ibid., 177.
99 In some cases, there appear to have been minor variations, such as slightly longer (8.5) weekday hours coupled with somewhat shorter (5.5) Saturday hours.
100 Roediger and Foner, *Our Own Time*, 234–37.
101 Whaples, *Hours of Work*, 10
102 Ibid. See also Roediger and Foner, *Our Own Time*, 222–37, esp. 233–37.
103 Ibid., 201.
104 Whaples, *Hours of Work*, 10

105 Ibid.
106 Ibid.
107 Peirce, *Canadian Industrial Relations*, 59. See also Benjamin Hunnicutt, *Work Without End: Abandoning Shorter Hours for the Right to Work* (Philadelphia: Temple UP, 1988), and Chris Nyland, *Reduced Worktime and the Management of Production* (Cambridge: Cambridge UP, 1989).
108 Sectoral evidence provided by Whaples, *Hours of Work*, at p. 4 suggests that shorter hours were not evenly spread across the American economy. His Census of Manufacturing figure for 1930 is 50.6 hours, a figure consistent with an 8.5-hour or even nine-hour day, with shorter hours on Saturday. This figure is only 0.6 hours shorter than the Manufacturing Census figure for 1920. In railroads, on the other hand, the 1930 weekly average was 42.9 hours, a figure more consistent with a 5.5-day week. And both bituminous and anthracite coal mining had seen drops of about six hours from their 1920 figures, to 33.3 and 37.0 hours, respectively. Further work is needed to determine how the Manufacturing Census figure for 1930 gibes with the finding by Giattino et al. of substantially shorter hours across the American economy.
109 Roediger and Foner, *Our Own Time*, 237 and Note 146, 351.
110 Whaples, *Hours of Work*, 10.
111 Ibid.
112 Roediger and Foner, *Our Own Time*, 241.
113 Whaples, *Hours of Work*, 10.
114 Ibid.
115 Roediger and Foner, *Our Own Time*, 245.
116 Ibid., 227. The exceptions included New York City firefighters and police, who won an eight-hour day through legislation, and New England telephone operators and Chicago soda clerks, who struck for a seven-hour day.
117 Ibid.
118 Benjamin Hunnicutt, *Kellogg's Six-Hour Day* (Philadelphia: Temple UP, 1996).
119 Roediger and Foner, *Our Own Time*, 231.
120 Ibid., 190. The Wobblies were no idle threat at the time, as they had recently led an unsuccessful shorter hours strike at the neighbouring Studebaker plant and had actually won shorter hours at three Detroit metal wheel factories during the preceding year.
121 For more detail, see Peirce, *Canadian Industrial Relations*, 62, and Sumner Slichter, "The Current Labor Policies of American Industry," *Quarterly Journal of Economics* 43 (May 1929).
122 Roediger and Foner, *Our Own Time*, 233.
123 Ibid., 233–34.
124 Ibid., 234.
125 See, for example, Benjamin Hunnicutt, *Free Time: The Forgotten American Dream* (Philadelphia: Temple UP), 114–118. See also Whaples, *Hours of Work*, 10–11.

126 Hunnicutt, *Free Time*, 113.
127 Quoted in Hunnicutt, *Free Time*, 114. See also Hunnicutt's more thorough discussion of that same "gospel" in *Free Time*, 114–16.
128 Whaples, *Hours of Work*, 11; Roediger and Foner, *Our Own Time*, 262. See also Hunnicutt, *Free Time*, 114–16.
129 For a brief discussion of this approach, see Whaples, *Hours of Work*, 11. For a more detailed and sophisticated discussion, see Hunnicutt, *Free Time*, 116–17.
130 Information on Hoover's food relief work is drawn from his Wikipedia biography. His efforts on behalf of all made hungry by the war, including Bolsheviks, earned him the praise of no less than Russia's Maxim Gorky.
131 Roediger and Foner, *Our Own Time*, 244.
132 Hunnicutt, *Free Time*, 116.
133 Ibid., 117.
134 Whaples, *Hours of Work*, 11; Hunnicutt, *Free Time*, 116. For a thorough and fascinating discussion of the Kellogg experiment, which would last until the 1970s, see Hunnicutt's *Kellogg's Six-Hour Day*.
135 Hunnicutt, *Free Time*, 117.
136 Ibid.
137 Ibid.
138 Roosevelt's pledge to repeal Prohibition, which had by this time become both massively unpopular and completely unenforceable, served as the "icing on the cake" in this election.
139 Whaples, *Hours of Work*, 11.
140 Ibid. See also Roediger and Foner, *Our Own Time*, 246.
141 Roediger and Foner, *Our Own Time*, 246.
142 Ibid.
143 Hunnicutt, *Free Time*, 117.
144 Ibid., 118.
145 Ibid.
146 Ibid.
147 Whaples, *Hours of Work*, 11.
148 Roediger and Foner, *Our Own Time*, 249.
149 Ibid.
150 Ibid., 250–51.
151 Ibid., 249.
152 Ibid., 249–50.
153 Ibid.
154 Peirce, *Canadian Industrial Relations*, 95–96.
155 Hunnicutt, *Free Time*, 119.
156 Ibid.
157 Ibid.
158 Ibid., 120.

Notes

159 Roediger and Foner, *Our Own Time*, 252–53.
160 Whaples, *Hours of Work*, 11.
161 Roediger and Foner, *Our Own Time*, 252–53.
162 Ibid.
163 Quoted in Roediger and Foner, *Our Own Time*, 255.
164 Ibid.
165 Except as otherwise noted, the discussion of the FLSA's minimum wage and maximum hours provisions and enforcement mechanisms has been drawn from Roediger and Foner, *Our Own Time*, 255–56.
166 Ibid., 256.
167 Ibid., 259.
168 Ibid., 273–74.
169 Ibid., 273.
170 Peirce, *Canadian Industrial Relations*, 155–56. See also Jon Peirce, "George Meany and the Decline of the American Labour Movement" (St. John's: Memorial University School of Business Working Paper, 1995).
171 Cited in Roediger and Foner, *Our Own Time*, 274.
172 Ibid.
173 Ibid., 274–75.
174 Ibid., 261.
175 My father, an architect who attended architecture school on the American GI Bill, was one of the beneficiaries of the post-war construction boom, designing many homes, schools, and churches in and around Norwalk, CT through the 1950s.
176 Except as otherwise noted, material for this paragraph has been drawn from Roediger and Foner, *Our Own Time*, 262.
177 Ibid.
178 Ibid., 269.
179 Ibid., 269–70.
180 Ibid., 269–70.
181 Ibid., 270.
182 Ibid., 258.
183 Ibid., 268.
184 Ibid., 266.
185 Peirce, *Canadian Industrial Relations*, 68.
186 Ibid., 123.
187 Jon Peirce, "Working People: Does No One Give a Damn Anymore?" *Toronto Star*, May 2, 2013. The piece has been reprinted in Jon Peirce, *Social Studies: Collected Essays, 1974–2013* (Victoria: Friesen, 2014) at 148–150. It's important to note that while at first, "right-to-work" provisions were used only in Southern or rural Midwestern states, by the early years of the present century they had spread to the country's industrial heartland, reaching Indiana in 2012 and Michigan, the birthplace of modern industrial

unionism, in 2013, a development that doesn't augur well for the growth or even survival of the American labour movement.
188 Roediger and Foner, *Our Own Time*, 268.
189 If you can believe this — I still find it hard to — those rates were about 3 percent, which is almost certainly lower than they would have been prior to the legalization of collective bargaining through the Wagner Act. See Peirce, "Working People: Does No One Give a Damn Anymore?" 148–50.
190 It did not succeed in this objective, as Republican presidential candidate Mitt Romney was able to carry the state by about two points, making it one of two states, along with Indiana, that Barack Obama carried in 2008 but not in 2012.

Chapter 3: Historical Development of Work Hours II: Canada

1 John Godard, *Industrial Relations: The Economy and Society* (Toronto: McGraw-Hill Ryerson, 1994), 101–2, cited in Jon Peirce, *Canadian Industrial Relations*, 2nd ed. (Toronto: Pearson, 2003), 82.
2 Ruth Bleasdale, "Class Conflict on the Canals of Upper Canada in the 1840s," *Labour/Le Travailleur* 7 (Spring 1981), cited in Peirce, *Canadian Industrial Relations*, 83.
3 See, among others, Daniel Drache, "The Formation and Fragmentation of the Canadian Working Class," *Studies in Political Economy* 15 (Fall 1984), 43–89; Carla Lipsig-Mumme, "Labour Strategies in the New Social Order: A Political Economy Perspective," in *Union-Management Relations in Canada*, ed. Morley Gunderson and Allen Pornak, 3rd ed. (Toronto: Addison Wesley, 1995); and Charles Lipton, *The Trade Union Movement of Canada* (Toronto: NC Press, 1973), all cited in Peirce, *Canadian Industrial Relations*, 81.
4 Lipton, *Trade Union Movement of Canada*, and Craig Heron, *The Canadian Labour Movement: A Short History* (Toronto: Lorimer, 1989), cited in Peirce, *Canadian Industrial Relations*, 81. The term "international" is actually something of a misnomer, since "international" unions are in reality U.S.-based unions with some Canadian members. Almost never do such unions have members from any country other than the United States or Canada.
5 Heron, *Canadian Labour Movement*, 14–15, cited in Peirce, *Canadian Industrial Relations*, 85.
6 Godard, *Industrial Relations*, 105, cited in Peirce, *Canadian Industrial Relations*, 85.
7 Gregory Kealey and Bryan Palmer, *Dreaming of What Might Be: The Knights of Labor in Ontario, 1880–1900* (Cambridge: Cambridge UP, 1982), cited in Peirce, *Canadian Industrial Relations*, 86.
8 Unions at the time were still legally treated as conspiracies in restraint of trade, with some Canadian jurisdictions providing jail terms for those entering into union contracts. See Peirce, *Canadian Industrial Relations*,

83. See also Desmond Morton, "The History of the Canadian Labour Movement," in *Union-Management Relations in Canada*, ed. Gunderson and Pornak, 134, cited in Peirce, *Canadian Industrial Relations*, 85.
9   Heron, *Canadian Labour Movement*, 17, quoted in Peirce, *Canadian Industrial Relations*, 85.
10 Leifer Magnusson, "First Canadian Industrial Conference," in L. Magnusson, E. Stewart, and A. Maylander, "Industrial Relations," *Monthly Labor Review* 9, no. 5 (September 1919), 51–62, esp. 54–55.
11 See, among many others, Patrick Ward," Frederick Taylor's Principles of Scientific Management Theory," Nanoglobals, October 3, 2021, nanoglobals.com/glossary/scientific-management-theory-of-frederick-taylor/
12 See, among others, Peirce, *Canadian Industrial Relations*, 59.
13 Material on the Blum government's work hours achievement has been drawn from Pierre Birnbaum, *Léon Blum and the Forty-Hour Work Week*, trans. Pamela Weidman, Yale University Press, July 30, 2015, yalebooks.yale.edu/2015/07/30/leon-blum-and-the-forty-hour-workweek/
14 Peirce, *Canadian Industrial Relations*, 97.
15 Ibid., 97–98.
16 Godard, *Industrial Relations: The Economy and Society*, cited in Peirce, *Canadian Industrial Relations*, 98. The union density rate is the percentage of paid non-agricultural workers belonging to unions at any given time in any given jurisdiction. It would not be until 1953 that the Canadian union density rate, which is now about three times that of the United States, would overtake the American rate, at 33.0 to 32.5 percent. See Peirce, *Canadian Industrial Relations*, Table 5.1, 123.
17 Gerard Mayer, "Union Membership Trends in the United States," *CRS Report for Congress*, August 2004, sgp.fas.org/crs/misc/RL32553.pdf.
18 See, for example, "President Consults Murray on Congress," *New York Times*, July 22, 1948, 9. The "Murray" referred to here was Congress of Industrial Organizations president Philip Murray.
19 Precise information on dates of adoption of shorter work hours laws in Canadian jurisdictions is hard to come by. The most I have for the post-war period in Canada is a Wikipedia statement, from its article "Eight-Hour Day," (en.wikipedia.org/wiki/Eight-hour_day) to the effect that Canada adopted an eight-hour day in the 1960s. This is a sharp contrast to the fulsome information provided about the United States in that same article. Indeed, information is more complete on European and even Latin American countries.
20 Growing up in suburban New York in the 1950s, I was not aware of any who did.
21 A significant literature on work-sharing built up during the 1980s. See, among many others, N. Meltz, F. Reid and G. Swartz, *Sharing the Work: An Analysis of the Issues in Worksharing and Jobsharing* (Toronto: University of Toronto Press, 1981).

Chapter 4: Historical Development of Work Hours III: Work Hours Around the World

1. In Charlie Giattino, Esteban Ortiz-Ospana and Max Roser, "Working Hours," *OurWorldinData*, 2013, revised December 2020, ourworldindata.org/working-hours.
2. Wikipedia, "Eight-hour Day," *Wikipedia*, en.wikipedia.org/wiki/Eight-hour_day.
3. Except for the ILO material, material in this paragraph has been drawn from Giattino et al., "Working Hours."
4. Stephan Bauer, "The Road to the Eight-Hour Day," trans. Alfred Maylander, *Monthly Labor Review* 9, no. 2 (August 1919), 41–65. Ironically, the signatories to this convention did not include the United States, even though the meeting at which the convention was passed was held in Washington, D.C.
5. Livia Gershon, "Why Europeans Have Such Long Summer Vacations," *JSTOR Daily*, July 28, 2018, daily.jstor.org/why-europeans-have-such-long-summer-vacations, notes that by the 1980s, a number of European countries were mandating five weeks of vacation for workers.
6. Wikipedia, "Eight-Hour Day."
7. Ibid.
8. This use has been cited by the *Oxford English Dictionary*, according to the Wikipedia article on the weekend, Wikipedia, "Workweek and Weekend," *Wikipedia*, wikipedia.org/wiki/Workweek_and_weekend.
9. The ILO study attracted considerable media attention. See, for instance, Reuters staff, "Over 600 Million Worldwide Work Excessive Hours: ILO," *Reuters*, June 7, 2007, reuters.com/article/us-employment-ilo-hours-idUSL075137920070607.
10. Wikipedia, "Working Hours in South Korea," *Wikipedia*, en.wikipedia.org/wiki/Working_hours_in_South_Korea. All material for this paragraph has been drawn from this Wikipedia article.
11. Lawyers and Jurists, "Introduction to the Bangladesh Labour Act, 2006," Chapter 9, *Lawyers and Jurists*, lawyersnjurists.com/article/introduction-bangladesh-labor-code-2006.
12. Replicon, "Sri Lanka Employment Law," *Replicon*, April 27, 2022, replicon.com/regulation/sri-lanka/.
13. Huileng Tan, "South Korea's Incoming President Once Criticized His Country's 52-Hour Work Week and Said People Should Be Allowed to Work 120 Hours a Week," *Insider*, March 10, 2022, businessinsider.com/koreas-new-president-people-work-120-hours-a-week-2022-3.
14. Ibid.
15. Andrew Jeong, "South Korea Proposes 69-Hour Work Week, Up from an Already Long 52," *Washington Post*, March 11, 2023.

Notes

16 SBR staff reporter, "Singapore Named Most Overworked Country in APAC," *Singapore Business Review*, June 2022, sbr.com.sg/hr-education/in-focus/singapore-named-most-overworked-country-in-apac.
17 Guide Me Singapore.Hawksford, "Guide to Singapore Employment Act," *Guide Me Singapore*, guidemesingapore.com/business-guides/managing-business/hr-management/guide-to-singapore-employment-act.
18 Ibid.
19 Material in this paragraph has been drawn from the *Singapore Business Review* article cited above.
20 Indeed editorial staff, "A Guide to Work Hours in Hong Kong (with types of Schedules)," *Indeed*, July 20, 2021, hk.indeed.com/career-advice/career-development/work-hours.
21 Paul Arkwright, "Hong Kong World's Most Overworked City," *HR Magazine*, March 15, 2022.
22 Ibid.
23 Ibid.
24 Yip Wai-yee, "China Steps in to Regulate Brutal '996' Work Culture," BBC, September 2, 2021, bbc.com/news/world-asia-china-58381538.
25 Wikipedia, "996 Working Hours System," *Wikipedia*, en.wikipedia.org/wiki/996_working_hour_system.
26 Quoted in Yip, "China Steps in."
27 Wikipedia, "996 Working Hours System."
28 These and other horrific incidents are cited in both Yip, "China Steps in," and Wikipedia, "996 Working Hours System."
29 Yip, "996 Working Hours System."
30 Ibid.
31 Ibid.
32 Ibid.
33 Kaizen, "Working Hours and Overtime Regulations in Vietnam," *Kaizen*, kaizencpa.com/Knowledge/info/id/1113.html.
34 ILO Country Office for Vietnam Policy, "Working Hours in Viet Nam," *International Labour Organization*, September 2019, ilo.org/wcmsp5/groups/public/---asia/---ro-bangkok/---ilo-hanoi/documents/publication/wcms_730898.pdf.
35 ILO Country Office for Vietnam Policy, "Working Hours in Viet Nam," Figure 4.
36 Saigon Heritage, "Business Hours in Vietnam," *Saigon Heritage*, October 23, 2022, saigonheritage.com/travel-tips/business-hours-in-vietnam.
37 Sandeep Patel, "The Thailand Guide: All About Employment Laws, Taxes, and Benefits," *Skuad*, December 8, 2020, skuad.io/blog/thailand-guide-employment-laws-taxes-benefits.

38 Lawyers & Jurists, "Introduction to the Bangladesh Labour Act, 2006," Chapter 9.
39 Anike Marike Chowdhury, "Employee's Rights in Workplace in Bangladesh," *IR Global*, August 31, 2021, irglobal.com/article/employees-rights-at-workplace-in-bangladesh.
40 Replicon, "Sri Lanka Employment Law," *Replicon*, April 27, 2022, replicon.com/regulation/sri-lanka.
41 Heather Chen, "This Country Wants a Four-Day Week. But It's Not About Making Workers Happy," CNN, June 15, 2022, cnn.com/2022/06/15/asia/sri-lanka-crisis-food-four-day-week-intl-hnk/index.html.
42 Marian Garibay, "What Is the Standard Work Week in Mexico?" *American Industries*, October 13, 2022, americanindustriesgroup.com/blog/what-is-the-standard-work-week-in-mexico.
43 Ibid.
44 Replicon, "Costa Rican Employment Law," *Replicon*, April 27, 2022, replicon.com/regulation/costa-rica.
45 Qcostarica, "Which Nationalities Work the Longest Hours? Costa Rica Is Second," *Qcostarica*, February 13, 2018, qcostarica.com/which-nationalities-work-the-longest-hours-costa-rica-is-second.
46 Wikipedia, "Eight-Hour Day." The initial Uruguayan law was not binding on all enterprises.
47 WorkMotion, *Uruguay*, *WorkMotion*, workmotion.com/countries/uruguay.
48 Legal Team Uruguay, "Employment Law in Uruguay: A Guide," *Biz Latin Hub*, updated August 20, 2022, bizlatinhub.com/employment-law-uruguay.
49 Material for this paragraph has been drawn from the two following sources: L&E Global, "Employment Law in Brazil: Working Conditions," *L&E Global*, July 26, 2022, leglobal.law/countries/brazil/employment-law/employment-law-overview-brazil/03-working-conditions/; and Deloitte, "'Relacoes Traballhistas': Compensation, Labor Rights and Benefits," *Deloitte*, December 2020, www2.deloitte.com/br/en/pages/living-and-working/articles/labor-relations.html.
50 International Organization of Employers, "Colombia: A New Law that Reduces Weekly Working Hours from 48 to 42," Industrial Relations and Labour Law Newsletter, *International Organization of Employers*, August 2021, industrialrelationsnews.ioe-emp.org/industrial-relations-and-labour-law-august-2021-1/news/article/colombia-a-new-law-that-reduces-the-weekly-working-hours-from-48-to-42.
51 Reuters, "Chile Approves Bill Cutting Work Week to 40 Hours from 45," Reuters, April 11, 2023, reuters.com/world/americas/chile-approves-bill-cutting-work-week-40-hours-45-2023-04-11.
52 Replicon, "Slovakia Employment Law," *Replicon*, updated July 23, 2023, replicon.com/regulation/slovakia.

53 Replicon, "Hungary Employment Law," *Replicon*, May 10, 2022, replicon.com/regulation/hungary.
54 Replicon, "Bulgaria Employment Law," *Replicon*, December 30, 2022, replicon.com/regulation/bulgaria.
55 Wikipedia, "Eight-Hour Day."
56 Replicon, "Russia Employment Law," *Replicon*, September 19, 2021, replicon.com/regulation/russia. Except as otherwise noted, all the rest of the material on Russia has been drawn from this article.
57 Wikipedia, "Israeli Labor Law," *Wikipedia*, en.wikipedia.org/wiki/Israeli_labor_law.
58 Replicon, "Turkey Employment Law," *Replicon*, replicon.com/regulation/turkey.
59 Hurriyet Daily News, "Most Employees Working Very Long Hours in Turkey," *Hurriyet Daily News*, May 2, 2017, hurriyetdailynews.com/most-employees-working-very-long-hours-in-turkey--112615.
60 Labour Guide, "Hours of Work and Overtime." *Labour Guide*, labourguide.co.za/employment-condition/working-hours-and-overtime.
61 Niall McCarthy, "Contrary to What Most People Think, Greeks Work the Longest Hours in Europe," *Forbes*, March 13, 2015, forbes.com/sites/niallmccarthy/2015/03/13/contrary-to-what-most-people-think-greeks-work-the-longest-hours-in-europe-infographic.
62 Rob Smith, "This Country Works the Longest Hours in Europe," *World Economic Forum*, "Work Force and Employment," February 20, 2018, weforum.org/agenda/2018/02/greeks-work-longest-hours-in-europe.

Chapter 5: A Special Decade: Work Hours and the 1920s

1 Wikipedia, "International Labour Organization," *Wikipedia*, en.wikipedia.org/wiki/International_Labour_Organization. Except as otherwise noted, all material on the founding of the ILO has been drawn from this article.
2 Stephan Bauer, "The Road to the Eight-Hour Day," *Monthly Labor Review* 9, no. 2 (August 1919), 63–64.
3 Ibid., 64.
4 Ibid., 50.
5 Ibid., 53.
6 Ibid., 54.
7 Ibid.
8 At Du Pont, Taylor's philosophy took hold to such an extent that the plant manager bought half a dozen copies of Taylor's *Principles* for use by his management team. See Donald Stabile, "The Du Pont Experiments in Scientific Management: Efficiency and Safety," *Business History Review* 61, no. 3 (1987), 366–69. In the spirit of Taylor, Du Pont even established an "efficiency division."
9 David Ahlstrom, "The Hidden Reason Why the First World War Matters Today: The Development and Spread of Modern Management," *Brown*

Journal of World Affairs 21, no. 1 (Fall/Winter 2014), 201–18, esp. p. 202.
10 Ibid., 206. See also Jon Peirce, *Canadian Industrial Relations*, 2nd ed., (Toronto: Pearson, 2003), 57–59.
11 See Chris Nyland, *Reduced Worktime and the Management of Production* (Cambridge: Cambridge UP, 1989).
12 H.N. Vernon, *Industrial Power and Efficiency* (New York: Dutton, 1921), cited in Edwin Lake, "The Ideas of Frederick W. Taylor: An Evaluation," *Academy of Management Review* 7, no. 1 (1982), 17.
13 This evolution, as it occurred between 1913 and 1920, is thoroughly, even minutely traced in Alfred Maylander and Josephus Daniels, "Wages and Hours of Work," *Monthly Labor Review* 11, no. 4 (October 1920), 75–150.
14 Alfred Maylander, "Wages and Hours of Work: Tendency Toward a Shorter Work Week," *Monthly Labor Review* 11, no. 1 (July 1920), 98.
15 See Paul Malles, *Canadian Labour Standards in Law, Agreement, and Practice* (Ottawa: Supply and Services Canada, 1976), quoted in Peirce, *Canadian Industrial Relations*, 59.
16 Leifer Magnusson, "First Canadian Industrial Conference," in L. Magnusson, E. Stewart, and A. Maylander, "Industrial Relations," *Monthly Labor Review* 9, no. 5 (September 1919), 51–62, esp. 54–55.
17 Wikipedia, "International Labour Organization."
18 See Hunnicutt, *Kellogg's Six-Hour Day* (Philadelphia: Temple UP, 1996).
19 For a detailed look at John Harvey Kellogg's workaholism, as well as a rattling good read and an intriguing portrayal of the early twentieth century's excesses both in indulgence and in abstinence, see T.C. Boyle, *The Road to Wellville* (New York: Viking, 1993).
20 Hunnicutt, *Kellogg's Six-Hour Day*, 39.
21 Ibid., 38–41.
22 Ibid., 35.
23 Ibid., 18–19.
24 The party line among most Democrats and even a few Republicans was that Hoover was primarily responsible for the evils of the Great Depression because of his inability or unwillingness to take strong action to deal with it.
25 This is the view of him presented by the Herbert Hoover Presidential Library and Museum. See "Years of Enterprise 1921–1928," *Herbert Hoover Presidential Library and Museum*, hoover.archives.gov/exhibits/years-enterprise-1921-1928.
26 As Matthew Schaefer notes in "Hoover and 20th Century Presidents: Calvin Coolidge" (*Herbert Hoover Presidential Library and Museum*, February 19, 2020, hoover.blogs.archives.gov/2020/02/19/hoover-and-20th-century-presidents-calvin-coolidge), Hoover and Coolidge differed sharply in their views as to the appropriate role and scope of government, with Hoover seeing a strong positive role for government and Coolidge taking a minimalist view.

Notes

Coolidge sardonically labelled Hoover "Wonder Boy." Schaefer's article, dated February 19, 2020, was published in the blog of the Herbert Hoover Library and Museum.

27 See, among many others, World Food Program USA, "American Food Heroes: Herbert Hoover," *World Food Program USA*, July 2, 2021, wfpusa.org/articles/historys-hunger-heroes-herbert-hoover. During the First World War, Hoover set up a large food relief effort in Belgium — the first of its kind and scope. After the war, as program director of the American Relief Administration (ARA), he targeted aid to prevent famine in Soviet Russia and the first American relief ships docked there in September 1921. Within a year, the ARA was feeding nearly eleven million people a day in nineteen-thousand kitchens across the country.

28 On Hoover's specific work with the steel industry, see Robert Zieger, "Herbert Hoover, the Wage-Earner, and the New Economic System, 1919–1929," *Business History Review* 51, no. 2 (Summer 1977), 161–89. For a more general account of Hoover's workplace philosophy, see Zieger's "Labor, Progressivism, and Herbert Hoover in the 1920s," *Wisconsin Magazine of History* 58, no. 3 (Spring 1975), 196–208.

29 Zieger, "Herbert Hoover, the Wage-Earner, and the New Economic System," 166.

30 Evan Metcalf, "Secretary Hoover and the Emergence of Macroeconomic Management," *Business History Review*, 49, no. 1 (Spring 1975), 60–80, esp. 64.

31 Peirce, *Canadian Industrial Relations*, 92. See also Zieger, "Herbert Hoover, the Wage-Earner, and the New Economic System," 181.

32 On Taylor, see Lake, "The Ideas of Frederick W. Taylor," 15–17, and Louis Fry, "The Maligned F.W. Taylor: A Reply to His Many Critics," *Academy of Management Review* 9, no. 3 (July 1976), 126. On Hoover, see Zieger, "Herbert Hoover, the Wage-Earner, and the New Economic System," 166.

33 Zieger, "Herbert Hoover, the Wage-Earner, and the New Economic System," 177.

34 Hunnicutt, *Kellogg's Six-Hour Day*, 17–21.

35 Ibid., 20–21.

36 Ibid., 18.

37 Ibid., 57.

38 Ibid., 21.

39 Ibid., 59.

40 Benjamin Hunnicutt, *Free Time: The Forgotten American Dream* (Philadelphia: Temple UP, 2013), 113.

41 Ibid.

42 Most notably through the introduction of a thirty-five-hour bill by Michigan Representative John Conyers in 1977. Regrettably, despite two years of political manoeuvring, the bill never even reached the floor of the House — a

House controlled by Democrats. See David Roediger and Philip Foner, *Our Own Time*, 273–74.
43 Reportedly, the troop ships used to bring young men home from the Front were a major source of spread for the so-called Spanish flu.
44 Andrew Barnes with Stephanie Jones, *The 4 Day Week* (London: Piatkus, 2020). See esp. 71–100.
45 On Iceland, see BBC, "Four-Day Week 'An Overwhelming Success' in Iceland," BBC, July 6, 2021, bbc.com/news/business-57724779. On New Zealand, see Elisabeth Buchwald, "The Pandemic Is Inspiring Some Companies to Test 4-Day Work Week — but Will It Hurt Productivity?" *Market Watch*, July 8, 2021, marketwatch.com/story/the-pandemic-is-inspiring-kickstarter-and-unilever-to-test-four-day-workweeks-but-will-it-hurt-productivity-11625609807. On Scotland, see Jack Kelly, "Scotland Joins Growing Global Movement Toward a Four-Day Work Week," *Forbes*, September 3, 2021, forbes.com/sites/jackkelly/2021/09/03/scotland-joins-the-growing-global-movement-towards-a-four-day-workweek/?sh=2bbd87b0295f. On Spain, see Rosie Frost, "Could Spain's Four-Day Working Week Save the Planet?" euronews.green, February 15, 2022, euronews.com/green/2021/03/16/why-a-four-day-working-week-could-save-us-and-the-planet. On the United Kingdom, see Brian McGleenon, "Why UK Businesses Are Experimenting with a Four Day Week," *Evening Standard*, January 24, 2022, standard.co.uk/business/four-day-week-uk-joe-o-connor-mark-mullen-atom-bank-b977847.html.
46 The rules around the "Four Day Week" models chosen in the U.K. pilots were quite loose. The only requirements were a substantial reduction in work hours and retention of 100 percent of the previous wage or salary. A wide variety of different weeks were used during the pilots. The pilot's Research Report cites at least five different types of shorter week.
47 On the recent decline and weakness of the labour movement, see among others A.J. Veal, *Whatever Happened to the Leisure Society?* (np: Routledge, 2018), 279. Here Veal cites French political economist Thomas Piketty, whose book *Capital* (Cambridge, MA: Belknap Press, 2014) has noted that in recent years the bulk of the benefits from productivity improvements have gone to owners rather than to workers.
48 On Leverhulme, see Hunnicutt, *Kellogg's Six-Hour Day*, 27–29.

Chapter 6: Technology, Work Intensification, Stress, and Distress
1 See, among many others, Economic Council of Canada, "Working with Technology," (Ottawa: Supply and Services Canada, 1987).
2 On de-skilling, see, among many others, Jenny Odell, *Saving Time* (London: Bodley Head, 2023), 31–36. For an older but still extremely useful treatment,

Notes

see Harry Braverman, *Labor and Monopoly Capital: The Degradation of Work in the Twentieth Century* (New York: Monthly Review Press, 1998).

3   Erich Fein, Natalie Skinner, and M. Anthony Machin, "Work Intensification, Work-Life Interference, Stress, and Well-Being in Australian Workers," *International Studies of Management and Organization* 47, no. 4 (September 2017), 369.

4   "Information and Communication Technology Use, Work Intensification, and Employee Strain and Distress," *Sage* 28, no. 4, March 10, 2014.

5   Francis Green, "Work Intensification, Discretion, and the Decline in Well-Being at Work," *Eastern Economic Journal* 30, no. 4 (2004), 615–25.

6   Johanna Bunner, Roman Prem, and Christian Korunka, "How Work Intensification Relates to Organization-Level Safety Performance: The Mediating Roles of Safety Climate, Safety Motivation, and Safety Knowledge," *Frontiers in Psychology*, December 17, 2018, frontiersin.org/articles/10.3389/fpsyg.2018.02575/full.

7   Or who, like the present writer during his union job with the Professional Institute, represents workers who have been put into such a situation.

8   Kat Eschner, "In 1913, Henry Ford Introduced the Assembly Line. Workers Hated It," *Smithsonian Magazine*, December 1, 2016, smithsonianmag.com/smart-news/one-hundred-and-three-years-ago-today-henry-ford-introduced-assembly-line-his-workers-hated-it-180961267.

9   Checkify, "Henry Ford Assembly Line: How Processes Increased Productivity," *Checkify*, checkify.com/blog/henry-ford-assembly-line.

10 Katy Booter, "Science, Technology and Society: A Student-Led Exploration," in *Industrial Revolution (1800s–1940s), Press Books*, pressbooks.pub/anne1/chapter/assembly-line.

11 Eschner, "In 1913, Henry Ford …"

12 *America's Assembly Line* (Cambridge: MIT Press, 2013), 102, quoted in Booter, "Science, Technology and Society."

13 Ibid. Note that many such examples of soul-destroying factory work can be found in Studs Terkel's monumental collection, *Working*.

14 In 1982 an Apple Mac, the computer on which I would eventually learn, cost $2,495, which is well over $6,000 adjusted for inflation. See Evan Comen, "Check Out How Much a Computer Cost the Year You Were Born," *24/7 Wall Street*, October 3, 2018, 247wallst.com/special-report/2019/06/07/cost-of-a-computer-the-year-you-were-born. The $2,495 would have represented slightly over one-sixth of my gross salary as an assistant professor of English at Queen's.

15 For more detail, see Craig Brod's *Technostress: The Human Cost of the Computer Revolution* (Reading, MA: Addison-Wesley, 1984).

16 Ibid., 16.

17 Ibid., 30–32.

18 Ibid., 16–17.

19   Ibid., 17.
20   See, for example, Ibid., 15–16 and 18.
21   Ibid., 18.
22   Ibid.
23   Some of these concerns are discussed in Lawrence Archer, "I Saw What You Did and I Know Who You Are," *Canadian Business*, November 1985, at p. 76 and following. At p. 83 of this article, Archer quotes computer designer Stephen Hollander's statement to an Ontario Federation of Labour convention, to the effect that "More than 100 pieces of equipment described by George Orwell in *Nineteen Eighty-Four* now exist."
24   Brod, *Technostress*, 29.
25   Ibid., 44–45.
26   Ibid., 47.
27   Ibid., 53.
28   Ibid.
29   Ibid., 46.
30   See, among many others, Juliet B. Schor, *The Overspent American: Why We Want What We Don't Need* (New York: Harper, 1998), 19–20. For Canada, see Bruce O'Hara, *Enough Already: Breaking Free in the Second Half of Life* (Vancouver: New Star Books, 2004), 33.
31   See Jon Peirce, *Collective Bargaining over Technological Change in Canada: A Quantitative and Historical Analysis* (Ottawa: Economic Council of Canada Discussion Paper #338, 1987), Tables 1 and 7.
32   Ibid., Table 7.
33   Ibid.
34   Ibid., Table 1.
35   Dennis Chamot and Kevin Murphy, "Technological Change Clauses in Collective Bargaining Agreements," in *The Critical Communications Review*, vol. 1, ed. Vincent Mosco and Janet Wasko (Norwood, NJ: Ablex, 1983), 245–78.
36   See Peirce, *Collective Bargaining over Technological Change*, 106, Note 39.
37   Ibid., 56 and Note 48.
38   Ibid., 57 and Table 9.
39   Ibid., 35 and Note 30.
40   Ibid., 32.
41   Ibid., 33.
42   Ibid., 33–34.
43   Ibid., 36 and Note 31.
44   Ibid., 31.
45   Ibid., 32 and Note 26.
46   For a description of this monstrous device, see Jenny Odell, *Saving Time: Discovering a Life Beyond the Clock* (London: Bodley Head, 2023), 24.
47   Ibid., 40.

Notes

48 Ibid., 88–94.
49 See among others, René Riedl, "On the Stress Potential of Videoconferencing: Definition and Root Causes of Zoom Fatigue," *Electronic Markets* 32 (December 6, 2021), link.springer.com/article/10.1007/s12525-021-00501-3.
50 Brian Dean, in *Backlink*, January 6, 2022. Dean's statistics on Zoom use were drawn from the company itself.
51 Betsy Hoffman and Jon Peirce, "Prof with Parkinson's," in *Plague Take It: A COVID Almanac by and About Elders*, ed. Jon Peirce and Ann McMillan (Ottawa: Loose Cannon Press, 2021), 300–302.
52 Peter Alexander, "A Dagger to the Heart of the Performing Arts," in *Plague Take It*, 392–97.
53 Paul Lenarczyk, "The Kitchen Party Piece," in *Plague Take It*, 398–99.
54 During 2020 alone, Colleen Naomi offered some twenty-four online workshops in acting, scriptwriting, and various other subjects. Even as the pandemic has eased, she has continued to offer online scriptwriting workshops; I myself have taken four of them. See her "Theatre in a COVID World," in *Plague Take It*, 403–5.
55 Harold Tausch, "COVID, Technology, and Me," in *Plague Take It*, 342–45, and Jon Peirce, "Theatre During the Pandemic: A Community Theatre Actor's Perspective," in *Plague Take It*, 406–10.
56 Bill Newmann and Jon Peirce, "Easing the Final Slide: Harder Since the COVID-19 Pandemic," in *Plague Take It*, 307.
57 Denise Giroux, "Zooming Our Way into Oblivion," in *Plague Take It*, 326.
58 Ruth Hawkins, "It's OK to not be OK," in *Plague Take It*, 298–99.
59 Ibid., 298.
60 Riedl, "On the Stress Potential of Videoconferencing." Except as otherwise noted, all material in this and the two following paragraphs has been drawn from this article.
61 Hoffman and Peirce "Prof with Parkinson's" in *Plague Take It*, 300.
62 Ibid.

Chapter 7: The "Great Resignation" and Its Effects on Work Hours

1 As noted by Workplace Reduction Center of Excellence co-founder Joe O'Connor in an interview in March 2023, some firms have begun offering four-day weeks at full pay as an incentive to bring workers back into the office after long periods of working from home.
2 Sarah Jaffe, *Work Won't Love You Back* (New York: Bold Type Books, 2021).
3 Amy Fontinelle, "What Is the Great Resignation? Causes, Statistics and Trends," *Investopedia*, May 5, 2022, investopedia.com/the-great-resignation-5199074.
4 Ibid.
5 Ibid. Fontinelle's job openings data were drawn from the Federal Reserve Bank of St. Louis.

6. On the response of Canadian workers, see, among others, Grace McGrenere, "The Great Resignation & Canadian Workers," *Leveller*, February 1, 2022, leveller.ca/2022/02/the-great-resignation-in-canada.
7. Fontinelle, "What Is the Great Resignation."
8. Ibid. See also Wikipedia, "Great Resignation," *Wikipedia*, en.wikipedia.org/wiki/Great_Resignation.
9. Except for the first sentence, all material in this paragraph has been drawn from Fontinelle's article.
10. David Miller and Haley Yamada, "The Great Resignation: Its Origins and What It Means for Future Business," *ABC News*, May 3, 2022, abcnews.go.com/US/great-resignation-origins-means-future-business/story?id=84222583.
11. Except as otherwise noted, material in this paragraph has been drawn from Jaffe, *Work Won't Love You Back*, xii–xiii. See also Ivana Davidovic, "'Lying Flat:' Why Some Chinese Are Putting Work Second," BBC, February 16, 2022, bbc.com/news/business-60353916.
12. Meera Navlakha, "People Aren't Ready to Quit Quitting," *Mashable*, April 22, 2022, mashable.com/article/2022-great-resignation-continues.
13. Bartleby, "How to Manage the Great Resignation," *Economist*, November 27, 2021, updated December 2, 2021, economist.com/business/2021/11/27/how-to-manage-the-great-resignation.
14. Simone Phipps, "What Exactly Is 'The Great Resignation'?" *Middle Georgia State University*, April 21, 2022, mga.edu/news/2022/04/what-is-the-great-resignation.php.
15. Ibid.
16. Ibid.
17. Julia Horowitz, "The Great Resignation Is Taking Root Around the World," *CNN Business*, March 30, 2022, cnn.com/2022/03/30/economy/great-resignation-uk-australia-europe/index.html. Except for the first sentence, all the material in this paragraph has been drawn from Horowitz's article.
18. Kristy Carscallan and Doron Melnick, "Where the Great Resignation Might be Headed in Canada," *Globe and Mail*, March 16, 2022. Material for this paragraph has been drawn from this article.
19. McGrenere, "The Great Resignation and Canadian Workers."
20. Canadian membership data have been drawn from Statistics Canada, "Union Membership by Industry, 2017–2021." U.S. membership data have been drawn from a January 22, 2022, news release of the Bureau of Labor Statistics. It is worth noting that while Canadian rates have held relatively steady over the past few decades, U.S. rates, according to the BLS news release, are only about half what they were in 1983.
21. I find it more than a little surprising that none of the discussions I have seen on the Great Resignation have included any mention of unions or unionization.

Notes

22 For a much more thorough elucidation of the arguments advanced here, see Richard Freeman and James Medoff, *What Do Unions Do?* (New York: Basic Books, 1979). After more than forty years, this book remains, in my opinion, the single best treatment of the subject.
23 Quoted in Horowitz, "The Great Resignation Is Taking Root Around the World."
24 Labour economist Gordon Betcherman, quoted in Alistair Steele, "Where Have All the Workers Gone? Don't Blame COVID, Economists Say," CBC, July 23, 2022, www.cbc.ca/news/canada/ottawa/ottawa-workers-covid-retirements-1.6529325.
25 Ibid.
26 Carleton University business professor Ian Lee, quoted in Steele, "Where Have All the Workers Gone?"
27 Emma Goldberg, "All of Those Quitters? They're at Work." *New York Times*, May 13, 2022, nytimes.com/2022/05/13/business/great-resignation-jobs.html.
28 Horowitz, "The Great Resignation Is Taking Root."
29 Kate Morgan, "The Great Resignation: How Employers Drove Workers to Quit," BBC, July 1, 2021, bbc.com/worklife/article/20210629-the-great-resignation-how-employers-drove-workers-to-quit.
30 See, among many others, StreetsblogMass, "T Reacts to Ongoing Driver Shortage with More Bus Service Cuts."" *Streetsblog Mass*, June 7, 2023, mass.streetsblog.org/2023/06/07/t-reacts-to-ongoing-driver-shortage-with-more-bus-service-cuts. This is but one of at least two dozen articles I have seen on this subject since the middle of 2021.
31 Taylor Dolven, "The MBTA Cut Bus Service Because it Doesn't Have Enough Drivers. In Lawrence, Higher Pay Has Led to More Drivers and More Frequent Service," *Boston Globe*, September 4, 2022, bostonglobe.com/2022/09/04/metro/mbta-cut-bus-service-because-it-doesnt-have-enough-drivers-lawrence-higher-pay-has-led-more-drivers-more-frequent-service.
32 Stephen Jones, "Why Are so Many Flights Being Cancelled? Aviation Analysts Say It's Due to Airlines' Inability to Plan Amid a Tight Labor Market," *Business Insider*, July 23, 2022, businessinsider.com/airlines-labor-shortage-cancelling-flights-aviation-jobs-market-2022-6.
33 Ibid.
34 Kate Duffy, "Nearly 950 U.S. Flights Were Cancelled and More than 7700 Were Delayed on Sunday as Travel Chaos Took Its Toll," *Business Insider*, August 8, 2022, businessinsider.in/Nearly-950-US-flights-were-cancelled-and-more-than-7700-were-delayed-on-Sunday-as-travel-chaos-took-its-toll/articleshow/93430442.cms.
35 Jones, "Why Are So Many Flights Being Cancelled?"
36 Quoted in Steele, "Where Have All the Workers Gone?"
37 Also quoted in Steele's article.

38 Taylor Telford, "'Quiet Quitting' Isn't Really About Quitting. Here Are the Signs," *Washington Post*, August 21, 2022, washingtonpost.com/business/2022/08/21/quiet-quitting-what-to-know. Material for this paragraph and, except as noted, for the entire sub section on "quiet quitting" has been drawn from Telford's article.

39 Baumgartner and Grasso are both quoted in Telford, "Quiet Quitting."

40 Jack Kelly, "You May Be Quiet Quitting, But Could Your Boss be Quietly Firing You?" *Forbes*, August 25, 2022, forbes.com/sites/jackkelly/2022/08/25/you-may-be-quiet-quitting-but-could-your-boss-be-quietly-firing-you/?sh=7fe5741f3c0d.

41 Also quoted in Telford, "Quiet Quitting Isn't Really About Quitting."

Chapter 8: The Right to Disconnect

1 I was, at the time, research director of the Advisory Committee on Labour-Management Relations in the (Canadian) federal public service. The committee was generally known as the Fryer Committee, after its head, John Fryer.

2 I can only conclude that these ads must be working; otherwise, the technology companies wouldn't be able to afford to continue to have them run on prime-time TV (as during the intermissions of hockey games).

3 Wikipedia, "El Khomri law," *Wikipedia*, en.wikipedia.org/wiki/El_Khomri_law.

4 Christopher Jordan, "The Situation in Germany," in "Switching On to Switching Off: Disconnecting Employees in Europe," ed. Caroline Froger-Michon and Christopher Jordan, *CMS Law Now*, May 9, 2018, cms-lawnow.com/en/ealerts/2018/09/switching-on-to-switching-off-disconnecting-employees-in-europe. Except as otherwise noted, material in this section on Germany has been drawn from Jordan's article.

5 Ibid.

6 Wikipedia, "Right to Disconnect," *Wikipedia*, en.wikipedia.org/wiki/Right_to_disconnect. Section on Germany.

7 Ibid., and Jordan, "The Situation in Germany."

8 Caroline Froger-Michon and Christopher Jordan, "Switching On to Switching Off," *CMS Law-Now*, (September 2018)

9 Wikipedia, "Right to Disconnect," *Wikipedia*, en.wikipedia.org/wiki/Right_to_disconnect. Section on Germany.

10 Wikipedia, "Right to Disconnect," *Wikipedia*, en.wikipedia.org/wiki/Right_to_disconnect. Section on France. Except as otherwise noted, material in this section on France has been drawn from the Wikipedia article.

11 The Wikipedia article lists operating with countries in different time zones or work schedules entailing night or weekend work as such special circumstances.

12 Material for this paragraph has been drawn from Caroline Froger-Michon, "The Situation in France," in "Switching On to Switching Off."

Notes

13 Wikipedia, "Right to Disconnect," *Wikipedia*, en.wikipedia.org/wiki/Right_to_disconnect. Section on Italy.

14 Wikipedia, "Right to Disconnect," *Wikipedia*, en.wikipedia.org/wiki/Right_to_disconnect. Section on Slovakia.

15 Material for this section has been drawn from Dinah Wisenberg Brin, "France and Spain: Right to Disconnect Spreads," *SHRM*, May 20, 2019, shrm.org/resourcesandtools/legal-and-compliance/employment-law/pages/global-france-spain-right-to-disconnect.aspx.

16 Garrigues News Room, "Remote Work in Latin America: COVID-19 Prompts New Legislation," *Garrigues*, January 20, 2021, garrigues.com/en_GB/new/remote-work-covid-19-prompts-new-legislation-latin-america. Except as otherwise indicated, all material on the right to disconnect in Chile is drawn from this article.

17 Charles Chau, "Bill for 'Right to Disconnect' Filed in the Philippines," *hrmasia*, February 4, 2022, hrmasia.com/bill-for-right-to-disconnect-filed-in-the-philippines. Except as otherwise noted, all material on the right to disconnect in the Philippines is drawn from this article.

18 Staff, "Right to Disconnect," *Philippine Daily Inquirer*, January 30, 2022, opinion.inquirer.net/149212/right-to-disconnect.

19 Ibid.

20 Government of Canada, *Final Report of the Right to Disconnect Advisory Committee* (Ottawa: Employment and Social Development Canada, Labour Standards Program, 2021).

21 Government of Ontario, "Your Guide to the *Employment Standards Act*: Written Policy on Disconnecting from Work," originally published February 18, 2022, updated July 21, 2022, Government of Ontario, ontario.ca/document/your-guide-employment-standards-act-0/written-policy-disconnecting-from-work. See also Jim Wilson, "Ontario's Right-to-Disconnect Law Takes Effect," *Canadian HR Reporter*, June 6, 2022.

22 Government of Ontario, "Your Guide to the *Employment Standards Act*." Except where otherwise noted, all information in the remainder of this section is drawn from this document.

23 Quoted in Wilson, "Ontario's Right-to-Disconnect Law Takes Effect."

24 Ilana Belfer, "A New Quebec Bill Would Make It Illegal for Your Boss to Bug You Outside Work Hours," *MTL Blog*, December 16, 2021, mtlblog.com/new-quebec-bill-illegal-boss-bug-outside-work-hours. See also Canadian Press (staff), "The Right to Disconnect After Work: Quebec Should Follow Ontario's Lead, Says QS," CTV, December 10, 2021, montreal.ctvnews.ca/the-right-to-disconnect-after-work-quebec-should-follow-ontario-s-lead-says-qs-1.5702037.

25 See Antoine Guilman and Paul Cote-Lepine, "The 'Right to Disconnect': Will Employees Be Able to Pull the Plug?" *Fasken*, April 2018, fasken.com/en

/knowledge/2018/04/droit-a-la-deconnexion-droit-de-tirer-la-plug, for an analysis of this bill from a management labour law perspective.
26. CBC, "Quebec Should Regulate Right to Disconnect, Young Lawyers' Association Says," *CBC News*, Feb. 21, 2023, cbc.ca/news/canada/montreal/right-to-disconnect-jeune-barreau-quebec-1.6754798.
27. At the time of writing (January 2023).

Chapter 9: Hybrid Workplaces and Their Implications for Work Hours

1. Sarah Rubenstein, "Class of 1992 Notes," *Amherst* (Fall, 1992), 105.
2. For an interesting and useful discussion of the initial impact of the shutdown on Canadian federal government workers and the union staff whose job it is to represent those workers, see Denise Giroux, "Zooming Our Way into Oblivion," in *Plague Take It*, 322–33, esp. 322–26.
3. Charlie Warzel and Anne Helen Petersen, *Out of Office: The Big Problem and Bigger Promise of Working from Home* (New York: Knopf, 2021), 225.
4. Ibid.
5. On the effects of large daily doses of Zoom, see also Giroux, "Zooming Our Way into Oblivion," and Ruth Hawkins, "It's OK if I'm Not OK," in *Plague Take It*, 298–99.
6. For a thorough and perceptive discussion, see Denise Giroux, "Zooming Our Way into Oblivion." Prior to her retirement in 2021, Giroux was a union labour relations officer representing professionals in the Canadian federal public service.
7. Ibid., 326.
8. Ibid.
9. Ibid.
10. Pete Evans, "As Employees Return to the Office, the Much-Touted Hybrid Model Faces Acid Test: Does It Work?" *CBC News*, March 23, 2022, updated March 24, cbc.ca/news/business/hybrid-work-office-return-1.6393222.
11. As of early March, at a time when according to Statistics Canada inflation was running at 5.2 percent, the government was offering just 8.25 percent over four years — an amount significantly less than half the inflation rate!
12. Falling into the latter category is the Royal Bank of Canada (RBC), which without ending hybrid work, which its chairman believes is here to stay, has asked employees to be on site three or four days a week as of May 1, 2023. Similarly, Amazon CEO Andy Jassy has issued a memo to employees telling them they will have to spend at least three days a week in office as of May 1. For more details, see, Samfira Tumarkin, "RBC Wants Employees In Office Three or Four Days a Week Starting May 1," Samfira Tumarkin, March 22, 2023, stlawyers.ca/blog-news/rbc-employees-return-office.
13. See among others Danielle Newman, "If You Work from Home Monday and Friday, There's a Tawdry Nickname for You," *CBC News*, July 6, 2022, cbc.ca/radio/costofliving/monday-friday-wfh-nsfw-1.6500507.

Notes

14 It is early March 2023 as this chapter is being written.
15 Unfortunately, considerations of space preclude my broadening this discussion beyond North America.
16 Victoria Wells, "The Great Resignation Isn't Over Yet: Workers Say They'll Quit if They Don't Get the Flexibility They Want," *Financial Post*, March 18, 2022, financialpost.com/fp-work/the-great-resignation-isnt-over-yet-workers-say-theyll-quit-if-they-dont-get-the-flexibility-they-want.
17 Canadian Press, "Return to In-Person Work a Contentious Issue among Federal Public Servants," *Globe and Mail*, December 12, 2022, theglobeandmail.com/canada/article-return-to-in-person-work-a-contentious-issue-among-federal-public.
18 Mona Fortier (Treasury Board president), cited in Jennifer Carr and Greg Phillips, op-ed in *Ottawa Citizen*, January 16, 2023.
19 Cindy Davis, "Musk Decrees the End to Work from Home (and More) for Twitter Employees. Employees Leave in Droves. Implications for Remote Work?" *AV Technology*, November 18, 2022, avnetwork.com/news/musk-decrees-the-end-to-work-from-home-and-more-for-twitter-employees-implications-for-hybrid-work.
20 Under normal circumstances, this would be an unexceptional declaration. But the circumstances around public service work during the pandemic have been anything but normal. Through the worst part of the pandemic, the vast majority of Canadian federal government employees were working from home — their own homes — often using their own equipment to do so. Even once the new policy takes effect, the vast majority will be working from their own homes about half the time, still, to a large extent, using their own equipment. It seems a stretch, to put it mildly, to say that what people do in their own homes with their own equipment is a unilateral management right.
21 Government of Canada, "Common Hybrid Work Model for the Federal Public Service," December 16, 2022, Government of Canada, canada.ca/en/government/publicservice/staffing/common-hybrid-work-model-federal-public-service.html.
22 Jack Aldane, "Select IT Staff Exempt from Canadian Government Return-to-Office Mandate," *Global Government Forum*, January 26, 2023, globalgovernmentforum.com/select-it-staff-exempt-from-canadian-government-return-to-office-mandate-us-revitalises-agency-internship-programmes-workforce-management-news-in-brief.
23 Canadian Press, "Public Service Union to File Labour Board Complaint Over Hybrid Work Plan," *CTV News*, December 21, 2022, ottawa.ctvnews.ca/public-service-union-to-file-labour-board-complaint-over-hybrid-work-plan-1.6204651.
24 Public Service Alliance of Canada, "PSAC Is Filing Policy Grievances Over Government's Flawed Hybrid Work Plan," Public Service Alliance of Canada, January 30, 2023, psacunion.ca/psac-filing-policy-grievances-over-governments.
25 My employer for nearly eleven years, from 2001 through the end of 2011.

26 In this connection, it is worth noting that business groups like the Ottawa Chamber of Commerce had for some time prior to the announcement of the new policy been calling for a resumption of in-person work for federal public servants. Both the Chamber of Commerce and the newly elected mayor of Ottawa, Mark Sutcliffe, praised the new policy. See Mike Lapointe, "Chamber of Commerce, Ottawa Mayor Applaud Federal Public Servants' Hybrid Return to Work, But Unions Plan to Fight Back," *Hill Times*, December 19, 2022, hilltimes.com/story/2022/12/19/treasury-board-mandates-federal-public-servants-to-return-to-office-two-to-three-days-a-week/359384.

27 This would have been the case for my daughter Lauren, an employee of the Department of Indian and Northern Affairs, had she not received a medical exemption allowing her to continue working from home.

28 Except as otherwise noted, material for this and the succeeding paragraphs is drawn from Christian Paas-Lang, "The Hybrid Model of Parliament Is Once Again Under the Microscope. Is It Here to Stay?" *CBC News*, October 9, 2022, cbc.ca/news/politics/hybrid-parliament-procedure-study-1.6611154. Excerpt from Christian Paas-Lang, "Minority Report," *CBC News*, October 9, 2022, subscriptions.cbc.ca/newsletter_static/messages/politicsnewsletter/2022-10-09.

29 Mark Nielsen, "Hybrid Parliament Draws Mixed Reviews from Northern B.C. MPs," *Prince George Citizen*, June 28, 2022, princegeorgecitizen.com/local-news/hybrid-parliaments-draw-mixed-reviews-from-northern-bc-mps-5523815.

30 Discussion current as of early 2023. Rota stepped down from the Speakership in September 2023.

31 I have personally attended two such parties, for the launches of *Chicken Soup for the Soul* anthologies.

32 Christopher Reynolds, "Parliamentary Hearings Over Zoom an Ongoing Headache for Interpreters," *CBC News*, January 20, 2021, cbc.ca/news/politics/parliamentary-translators-survey-1.5879907.

33 Davis, "Musk Decrees the End to Work from Home (and More) for Twitter Employees." Except as otherwise noted, all material for the discussion of Twitter's new remote work policy is drawn from Davis's article.

34 Ibid.

35 Alex Hern and Dan Milno, "Rise in Twitter Outages Since Musk Takeover Hints at More Systemic Problems," *Guardian*, March 8, 2023, theguardian.com/technology/2023/mar/08/spike-in-twitter-outages-since-musk-takeover-hint-at-more-systemic-problems.

36 Luke Hurst, "Elon Musk Backtracks After Publicly Mocking Twitter Employee Who Asked if He Still Had a Job," euronews.com, March 8, 2023, euronews.com/next/2023/03/08/elon-musk-backtracks-after-publicly-mocking-twitter-employee-who-asked-if-he-still-had-a-j.

37 Gina Martinez and Stephen Lepore, "You Can't Tell Me You're Afraid of COVID on Monday and I See You in a Club on Sunday: Eric Adams Demands NYC

Notes

Workers Return to Offices as It's Revealed Manhattan Offices Are Just 28% Full," *Daily Mail*, February 17, 2022, dailymail.co.uk/news/article-10524065/Pressure-grows-NYC-firms-end-business-killing-WFH-rules.html.

38 Gregory Kuste, Jo Constantz and Bloomberg, "NYC's Mayor Is Backpedaling on His Return-to-Office Demand Because the City Can't Fill Enough Jobs," *Fortune*, February 16, 2023, fortune.com/2023/02/16/return-to-office-nyc-job-vacancies-mayor-eric-adams-changes-strategy-remote-work-hybrid.

39 For an interesting and far-reaching discussion of ideas around post-pandemic office redesign in Canada, see CBC, "Design Experts Reshape the Workspace as Pandemic Restrictions Ease Across Canada," *The Current*, originally posted March 11, 2022, most recently updated August 24, 2022, cbc.ca/radio/thecurrent/the-current-for-feb-25-2022-1.6364228/design-experts-rethink-the-workspace-as-pandemic-restrictions-ease-across-canada-1.6373245.

40 In this connection, it's important to note that "appreciating nature" was one of several things the Kellogg's workers interviewed by Benjamin Hunnicutt reported doing more of thanks to their shorter work weeks. Hunting and fishing, along with gardening and farming, were among the most popular activities benefiting from the extra time. See Benjamin Hunnicutt, *Kellogg's Six-Hour Day*, esp. p. 81.

41 Warzel and Petersen, *Out of Office*, 157.

42 Ibid.

Chapter 10: What's Been Happening Lately on the Shorter Hours Scene?

1 That think tank was CSTIER (Centre for the Study of Training, Investment, and Economic Restructuring).

2 Jon Peirce, "It's Late: Still at Work?" *Christian Science Monitor*, December 11, 1997. The piece was later reprinted in my essay collection, *Social Studies* (Victoria: Friesen, 2014), at 145–147. Except as otherwise noted, all material in this paragraph has been drawn from the aforementioned *Monitor* article.

3 4 Day Week Global, 4 Day Week UK, and Autonomy, "The Results Are in: The UK's 4 Day Week Pilot." *Research Report of the UK Trials Conducted June–December 2022*, released in February 2023. Hereafter referred to as *Research Report*.

4 Statement by Joe O'Connor, director of Reduced Work Time Center of Excellence, in interview April 3, 2023.

5 *Research Report*. See esp. 4–5.

6 Ibid., 12.

7 Ibid., 17–19.

8 Ibid., 17.

9 Ibid., 17–19.

10 Ibid., 19–20.

11 This form of shorter work week would seem particularly well-suited to highly seasonal businesses such as restaurants or tourist hotels.
12 This is a form of shorter work week highly and repeatedly recommended by Barnes and Jones in *The 4 Day Week*.
13 *Research Report*, 25.
14 Ibid., 32.
15 Ibid., 27.
16 Ibid., Executive Summary.
17 Ibid.
18 Ibid., 30.
19 Ibid., Executive Summary. Except as otherwise noted, all employee results discussed in this paragraph and the next are drawn from this Executive Summary.
20 *Research Report*, 36.
21 Ibid., 60.
22 Ibid., 45.
23 I can attest from personal experience that this innovation works. I try to do the same thing every Sunday for the forthcoming week. When I do, I have a much more productive week than when I don't.
24 *Research Report*, 57.
25 O'Connor, Joe (CEO of 4 Day Week) in discussion with author, April 3, 2023.
26 *Research Report*, 68.
27 Ibid., Schor, Juliet B. et al., *The Four Day Week: Assessing Global Trials of Reduced Work Time with No Reduction in Pay* (Auckland, NZ: Four Day Week Global, 2022). Except as noted, all material on this trial is drawn from the aforementioned report by Schor et al.
28 BBC, "Four Day Week 'An Overwhelming Success,' in Iceland," *BBC Business*, July 6, 2021, bbc.com/news/business-57724779. Except as otherwise noted, all material on the Icelandic trials has been drawn from this article.
29 Elisa Tarzia, "The 4-Day Work Week in Portugal: Is It Really Happening?" *Bridge In*, March 3, 2023, bridgein.pt/blog/4-day-work-week-in-portugal. All material for this paragraph has been drawn from Tarzia's article.
30 Luke Fraser, "Good News for 4-Day Work Week in South Africa," *Businesstech*, February 25, 2023, businesstech.co.za/news/business/667441/good-news-for-4-day-work-week-in-south-africa. All information in this paragraph has been drawn from Fraser's article.
31 It's worth noting that the trial was also announced in 4 Day Week Global's April 2023 newsletter.
32 Rodrigo Ghedin, "Is the Future of Work to Work Less? Brazilian Companies Try the Four-Day Work Week," *LABS (Latin America Business Stories)*, updated June 10, 2022, labsnews.com/en/articles/society/is-the-future-of-work-to-work-less-brazilian-companies-try-the-four-day-work-week. All material in this paragraph and the next is drawn from Ghedin's article.

Notes

33 Information about Haller has been drawn from his Wikipedia biography (Wikipedia, "Wilhelm Haller," *Wikipedia*, en.wikipedia.org/wiki/Wilhelm_Haller.)

34 I have met Willi Haller, who came to the Economic Council of Canada to give a talk during the mid-1980s, while I was working there. Regrettably, my high-school and university German had not survived well enough to enable me to comprehend the nuances of work scheduling that he was discussing in his written documents (mainly if not entirely written in German). But his passionate commitment to the shorter hours cause was evident, and it was clear just from a reading of the tables in his written articles that he had gone into the matter exceptionally thoroughly — quite possibly more thoroughly than anyone else then alive. I do remember that his documents included more different types of work schedule than I had ever seen before or would ever see again.

35 This list can be found at 4 Day Week, "4 Day Work Week Companies in Germany," 4 Day Week, 4dayweek.io/companies/germany.

36 Heidi Lee, "A Four-Day Work Week Can Be Life-Changing. Should Canadians Get One?" *Global News*, February 22, 2023, globalnews.ca/news/9501740/four-day-working-week-major-study.

37 Quoted in Lee, "Four-Day Work Week."

38 4 Day Week, Canada, available online at 4dayweek.io/country/canada.

39 Tyler Fleming and Josh Pringle, "Ottawa French Catholic School Board Piloting Four-Day Week at Two Schools," *CTV News*, March 23, 2023, ottawa.ctvnews.ca/ottawa-french-catholic-school-board-piloting-four-day-week-at-two-schools-1.6325897.

40 CBC News, "Ministry Rejects Ottawa School Board Plan for 4-Day Week." *CBC News*, May 5, 2023, cbc.ca/news/canada/ottawa/no-4-day-school-week-cecce-1.6820358.

41 Alex Treiber, "Four-Day Work Week Act, 2022, Passes First Reading," *McCarthy Tétreault*, February 26, 2023, mccarthy.ca/en/insights/blogs/canadian-employer-advisor/four-day-work-week-act-2022-passes-first-reading. Except as otherwise noted, material on the proposed Ontario legislation has been drawn from this article.

42 Irina Ivanova, "Four-Day Work Week Gains Support among Progressives in Congress," *CBS News*, December 8, 2021, cbsnews.com/news/4-day-workweek-congress-progressives.

43 Taylor Telford, "This Bill Could Make the Four-Day Work Week a Reality," *Washington Post*, March 8, 2023, washingtonpost.com/us-policy/2023/03/08/four-day-workweek-bill-takano. Except as otherwise noted, all remaining material on the proposed U.S. legislation has been drawn from Telford's article.

44 "California's 4-Day Work Week Bill: What Happened to It," In "4-Day Work Week: The Complete Overview," *Buildremote*, October 15, 2022,

buildremote.co/four-day-week/complete-overview. Except as otherwise noted, all material on California's bill has been drawn from this article.
45 This is cited in O'Loughlin's article.
46 Devan McGuinness, "Pennsylvania Workers Could Get a 4-Day Work Week," *Fatherly*, March 2, 2023, fatherly.com/news/pennsylvania-workers-could-get-a-4-day-workweek. Except as otherwise noted, all material on Pennsylvania's proposed legislation is drawn from this article.
47 Luke Hurst, "Workers in Belgium Can Now Switch to a Four-Day Week — but They Won't be Working Fewer Hours," *euronews.next*, November 21, 2022, euronews.com/next/2022/11/21/workers-in-belgium-can-now-switch-to-a-four-day-week-but-they-wont-be-working-fewer-hours.
48 Economic Times, "Belgium Announces 4-Day Work Week," *Economic Times*, February 11, 2022, economictimes.indiatimes.com/nri/work/belgium-announces-4-day-work-week-right-to-disconnect-after-office-hours.
49 Hurst, "Workers In Belgium Can Now Switch."
50 Ibid. See also, Economic Times, "Belgium Announces 4-Day Work Week."
51 BBC News, "Peter Dowd, MP Calls for Four-Day Working Week Without Cut in Pay." BBC, October 18, 2022, bbc.com/news/uk-england-merseyside-63297871.
52 Henry O'Loughlin, "20 Countries with 4-Day Work Week (Trial, Proposal, Law)," *Buildremote*, July 3, 2023. buildremote.co/four-day-week/4-day-work-week-countries.

Chapter 11: Recommendations
1 See, for example, Jon Peirce, *Canadian Industrial Relations*, 2nd ed. (Toronto: Pearson, 2022), 196–97.
2 See, among others, David R. Roediger and Philip S. Foner, *Our Own Time: A History of American Labor and the Working Day* (New York; London: Verso, 1989), 178.

Conclusion
1 In an important new book, *Saving Time: Discovering a Life Beyond the Clock* (London: Bodley Head, 2023), visual artist and writer Jenny Odell invites us to discover many different time rhythms beyond the clock-driven ones typically imposed by employers. Awareness of these many alternative rhythms, Odell argues, will help enable us "to imagine a source of meaning outside the world of work and profit, and to understand that the trajectory of our lives — or the life of the planet — is not a foregone conclusion."

Appendix A: Profile of Joe O'Connor: He Works so You Can Work Less
1 The results of those trials were discussed at some length in Chapter 10, "What's Been Happening Lately on the Shorter Hours Scene."
2 From personal experience, I can attest that this is definitely true for me.

Bibliography

Books, Monographs, and Major Reports

Autonomy, 4 Day Week UK, and 4 Day Week Global. "The Results Are In: The UK's Four-Day Week Pilot," *Research Report of the UK Trials Conducted June–December 2022*. Released in February 2023.

Barnes, Andrew, and Stephanie Jones. *The 4 Day Week: How the Flexible Work Revolution Can Increase Productivity, Profitability and Wellbeing, and Help Create a Sustainable Future*. London: Piatkus, 2020.

Brod, Craig. *Technostress: The Human Cost of the Computer Revolution*. Reading, MA: Addison-Wesley, 1984.

Ferriss, Timothy. *The 4-Hour Workweek*, expanded and updated edition. New York: Harmony Books, 2009.

Giattino, Charlie, Esteban Ortiz-Ospina, and Max Roser. "Working Hours," *Our World in Data*, last modified 2020, ourworldindata.org/working-hours.

Government of Canada. "Final Report of the Right to Disconnect Advisory Committee." Ottawa: Labour Standards Program, Employment and Social Development Canada, February 2022.

Hinrichs, Karl, William Roche, and Carmen Sirianni, eds. *Working Time in Transition: The Political Economy of Working Hours in Industrial Nations*. Philadelphia: Temple UP, 1991.

Hunnicutt, Benjamin. *Free Time: The Forgotten American Dream*. Philadelphia: Temple UP, 2013.

———. *Kellogg's Six-Hour Day*. Philadelphia: Temple UP, 1996.

———. *Work Without End*. Philadelphia: Temple UP, 1988.

Jaffe, Sarah. *Work Won't Love You Back*. New York: Bold Type Books, 2021.

O'Hara, Bruce. *Enough Already! Breaking Free in the Second Half of Life*. Vancouver: New Star Books, 2004.

———. *Working Harder Isn't Working*. Vancouver: New Star Books, 1993.

Peirce, Jonathan C. (Jon). *Canadian Industrial Relations*, 2nd ed. Toronto: Pearson Education Canada, 2002.

———. *The Case for a Shorter Work Week*. Ottawa: Carleton University Centre for the Study of Training, Investment, and Economic Restructuring, 2000.

———. *Collective Bargaining over Technological Change in Ottawa: A Quantitative and Historical Analysis*. Economic Council of Canada Discussion Paper #338. Ottawa: Economic Council of Canada, 1987.

———. *Social Studies: Collected Essays, 1974–2013*. Victoria: Friesen, 2014.

Peirce, Jonathan C. (Jon), and Ann McMillan, eds. *Plague Take It: A COVID Almanac by and About Elders*. Ottawa: Loose Cannon Press, 2021.

Reid, Donald. *Work and Leisure in the 21st Century*. Toronto and Dayton: Wall & Emerson, 1995.

Schor, Juliet. *The Overspent American*. New York: Harper, 1998.

———. *The Overworked American: The Unexpected Decline of Leisure*. New York: Basic Books, 1991.

Schor et al. *The Four Day Week: Assessing Global Trials of Reduced Work Time with No Reduction in Pay*. Auckland, NZ: Four Day Week Global, 2022.

Veal, Anthony. *Whatever Happened to the Leisure Society?* Milton Park, Abingden, U.K.; New York: Routledge, 2019.

Warzel, Charlie, and Anne Helen Petersen. *Out of Office: The Big Problem and Bigger Promise of Working from Home*. New York: Knopf, 2021.

Whaples, Robert. "Hours of Work in U.S. History." *EH.net*, eh.net/encyclopedia/hours-of-work-in-u-s-history.

Bibliography

Articles and Essays

Abdelrahman, M. "The Indefatigable Worker: From Factory Floor to Zoom Avatar." *Critical Sociology* 48, no. 1 (February 5, 2021): 75–90.

Anand, Shefali. "India: Retaining Talent amid the Great Resignation." *Society for Human Resource Management*, February 3, 2022, shrm.org/resourcesandtools/hr-topics/global-hr/pages/india-great-resignation.aspx.

Ayyagari, R., V. Grover, and R. Purvis. "Technostress: Technological Antecedents and Implications." *MIS Quarterly* 35, no. 4 (2011): 831–858.

Bailey, J. "Precarious or Precariat?" (review article). *International Socialist Review* 85 (September 2012). isreview.org/issue/85/precarious-or-precariat/index.html.

Bateman, Kayleigh. "Some Companies Are Trialling a Four-Day Work Week. Here's What They Discovered." World Economic Forum, January 31, 2022. weforum.org/agenda/2022/01/four-day-week-work-life-balance-trial.

Bateman, Tom. "Wales Could Become the Latest Country to Trial a Four-Day Week. Here's Why." *euronews.next*, last updated February 15, 2022, euronews.com/next/2022/02/14/a-four-day-week-in-wales-would-boost-productivity-and-improve-health-a-new-report-says.

Belfer, Ilana. "A New Quebec Bill Would Make It Illegal for Your Boss to Bug You Outside Work Hours." *MTL Blog*, last updated December 16, 2021, mtlblog.com/new-quebec-bill-illegal-boss-bug-outside-work-hours.

Brin, Dinah W. "Countries Experiment with Four-Day Work Week." *Society for Human Resource Management*, May 11, 2021, shrm.org/resourcesandtools/hr-topics/global-hr/pages/countries-experiment-with-four-day-workweek.aspx.

Buchwald, Elizabeth. "The Pandemic Is Inspiring Some Companies to Test 4-Day Work Weeks — but Will It Hurt Productivity?" *Market Watch*, last updated July 8, 2021, marketwatch.com/story/the-pandemic-is-inspiring-kickstarter-and-unilever-to-test-four-day-workweeks-but-will-it-hurt-productivity-11625609807.

Canadian Press (Staff). "The Right to Disconnect After Work: Quebec Should Follow Ontario's Lead, Says QS." *CTV News*, last updated December 10, 2021, montreal.ctvnews.ca/the-right-to-disconnect-after-work-quebec-should-follow-ontario-s-lead-says-qs-1.5702037.

Carbonaro, Giulia. "Is the 6-Hour Workday the Answer to a Better Work-Life Balance?" *euronews.next*, updated August 4, 2022, euronews.com/next/2022/07/27/is-the-6-hour-workday-the-answer-to-a-better-work-life-balance.

Carscallen, Kristy, and Doron Melnick. "Where the Great Resignation Might Be Headed in Canada, and What Employers Should Do About It." *Globe and Mail*, March 16, 2022, theglobeandmail.com/business/careers/leadership/article-where-the-great-resignation-might-be-headed-in-canada-and-what.

Christian, Alex. "The Great Resignation Is Here and No One Is Prepared." *Wired*, August 27, 2021, wired.co.uk/article/great-resignation-quit-job.

Clark, Pilita. "Get Ready for the Four-Day Working Week." *Irish Times*, January 24, 2022, irishtimes.com/business/work/pilita-clark-get-ready-for-the-four-day-working-week-1.4783786.

Coley, Ben. "How Shake Shack is Becoming an Employer of Choice." *QSR*, April 28, 2022, qsrmagazine.com/employee-management/how-shake-shack-becoming-employer-choice.

Daniel, Luke. "SA's Version of the 'Great Resignation' Is a Little Different — As Are Reasons for Leaving." *news24*, April 22, 2022, news24.com/news24/bi-archive/the-great-resignation-in-south-africa-2022-4.

Davidovic, Ivana. "'Lying Flat:' Why Some Chinese Are Putting Work Second." *BBC News*, February 16, 2022, bbc.com/news/business-60353916.

De Beer, Marthin. "The Workplace Reckoning in the Wake of the Great Resignation." *Fast Company*, May 21, 2022, fastcompany.com/90750532/the-workplace-reckoning-in-the-wake-of-the-great-resignation.

Dobson, Sarah. "Many Workers Regret Quitting during 'Great Resignation.'" *Canadian HR Reporter*, July 12, 2022, hrreporter.com/focus-areas/recruitment-and-staffing/many-workers-regret-quitting-during-great-resignation/368158.

Dujay, John. "Does Canada Need a 'Right-to-Disconnect' Law?" *Canadian HR Reporter*, June 21, 2021, hrreporter.com/focus-areas/culture-and-engagement/does-canada-need-a-right-to-disconnect-law/357385.

Dunn, Trevor. "Big Shift Back to In-Person Office Work Expected This Month in Toronto as COVID-19 Restrictions Lift." *CBC News*, March 1, 2022, cbc.ca/news/canada/toronto/big-shift-back-to-in-person-office-work-expected-this-month-in-toronto-as-covid-19-restrictions-lift-1.6367912.

Bibliography

Economist. "Evidence for the 'Great Resignation' Is Thin on the Ground." *Economist*, December 6, 2021, updated December 9, 2021, economist.com/finance-and-economics/evidence-for-the-great-resignation-is-thin-on-the-ground/21806659.

———. "How to Manage the Great Resignation." *Economist*, November 27, 2021, updated December 2, 2021, economist.com/business/2021/11/27/how-to-manage-the-great-resignation.

Ellis, Matt. "The Four-Day Work Week: Why It Works." *Zapier*, November 6, 2018, zapier.com/blog/four-day-work-week.

Evans, Pete. "As Employees Return to the Office, the Much-Hyped Hybrid Model Faces Acid Test: Does It Work?" *CBC News*, March 23, 2022, cbc.ca/news/business/hybrid-work-office-return-1.6393222.

Farrell, Chris. "How the Coronavirus Punishes Many Older Workers." *Forbes*, April 14, 2020, forbes.com/sites/nextavenue/2020/04/14/how-the-coronavirus-punishes-many-older-workers/?sh=654fb8bc202a.

———. "Older Workers and the 'Big Quit'." *Forbes*, July 23, 2021, forbes.com/sites/nextavenue/2021/07/23/older-workers-and-the-big-quit/?sh=12be7c2f3e47.

Financial Times (Editorial Board). "The Great Resignation Is Not Going Away." *Financial Times*, February 1, 2022, ft.com/content/857bdeba-b61b-4012-ab82-3c9eb19506df.

Finister, Marcus. "America's 'Great Resignation' Could Be an Opportunity for European Employers." *Forbes*, March 25, 2022, forbes.com/sites/forbesbusinesscouncil/2022/03/25/americas-great-resignation-could-be-an-opportunity-for-european-employers/?sh=4462c5223e10.

Fontinelle, Amy. "What Is the Great Resignation? Causes, Statistics and Trends." *Investopedia*, May 5, 2022, investopedia.com/the-great-resignation-5199074.

Froger-Michon, Caroline, and Christopher Jordan. "Switching On to Switching Off: Disconnecting Employees in Europe?" *CMS Law-Now*, September 5, 2018, cms-lawnow.com/en/ealerts/2018/09/switching-on-to-switching-off-disconnecting-employees-in-europe.

Frost, Rosie. "Could Spain's Four-Day Work Week Save the Planet?" *euronews.green*, March 16, 2021, last updated February 15, 2022, euronews.com/green/2021/03/16/why-a-four-day-working-week-could-save-us-and-the-planet.

———. "Why Iceland's Four-Day Week Trial Was an 'Overwhelming Success' for People and Planet." *euronews.green*, July 7, 2021, last updated February 15, 2022, euronews.com/green/2021/07/08/why-iceland-s-four-day-week-trial-was-an-overwhelming-success-for-people-and-planet.

Fuller, Joseph, and William Kerr. "The Great Resignation Didn't Start with the Pandemic." *Harvard Business Review*, March 23, 2022, hbr.org/2022/03/the-great-resignation-didnt-start-with-the-pandemic.

Ghicuic, Georgiana. "The Not So 'Great Revolution' Takes Over Europe." LinkedIn, November 15, 2021, linkedin.com/pulse/so-great-resignation-takes-over-europe-georgiana-gitschuk-phd.

Giroux, Denise. "Zooming Our Way into Oblivion." In *Plague Take It: A COVID Almanac by and About Elders*, ed. Jon Peirce and Ann McMillan. Ottawa: Loose Cannon Press, 2021, 322–33.

Goldberg, Emma. "All of Those Quitters? They're at Work." *New York Times*, May 13, 2022, nytimes.com/2022/05/13/business/great-resignation-jobs.html.

Government of Ontario. "Written Policy on Disconnecting from Work." Government of Ontario, ontario.ca/document/your-guide-employment-standards-act-0/written-policy-disconnecting-from-work.

Hawkins, Ruth. "It's OK if I'm Not OK." In *Plague Take It: A COVID Almanac by and About Elders*, ed. Jon Peirce and Ann McMillan. Ottawa: Loose Cannon Press, 2021, 298–99.

Hoffman, Betsy, and Jon Peirce. "Prof with Parkinson's Zooms Her Way Through Pandemic." In *Plague Take It: A COVID Almanac by and About Elders*, ed. Jon Peirce and Ann McMillan. Ottawa: Loose Cannon Press, 2021, 300–302.

Horowitz, Julia. "The Great Resignation Is Taking Root Around the World." *CNN Business*, March 30, 2022, cnn.com/2022/03/30/economy/great-resignation-uk-australia-europe/index.html.

HRPA Insights. "Is the Great Resignation Over? Not Even Close." HRPA, April 6, 2022, hrpa.ca/hr-insights/is-the-great-resignation-over-not-even-close.

Hudson, Paul. "Gen Z Isn't Looking for 'a Dream Job.' Here's What They Want Instead." *Fast Company*, July 27, 2022, fastcompany.com/90772850/gen-z-isnt-looking-for-a-dream-job-heres-what-they-want-instead.

Huet, Natalie. "Nearly Half of European Workers at High Risk of Mental Health Issues, New Poll Shows." *euronews.next*, February 11, 2022, euronews.com/next

Bibliography

/2022/11/02/nearly-half-of-european-workers-living-with-mental-health-issues-and-stress-new-poll-shows.

Hurst, Luke. "Four-Day Work Week: 3,300 Employees in the UK Start Biggest Trial of its Kind." *euronews.next*, June 6, 2022, euronews.com/next/2022/06/05/four-day-week-3-000-employees-in-the-uk-to-take-part-in-the-biggest-trial-of-its-kind.

Iacurci, Greg. "The Great Resignation Is Still Red Hot — but May Not Last." *CNBC*, May 3, 2022, cnbc.com/2022/05/03/the-great-resignation-is-still-red-hot-but-may-not-last.html.

Joly, Josephine. "Remote Work is Not an Option for Most Employees and One-Third are Ready to Quit, BCG Poll Shows." *euronews.next*, updated July 9, 2022, euronews.com/next/2022/07/09/remote-work-not-an-option-for-most-workers-and-one-third-are-ready-to-quit-bcg-poll-shows.

Joly, Josephine, Luke Hurst, and David Walsh. "Four-Day Week: Which Countries Have Embraced It and How's It Going So Far." *euronews.next*, June 6, 2022, euronews.com/next/2023/06/21/the-four-day-week-which-countries-have-embraced-it-and-how-s-it-going-so-far.

Kelly, Jack. "Scotland Joins the Growing Global Movement Toward a Four-Day Work Week." *Forbes*, September 3, 2021, forbes.com/sites/jackkelly/2021/09/03/scotland-joins-the-growing-global-movement-towards-a-four-day-workweek/?sh=6367cc45295f.

———. "You May be Quiet Quitting, but Could Your Boss Be Quietly Firing You?" *Forbes*, August 25, 2022, forbes.com/sites/jackkelly/2022/08/25/you-may-be-quiet-quitting-but-could-your-boss-be-quietly-firing-you/?sh=6c18ca723c0d.

Kemle, Andrew. "The 'Great Resignation' and Why Companies Need to Listen to Workers." *Toronto Star*, April 2, 2022, thestar.com/business/the-great-resignation-and-why-companies-need-to-listen-to-workers.

Kesslen, Ben. "A 'Right to Disconnect?' New York City Council Explores Protecting Off Hours." *NBC News*, January 26, 2019, nbcnews.com/news/us-news/right-disconnect-new-york-city-council-explores-protecting-hours-n963071.

Keynes, John Maynard. "Economic Possibilities for Our Grandchildren (1930)." John Maynard Keynes, *Essays in Persuasion* (New York: Harcourt Brace, 1932), 358–73.

Klein, Danny. "Inside Shake Shack's Employee Retention Strategy." *QSR*, June 2019, qsrmagazine.com/employee-management/inside-shake-shacks-employee-retention-strategy.

Lee, Heidi. "A Four-Day Work Week Can Be Life-Changing. Should Canadians Get One?" *Global News*, February 22, 2023, globalnews.ca/news/9501740/four-day-working-week-major-study.

Llach, Laura. "The Great Resignation: Is the American Workplace Coming to Europe?" *euronews.next*, December 1, 2021, euronews.com/next/2021/12/01/the-great-resignation-is-it-an-american-revolution-or-is-the-trend-coming-to-europe.

———. "Here's Why a Four-Day Working Week Trial in Spain Has Not Been a Runaway Success." *euronews.next*, July 16, 2022, euronews.com/next/2022/07/15/heres-why-a-four-day-working-week-trial-in-spain-has-not-been-a-runaway-success.

Loop. "'The Great Resignation' Trend Has Spread to Jamaica." *Loop Jamaica News*, November 21, 2021, jamaica.loopnews.com/content/great-resignation-trend-has-spread-jamaica.

McGleenon, Brian. "Why UK Businesses are Experimenting with a Four-Day Week." *Evening Standard*, January 24, 2022, standard.co.uk/business/four-day-week-uk-joe-o-connor-mark-mullen-atom-bank-b977847.html.

McGrenere, Grace. "The Great Resignation & Canadian Workers." *Leveller*, February 1, 2022, leveller.ca/2022/02/the-great-resignation-in-canada.

Microsoft Work Trend Index. "The Next Great Disruption Is Hybrid Work: Are You Ready?" *microsoft*, March 22, 2021, microsoft.com/en-us/worklab/work-trend-index/hybrid-work.

Miller, David, and Haley Yamada. "The Great Resignation: Its Origins and What It Means for Future Business." *ABC News*, May 3, 2022, abcnews.go.com/US/great-resignation-origins-means-future-business/story?id=84222583.

Morgan, Kate. "The Great Resignation: How Employers Drove Workers to Quit." *BBC Worklife*, July 1, 2021, bbc.com/worklife/article/20210629-the-great-resignation-how-employers-drove-workers-to-quit.

Nadkarni, Anuja. "NZ 'Disappointingly Slow' to Take Up Four-Day Week." *Newsroom*, July 14, 2021, newsroom.co.nz/disappointingly-slow-uptake-of-4-day-week.

Bibliography

Navlakha, Meera. "People Aren't Ready to Quit Quitting." *Mashable*, April 22, 2022, mashable.com/article/2022-great-resignation-continues.

Newman, Danielle. "If You Work from Home Monday and Friday, There's a Tawdry Nickname for You." *CBC Radio*, July 6, 2022, cbc.ca/radio/costofliving/monday-friday-wfh-nsfw-1.6500507.

Noakes, Jason, and Jeff Landmann. "The Great Resignation: A Global Risk?" *Norton Rose Fulbright*, December 13, 2021, nortonrosefulbright.com/en/knowledge/publications/cc03a277/the-great-resignation-a-global-risk.

O'Carroll, Aileen. "Three Things COVID Revealed About Working Time." *four day week*, July 19, 2021, fourdayweek.ie/three-things-covid-revealed-about-working-time.

Parker, Kim, and Juliana M. Horowitz. "Majority of Workers Who Quit a Job in 2021 Cite Low Pay, No Opportunities for Advancement, Feeling Disrespected." Pew Research Center, March 9, 2022, pewresearch.org/short-reads/2022/03/09/majority-of-workers-who-quit-a-job-in-2021-cite-low-pay-no-opportunities-for-advancement-feeling-disrespected.

Parker, Kim, Juliana M. Horowitz, and Rachel Minkin. "COVID-19 Pandemic Continues to Reshape Work in America." Pew Research Center, February 16, 2022, pewresearch.org/social-trends/2022/02/16/covid-19-pandemic-continues-to-reshape-work-in-america.

Peirce, Jon. "It's Late — Still at Work?" *Christian Science Monitor*, December 11, 1997, reprinted in Jon Peirce, *Social Studies: Collected Essays, 1974–2013*. Victoria: Friesen Press, 2014, 145–47.

———. "Working People: Does No One Give a Damn Anymore?" *Toronto Star*, May 2, 2013, reprinted in Jon Peirce, *Social Studies: Collected Essays, 1974–2013*. Victoria: Friesen Press, 2014, 148–50.

Phipps, Simone. "What Exactly Is 'The Great Resignation'?" *Middle Georgia State University News*, April 21, 2022, mga.edu/news/2022/04/what-is-the-great-resignation.php.

Piper, Dannielle. "Flexibility of Virtual Learning Prompts Some Post-secondary Students to Pursue More Online Learning." *CBC News*, March 5, 2022, cbc.ca/news/canada/online-learning-post-secondary-science-degrees-1.6364340.

Pusca, Delia. "Has the 'Great Resignation' Reached Europe as Well?" *Pluria*, February 2, 2022, remote.pluria.co/has-the-great-resgnation-reached-europe.

Rauch, Erik. "Productivity and the Work Week." No publication. No date. Available at groups.csail.mit.edu/mac/users/rauch/worktime/. Downloaded March 2022.

Red Thread. "Key Findings from Microsoft Work Trend Index for 2020." *Red Thread*, red-thread.com/blog/microsoft-work-trend-index.

Riedl, René. "On the Stress Potential of Videoconferencing: Definition and Root Causes of Zoom Fatigue." *Electronic Markets* 32 (2021), December 6, 2021, link.springer.com/article/10.1007/s12525-021-00501-3.

Ritchell, Tiana, Richard Manns, and Jordan O'Connor. "Look Out for These Three Talent Retention Myths." *DoChangeRight.com*, September 21, 2021, dochangeright.com/the-great-resignation-is-here-look-out-for-these-three-talent-retention-myths.

Roy, Eleanor Ainge. "Jacinda Ardern Flags Four-Day Working Week as a Way to Rebuild New Zealand after COVID-19." *Guardian*, May 20, 2020, theguardian.com/world/2020/may/20/jacinda-ardern-flags-four-day-working-week-as-way-to-rebuild-new-zealand-after-covid-19.

Russell, Bertrand. "In Praise of Idleness." *Harper's*, October 1932, harpers.org/archive/1932/10/in-praise-of-idleness.

Ryall, Julian. "Japan Proposes Four-Day Working Week." DW, June 22, 2021, dw.com/en/japan-work-life-balance/a-57989053.

Schachter, Harvey. "Could You Live with a 30-Hour Work Week?" *Globe and Mail*, November 28, 2013, theglobeandmail.com/report-on-business/careers/career-advice/life-at-work/could-you-live-with-a-30-hour-work-week/article15619217.

———. "Do We Really Want a Shorter Work Week?" *Globe and Mail*, May 24, 2012, theglobeandmail.com/report-on-business/careers/career-advice/do-we-really-want-a-shorter-work-week/article4209573.

———. "Get Over It. There Is No Work-Life Balance, Just Work." *Globe and Mail*, February 28, 2013, theglobeandmail.com/report-on-business/careers/career-advice/life-at-work/get-over-it-there-is-no-work-life-balance-just-work/article9113494.

———. "A Strategy for Doing Your Best Work When You're at Your Best Self." *Globe and Mail*, November 25, 2021, theglobeandmail.com/business/careers/management/article-a-strategy-for-doing-your-best-work-when-youre-at-your-best-self.

Bibliography

Schachter-Snipper, Lanie. "Workplace Mental Health." *lanie schachter-snipper*, lssmentalhealth.com/consulting.

Sirianni, Carmen. "The Self-Management of Time in Post-Industrial Society," in *Working Time in Transition: The Political Economy of Working Hours in Industrial Nations*, ed. Karl Hinrichs, William Roche, and Carmen Sirianni. Philadelphia: Temple UP, 1991.

Spanjaart, Jasper. "Will 'The Great Resignation' Blow Over to Europe?" *Totalent*, July 18, 2021, totalent.eu/will-the-great-resignation-blow-over-to-europe.

Steele, Alistair. "Where Have All the Workers Gone? Don't Blame COVID, Economists Say." *CBC News*, July 23, 2022, cbc.ca/news/canada/ottawa/ottawa-workers-covid-retirements-1.6529325.

Telford, Taylor. "'Quiet Quitting' Isn't Really About Quitting. Here Are the Signs." *Washington Post*, August 21, 2022, washingtonpost.com/business/2022/08/21/quiet-quitting-what-to-know.

Tharoor, Ishaan. "The 'Great Resignation' Goes Global." *Washington Post*, October 18, 2021, washingtonpost.com/world/2021/10/18/labor-great-resignation-global.

Thompson, Derek. "The Five-Day Work Week is Dying." *Atlantic*, February 23, 2022, theatlantic.com/ideas/archive/2022/02/work-from-home-revolution/622880.

———. "Why Americans Care About Work So Much." *Atlantic*, March 31, 2023, theatlantic.com/ideas/archive/2023/03/work-revolution-ai-wfh-new-book/673572.

Tran, Cindy. "Why the Pandemic Had These Young People Quitting Their Jobs." *CBC News*, May 5, 2022, cbc.ca/news/canada/ottawa/young-people-quit-jobs-pandemic-1.6428222.

Vigliarolo, Brandon. "How the UK and EU Are Addressing the Great Resignation: Increased Pay." *Tech Republic*, February 3, 2022, techrepublic.com/article/how-the-uk-and-eu-are-addressing-the-great-resignation-increased-pay.

Weikle, Brandi. "Forget 9 to 5. These Experts Say the Time Has Come for the Results-Only Work Environment." *CBC Radio*, December 20, 2021, cbc.ca/radio/costofliving/results-only-work-environment-1.6290492.

Wells, Victoria. "The Great Resignation Isn't Over Yet: Workers Say They'll Quit if They Don't Get the Flexibility They Want." *Financial Post*, March 18,

2022, financialpost.com/fp-work/the-great-resignation-isnt-over-yet-workers-say-theyll-quit-if-they-dont-get-the-flexibility-they-want.

Wikipedia. "Great Resignation." *Wikipedia*, en.wikipedia.org/wiki/Great_Resignation.

Wilson, Jim. "Canada's Right-to-Disconnect Law Takes Effect." *Canadian HR Reporter*, June 6, 2022, hrreporter.com/focus-areas/culture-and-engagement/ontarios-right-to-disconnect-law-takes-effect/367209.

Wong, Daniel, Megan Mah, and Alfred Pepushaj, "Federal Advisory Committee Offers Insight into Disconnect from Work Policies for Employees." *Weirfoulds LLP*, February 16, 2022, weirfoulds.com/federal-advisory-committee-offers-insight-into-disconnect-from-work-policies-for-employees.

Yeung, Peter. "Spain's 4-Day Week a Game Changer." *Reasons to be Cheerful*, May 3, 2021, reasonstobecheerful.world/spain-four-day-work-week-national-government.

YPulse. "Why the Great Resignation Is Happening in Western Europe Too," November 2, 2021, ypulse.com/article/2021/11/02/why-the-great-resignation-is-happening-in-western-europe-too.

Yu, Andrea. "How a Four-Day Work Week Could Benefit Women." *Globe and Mail*, June 1, 2022, theglobeandmail.com/business/article-how-a-four-day-workweek-could-benefit-women.

Zimonjic, Peter. "Canada's Working-Age Population Is Older than Ever, StatsCan Says." *CBC News*, April 27, 2022, ici.radio-canada.ca/rci/en/news/1879202/canadas-working-age-population-is-older-than-ever-statscan-says.

Index

Figures and tables indicated by page numbers in italics

Abildgaard, Pernille, 223
Adams, Casey, 155
Adams, Eric, 173–74
Adamson Act (U.S., 1916), 37
AFL-CIO, 47, 49, 195. *See also*
 American Federation of Labor
Africa, 64, 86. *See also* Kenya; South
 Africa
agriculture, 22
Ahlstrom, David, 94
airlines, 128–29
Aldrich Report, 26
Alexander, Peter, 116–17
alternative work weeks, 217–18. *See also*
 four-day week; shorter work week
Amazon, 256n12
American Federation of Labor (AFL),
 30, 33, 37–38, 41–42, 48, 99, 100.
 See also AFL-CIO
American Relief Administration (ARA),
 246n27
Andrews, John B., 38–39
annualized work weeks, 184, 194,
 259n11
Archer, Lawrence, 249n23

Argentina, 145
Asia, 75–81. *See also specific countries*
assembly lines, 103, 105–7, 222
Association for Sustainable Democracy
 (Alda), 189
asynchronicity, 118
Aubry Law (Martine Aubry), *70*
Australia
 eight-hour day, 67, *68, 69*
 five-day week, 64
 four-day week, 198
 healthcare crisis, 15
 holiday leave and paid vacations,
  25, 65
 quiet quitting and, 123
 work hours, cross-national
  comparisons, *24,* 34–35, *58, 66*
Austria, *69*
automation, 103, 105, 186
Autonomy (think tank), 182–83, 189,
 224

baby boom, postwar, 48, 60, 100,
 239n175
Bachrach, Taylor, 169

Bagley, Sarah, 27
Bains, Parm, 169
Bangladesh, 21–22, *73*, 74, 75, 76, 80–81
Barber, Larissa, 155
Barnes, Andrew, 9–10, 11, 13, 101, 201, 223
 The 4 Day Week (with Jones), 181, 259n12
BASF, 138
Bauer, Stephen, 92, 93
Baumgartner, Natalie, 130
Bayer, 138
BDO, 78
Belgium
 four-day week, 199, 220
 right to disconnect, 141–42
 shorter work hours and productivity, 94
 work hours, cross-national comparisons, 21, 23, 34, 58, 65, *65*, 66
Belkin, Liuba, 156
Belmonte, Adriana, 231n34
Bennett, R.B. (Bennett government), 59
Bentham, Jeremy, 114
Bituminous Coal Conservation Act (U.S., 1935), 45
Black, Hugo, 42, 43
Blum, Léon, 46, 58–59, *69*, 71
BMW, 138
body language, 116, 118
Boric, Gabriel, 84–85
Boston, 28, 128
Boulet, Jean, 154
Brazil, 72, *73*, 74, 84, 190–91
Brenner, Harvey, 10
Britain. *See* United Kingdom
British Columbia, 16–17, 154
Brod, Craig, 108–10
Brown, George, 56–57
Brown, Lewis, 96, 97, 101
Buffer, 219

Bulgaria, *73*, 87
Bunner, Johanna, 105
Bury, Erin, 152

California, 17, 156, 196–97, 215, 221
Calkins, Blaine, 169–70
Canada
 climate change crisis, 16–17
 federal bargaining with unionized employees, 165–66, 256n11
 five-day week, 64
 four-day week, 193–94
 Great Resignation, 124–26, 127
 healthcare crisis, 13–16
 holiday leave and paid vacations, *25*, 53, 206
 hybrid work, Parliament debate, 160, 169–71, 174
 hybrid work, Treasury Board debate, 159–60, 165–69, 174, 257n20, 258nn26–27
 industrialization, 54, 56
 labour movement and unionization, 54, 59–60, 126, 240n8, 241n16, 252n20
 right to disconnect, 148–50, 151, 208
 scientific management and, 57
 shorter work hours, history of, 56–57, 95, 241n19
 U.S., comparison to, 53–54, *55*, 55–56, 58, 59–61
 work hours, cross-national comparisons, 21, *24*, 34, 37, *65*, 65–67
Canadian Association of Professional Employees (CAPE), 168
Canadian Union of Postal Workers (CUPW), 114
Canadian Union of Public Employees (CUPE) Local 2424, 114
Carleton University, 113, 114
Carr, Jennifer, 168–69

Index

Carscallen, Kristy, 124–25
Carter, Jimmy, 98
Carver, Thomas Nixon, 39
Castelo, Winnie, 148
cellphones, 133–36
Chamot, Dennis, 112
child labour, 45–46, 78, 83
Chile, 72, *73*, 74, 84–85, 145–46
China, 21, *73*, 74, 78–80, 123, 124
Chipeco, Joaquin, 147
Christopherson, Susan, 23
Civil War (U.S.), 28
climate change, 13, 16–18, 100. *See also* environment
Collins, Laurel, 169
Colombia, 72, *73*, 74, 84
Committee on Recent Economic Changes, 39, 100
Commons, John R., 12, 38–39
compressed work week, 194, 199, 215
computer technology, 104–5, 107–11, 115, 249n14
conditional hours reduction, 184, 259n12
Congress of Industrial Organizations (CIO). *See* AFL-CIO
Connery, William, 42, 45
consumption, gospel of, 39–40, 48–49, 96, 99–100
Conyers, John, 46–47, 247n42
Coolidge, Calvin, 97, 98, 246n26
Co-operative Commonwealth Federation (CCF), 59
Costa Rica, *73*, 74, 75, 83
Covid-19 pandemic
   1920s, comparison to, 100
   Great Resignation and, 121–22, 124, 127, 181
   health issues, work-related, and, 9, 11–12, 116
   healthcare crisis and, 14, 15–16
   remote work and, 161, 165
   work hours and, 182, 212, 218–19

Curium Solutions, 224
Czech Republic, *69*

Daimler, 138
Darrow, T.R., 99
Davis, Cindy, 172
death, from overwork, 76, 79
decentralized stoppage, 184
Denison Mines, 113
Denmark, 65, *65*, 66, 67, *69*, *70*
Depression, 39–40, 40–46, 59, 97, 246n24
De Sutter, Petra, 142
Deutsche Bank, 138
Deutsche Telekom, 138
Dowd, Peter, 201
DuPont, 94, 245n8
Duxbury, Linda, 165, 178

Eastern Europe, 72, 86–88. *See also specific countries*
Economic Council of Canada, 108, 111, 115–16
education
   four-day week, 193–94
   leisure studies, 207
   work hours studies, 207
eight-hour day, history of, 27–34, 63–64, 66, 67, *68*, 83, 87, 92–96, 106
El Khomri, Myriam, 139
El Khomri law (France), 137, 139–41
electronic monitoring (surveillance), 6, 109, 112, 113–15, 209
email, 138–39, 186
Employment Act (U.S., 1946), 48
England. *See* United Kingdom
environment
   climate change, 13, 16–18, 100
   four-day week and, 18–19, 214, 232n48
   hybrid work and, 177
E.ON, 138

Eschner, Kat, 106
Espinal, Rafael L., Jr., 155, 156
European Union (EU), *24, 70,* 144. *See also specific countries*
Evonik, 139
eye contact, 116, 118

Factory Act (U.K., 1833), *68*
Fair Labor Standards Act (FLSA, 1938), 45–46, 50, 58
Federal Public Works Act (U.S., 1912), 36
Federation of Organized Trades and Labor, 30
Fein, Erich, 104–5
Felt, Jeremy, 45
fifth-day stoppage, 184
Finland, 201
First World War, 36–37, 58, 91, 94, 205, 246n27
five-day week, 37–38, 64, 67, *69,* 186
Flex Jobs (flexjobs.com), 224
flextime, *69,* 191
Florence, P. Sargent, 39
Flórez, Raquel, 144
focus (heads-down) time, 186
Foner, Philip
  on Haymarket incident, 31
  on history of shorter work hours, 22–23, 26, 28, 32, 36, 37, 38, 49–50, 235n48
  on work hours, U.S. vs. Europe, 233n10
Foot, David, 231n28
Ford, Henry, 37, 38, 39, 58, 96, 100, 101, 103, 105–7, 110
Fortier, Mona, 166–67, 168
forty-hour week, 44–46, 49–50, 58–59, 60
four-day week
  Australia, 198
  Belgium, 199, 220
  Brazil, 190–91
  California, 196–97

Canada, 193–94
  environmental impacts, 18–19, 214, 232n48
  Finland, 201
  Iceland, 189, 220
  India, 199
  Ireland, 187–88
  Japan, 199
  Lithuania, 200
  Malta, 200
  Maryland, 197, 215
  models of, 184
  New Zealand, 201
  O'Connor on, 213–16
  O'Loughlin on, 218, 219–21
  Ontario, 194–95
  Pennsylvania, 198
  Portugal, 189–90
  as post-pandemic incentive, 178, 251n1
  rationale for, 181–82, 214
  Scotland, 200
  South Africa, 190
  Spain, 189, 200
  Sri Lanka, 81, 201
  Thailand, 201
  United Arab Emirates, 200
  United Kingdom, 182–87, 201, 221, 248n46
  U.S., 187–88, 195, 220–21
  Wales, 201
  See also shorter work week
4-Day Week Campaign, 225
4 Day Week Global, 182–83, 190, 193, 195, 213, 220, 221, 225
Four Day Week Ireland, 225
France
  Great Resignation, 124
  healthcare crisis, 15
  holiday leave and paid vacations, *25*
  right to disconnect, 136–37, 139–41
  shorter work hours, history of, 46, 63, *68, 69, 70,* 71

Index

work hours, cross-national comparisons, 21, *24*, 34, 35, 58, *65*, 66
work hours and productivity, 94
Fraser, Douglas, 47
Freeman, Richard
   What Do Unions Do? (with Medoff), 252n22
Frydenberg, Josh, 127
Fryer, John (Fryer Committee), 134–35, 254n1

Garcia, Christina, 196, 197
Garrison, William Lloyd, 28
Gen Z workers, 123
gender. *See* women workers
General Motors, 41
George, Claude, 34
Germany
   flextime and, *69*, 191
   holiday leave and paid vacations, *25*
   IG Metall, *70*, 71, 101, 137–38, 192, 207, 225
   right to disconnect, 137–39
   scientific management and, 57
   shorter work hours, 191–93
   shorter work hours, history of, *69*, *70*, 71
   work hours, cross-national comparisons, 21, *24*, 34, 37, 58, *65*, 66
   work hours and productivity, 94
Giattino, Charlie
   "Working Hours" study, 35, 55, 58, 63, 233n9
Gilbreth, Frank, 114
Giroux, Denise, 117, 256n6
Godard, John, 60
Goldberg, Emma, 128
Gompers, Samuel, 30, 32
Goodyear Tire, 41, 97
Gorky, Maxim, 238n130
government workers, 206

Grasso, Joe, 130
Great Britain. *See* United Kingdom
Great Depression, 39–40, 40–46, 59, 97, 246n24
Great Recession, 61
Great Resignation
   about, 5, 121, 211–12
   in Canada, 124–26, 127
   Covid-19 pandemic and, 121–22, 124, 127, 181
   demographics of, 123
   as global phenomenon, 123–24
   as Great Reshuffle, 127–28
   quiet quitting and, 123, 129–31
   staff shortages and, 128–29
   unionized workforce and, 126–27, 252n21
Greece, *73*, 74, 89–90
Green, Francis, 105
Green, William, 99
greenhouse gas emissions, 18–19. *See also* environment

Haller, Wilhelm (Willi), *69*, 110, 191, 260n34
Harvey, John, 96
Hawkins, Ruth, 117
Hay, Michelle, 130
Hayden, Anders, 179
Haymarket incident, 30–33, 235nn57–58
heads-down (focus) time, 186
health
   healthcare crisis, 13–16
   hybrid work and, 176
   mental health, 17–18, 108, 185
   overwork and, 9–10, 11–12
   technostress, 103–4, 108–10
   Zoom and other video conferencing technologies, 117–19, 170–71
Henkel, 138
"Henry's List" (O'Loughlin), 219
Hivemind Technologies, 192

Hoffman, Betsy, 118–19
holidays. *See* vacation leave and paid holidays
Hollander, Stephen, 249n23
Hong Kong, 72, *73*, 74, 78
Hoover, Herbert
  consumption, gospel of, and, 39, 100
  vs. Coolidge on role of government, 246n26
  Depression and, 40, 41, 97, 246n24
  relief work, 97–98, 238n130, 246n27
  reputation and legacy, 97–98
  shorter work hours and, 36, 41, 95, 98, 99, 101
Hopkins, Harry, 43
Horowitz, Julia, 124
Huberman, Michael, 23, 34, 35, 233n10
Hungary, *73*, 74, 86–87
Hunnicutt, Benjamin, 40, 42, 43, 44, 99, 223, 258n39
  Free Time, 39
hybrid work
  about, 5, 159, 174, 178
  benefits and challenges, 160–61, 162–63, 164, 174–77
  Canada, Parliament debate, 160, 169–71, 174
  Canada, Treasury Board debate, 159–60, 165–69, 174, 257n20, 258nn26–27
  environmental benefits, 19, 177
  future of, trying to predict, 161–62
  health and safety issues, 176
  home office issues, 164, 175–76
  New York City, 173–74
  privacy concerns, 174–75
  resistance to returning to office, 165–66
  right to disconnect and, 176
  Twitter (now X), 167, 171–73
  work hours and work schedules, 160, 163–65, 166

workplace dynamics and, 177
Zoom and other video conferencing technologies, 116–20, 170–71, 176

Iceland, 101, 189, 220
IG Metall, *70*, 71, 101, 137–38, 192, 207, 225
India, 124, 199
Indiana, 239n187, 240n190
Indonesia, 21
Industrial Disputes Investigation (IDI) Act (Canada, 1907), 59
Industrial Workers of the World (Wobblies), 38, 237n120
industrialization, 22–23, 25–26, 54, 56, 75–76
intensity of work, 104–7
International Labour Organization (ILO)
  about, 91–93
  Canada's right to disconnect committee and, 149
  eight-hour day convention, 58, 64, 67, *69*, 242n4
  on "excessive" work hours, 72, 242n9
  recommendation for new work hours conference, 208
  on Vietnamese work hours, 80
International Workingmen's Association, *68*
Ireland, 187–88
Israel, 88
Italy, 15–16, *25*, *65*, 66, 124, 142

Jackson, Ted, 179
Jacquemain, M.A., 17–18
Jaffe, Sarah, 122
Jamaica, *73*, 82, 85, 124
Japan, 23, *69*, 199
Jassy, Andy, 256n12
joint consultation committees, 115, 205

Index

Jones, Stephanie
 The 4 Day Week (with Barnes), 181, 259n12
Jones, Stephen, 129

Karpoche, Bhutila, 194, 215, 223
Kellogg, William K., 96–97, 99, 101
Kellogg Company, 38, 41, 107, 188, 204, 232n48, 258n39
Kenya, 144, 147
Keynes, John Maynard, 9
King, Mackenzie (King government), 59
Kingston Whig-Standard (newspaper), 107
Klotz, Anthony, 122–23
Knights of Labor, 30, 32–33, 56, 234n45, 235n48

labour movement and unionization
 activism, in Canada, for shorter work hours, 56–57
 activism, in U.S., for shorter work hours, 26–33, 36, 37–38, 41, 99, 234n21, 234n43, 237n116, 237n120
 activism, in Western world, for shorter work hours, 71
 in Canada, 54, 59–60, 126, 240n8, 241n16, 252n20
 and computer technology and tech-change-related issues, 110–11, 111–14, 115
 in Germany, 71
 Great Resignation and, 126–27, 252n21
 "international" unions, 54, 240n4
 in North Carolina, 50, 239n189
 vs. right-to-work provisions, 50, 239n187
 shorter work hours, end of engagement with, 48–50, 51, 111, 179–80
 shorter work hours, re-engagement recommendation, 207–8
 in U.S., 47, 60, 126, 155, 252n20
 weakening of, 12, 47, 50–51, 98, 110–11
Laplana, Joan Pons, 128
Latin America, 71–72, 81–85, 144. See also specific countries
Lawrence (MA), 128
leadership, for shorter work hours, 95–97, 101–2
League of Nations, 91, 95
Leduc, Alexandre, 153
Lee, Ian, 129
leisure movement, 24, 33, 39, 99
leisure studies, 207
Lenarczyk, Paul, 117
Leverhulme, Lord, 101
Life Work, Mental Health Index, 125
LinkedIn, 124
Lithuania, 200
Lockhart, Charlotte, 223
Logistics in Motion, 230n7
Low, Evan, 196
Lowell (MA), 27
Luelo, Catherine, 167–68
Luo Huazhong, 79, 123
Luxembourg, 142–43
"lying flat" movement, 79, 123

Ma, Jack, 79
Madsen, Dave, 198
Mah, Megan, 150
Malaysia, 220
Malta, 200
Manitoba Labour Division, 112–13
manufacturing sector, 26, 35–36, 236n108
Maritime Hours Law Act (U.S., 1936), 45
Maryland, 197, 215, 221
Massachusetts, 26, 27, 29, 37
Mavtek, 193

McCarthy, Eugene, 49
McGrenere, Grace, 125–26
Meany, George, 47, 49
Medoff, James
    What Do Unions Do? (with Freeman), 252n22
meetings, 163, 186
Melnick, Doron, 124–25
mental health, 17–18, 108, 185. *See also* health
Mexico, 21, 23, *24*, 81–83, 90, 220
Michigan, 239n187
Microsoft Work Trend Index, 11, 123
Millennial workers, 123
Minns, Chris, 23, 34, 35, 233n10
Mitterrand, François, *70*, 71
Mkandwire, Paul, 125–26
monotasking, 187
Motor Carrier Act (U.S., 1935), 45
multi-tasking, 118
Murdoch, Steven, 173
Murphy, Kevin, 112
Murray, Philip, 241n18
Musk, Elon, 171–73, 178
Myanmar, 220

Nadeau-Dubois, Gabriel, 153
Naomi, Colleen, 117, 251n54
National Association of Manufacturers, 43
National Industrial Conference, 57, 95
National Industrial Recovery Act (NIRA, 1933), 43–44
National Labor Relations Act (Wagner Act, 1935), 44
National Labor Union, 29
National War Labor Board (U.S.), 37
National War Labour Board (Canada), 59
Natixis, 141
Nectafy, 220
Netherlands, *65*, 66, *70*, 124
New York City, 30, 32, 144, 155–56, 173–74
New Zealand, *24, 25,* 66, 67, *68, 69,* 201
Newmann, Bill, 117
Nigeria, 220
night shifts, 87, 88
nine-hour leagues, 56
"996" work culture, 79
North Carolina, 50–51, 239n189, 240n190
Norway, 21–22, *70*
Nye, David, 106–7

O'Connor, Joe, 19, 178, 187, 193, 213–16, 223, 232n51, 251n1
Odell, Jenny
    Saving Time, 114, 262n1
office spaces, 162, 174–75, 177, 222
off-site employment. *See* hybrid work
O'Hara, Bruce, 9, 179
    Working Harder Isn't Working, 1–3
O'Loughlin, Henry, 196, 217–22, 224
on-call work, 10, 230n7
Ontario, 150, 151–53, 181, 194–95, 208
open-concept workplaces, 174–75
Orwell, George
    Nineteen Eighty-Four, 249n23
Ottawa Chamber of Commerce, 257n26
Ottawa-Carleton French Catholic School Board, 193–94
overtime
    Bangladesh, 80–81
    Brazil, 84
    China, 78
    Costa Rica, 83
    Greece, 89–90
    Hivemind Technologies, 192
    Hong Kong, 78
    Hungary, 86–87
    Jamaica, 85
    recommendations on, 204–5
    right to disconnect and, 145, 146

Index

Russia, 87
Slovakia, 86
South Africa, 89
South Korea, 76
Thailand, 80
Turkey, 88
unionized workplaces and, 126
Uruguay, 83–84
U.S., 37, 60–61
U.S. four-day week proposals and, 195, 196, 221
overwork
   climate crisis and, 16–18
   death from, 76, 79
   factors enabling, 12
   health issues from, 9–10, 11–12
   healthcare crisis and, 13–16
   perma-work culture and, 10–11
   productivity and, 12–13
Owen, Robert, *68*

panopticon, 114
Parsons, Albert, 31
Pennsylvania, 27, 198, 221
Pepushaj, Alfred, 150
Perkins, Frances, 42
perma-work culture, 10–11
Peru, 21, 146–47
Petersen, Anne Helen, 161–62, 177, 224
Philip II (king of Spain), 67, *68*
Philippines, 144, 147–48
Phillips, Greg, 168–69
Phillips, Wendell, 28
Phipps, Simone, 124, 128
Pielli, Chris, 198
Piketty, Thomas
   Capital, 248n47
Portugal, 89, 143, 189–90
Postal Act (U.S.), 45
Powderly, Terence, 32
Pragan, Otto, 49, 60
Pressbooks, 193
privacy, 174–75

productivity
   factors for, 131
   overwork and, 12–13
   scientific management research on, 57–58
   work hours and, 21–22, 28, 38–39, 58, 93–94
Professional Institute of the Public Service of Canada (PIPSC), 135, 168
Prohibition, 41, 238n138
Public Contracts Act (U.S., 1936), 45
Public Service Alliance of Canada (PSAC), 168
Puma, 138

Quebec, 17, 151, 153–54, 208
quiet quitting, 123, 129–31

Reagan, Ronald, 47
Registered Practical Nurses Association of Ontario, 13–14
Reid, Donald, 16
remote work, 217–18. *See also* hybrid work
research, work hours, 205, 209
Reuther, Walter, 48, 49
Riedl, René, 118
right to disconnect
   about, 5, 6, 136, 156–57, 212
   Argentina, 145
   Belgium, 141–42, 199
   British Columbia, 154
   Canada, 148–50, 151, 208
   Chile, 145–46
   European Union, 144
   France, 136–37, 139–41
   Germany, 137–39
   hybrid work and video conferencing technologies, 119–20, 176
   Italy, 142
   Kenya, 147
   Lumembourg, 142–43
   New York City, 155–56

O'Connor on, 215–16
O'Loughlin on, 221–22
Ontario, 151–53, 208
Peru, 146–47
Philippines, 147–48
Portugal, 143
Quebec, 151, 153–54, 208
quiet quitting and, 130–31
recommendation on, 208
Slovakia, 143
Spain, 143–44
U.S., 155–56
right-to-work provisions, 50, 239n187
Roediger, David
  on Haymarket incident, 31
  on history of shorter work hours, 22–23, 26, 28, 32, 36, 37, 38, 49–50, 235n48
  on work hours, U.S. vs. Europe, 233n10
Romney, Mitt, 240n190
Roosevelt, Franklin D. (Roosevelt administration), 40, 41–45, 60, 238n138
Rota, Anthony, 170
Royal Bank of Canada, 256n12
Rubenstein, Sarah, 160–61, 164
Russell, Bertrand, 9
Russia, 72, *73,* 87–88

salaries, 204
Schor, Juliet, 9, 10, 224
scientific management, 34, 57–58, 93, 94–95, 97, 205, 245n8
Scotland, 101, 200
Sears, 41
Second World War, 44, 46, 47–48, 64
Shoot, 190–91
Shopify, 220
shorter work week
  about, 5–6, 201–2
  author's CBC Opinion piece, 3, 180–81

  company initiatives vs. government mandates, 221
  enforcement, 206–7
  Germany, 191–93
  government workers, as example, 206
  joint consultation committees for, 205
  overtime, 204–5
  phase-in period, 206
  research recommendations, 205, 209
  salaries and, 204
  standard work week recommendation, 203–4
  See also four-day week
Siegel, Joshua, 198
Siemens, 139
Silas, Linda, 14
Singapore, 72, *73,* 74, 75, 77, 123
Slaughter, Jane, 47
Slovakia, *73,* 86, 143
Smart, Katharine, 14–15
Société Générale, 141
Society of Occupational Medicine, 9
South Africa, 89, 124, 190
South Korea, 72, *73,* 74, 75, 76–77
Spain
  four-day week, 101, 189, 200
  Great Resignation, 124
  right to disconnect, 143–44
  shorter work hours, history of, 67, 68
  work hours, cross-national comparisons, *65,* 66, 89
Spanish flu, 100, 247n43
split shift, 119, 163–64
Sri Lanka, *73,* 74, 75, 76, 81, 201
staff shortages, 128–29
staggered stoppage, 184
Standard Oil, 41
steel industry, 36, 63
Steele, Alistair, 127
stress. *See* health

Index

Stronge, Will, 189
Sugar Act (U.S., 1937), 45
Sumner, Charles, 28
surveillance (electronic monitoring), 6, 109, 112, 113–15, 209
Sutcliffe, Mark, 257n26
Sweden, 34, 58, 65, *65*, 66
Switzerland, 21, *65*, 66, 94

Taft-Hartley Act (1947), 50
Taiwan, *73*, 74
Takano, Mark, 195, 224
task lists, 187, 260n23
Tausch, Harold, 117
Taylor, Frederick (F.W.), 57, 94, 98, 114
  Principles of Scientific Management, 93, 245n8
Teagle, Walter, 41
technology
  cellphones, 133–36
  computer technology, 104–5, 107–11, 115, 249n14
  labour movement and tech-change-related issues, 110–11, 111–14, 115
  stress and, 103–4, 108–10
  surveillance (electronic monitoring), 6, 109, 112, 113–15, 209
  TV ads, 136, 254n2
  work intensification and, 104–7
  Zoom and other video conferencing technologies, 116–20, 170–71, 176
technostress, 103–4, 108–10. *See also* health
telecommuting, 85. *See also* hybrid work
telepressure, 155
ten-hour day, 26–28, 29, 66, *68*, 234n21, 234n43
Terkel, Studs
  Working, 249n13
Thailand, 72, *73,* 74, 75, 80, 201
Thibodeau, Patrick, 155

Thompson, Derek, 224
time, 211
time banking, 72, 86–87
Tolentino, Francis, 148
Trade Unions Act (Canada, 1872), 57
Treiber, Alex, 195
Truman, Harry S. (Truman administration), 60
Tugwell, Rexford, 43
Tulip (retail platform), 193
Turkey, 88–89
Twitter (now X), 167, 171–73

unionization. *See* labour movement and unionization
United Arab Emirates, 200
United Auto Workers (UAW), 49
United Brotherhood of Carpenters and Joiners, 33
United Kingdom
  four-day week, 182–87, 201, 221, 248n46
  Great Resignation, 123–24
  healthcare crisis, 15
  holiday leave and paid vacations, *25*
  productivity and work hours, 94
  quiet quitting, 123
  scientific management and, 57
  shorter work hours, history of, 67, *68*
  work hours, cross-national comparisons, 23, *24,* 34–35, 58, *65*, 66
United States of America
  Canada, comparison to, 53–54, *55,* 55–56, 58, 59–61
  Civil War, 28
  climate crisis, 16–17
  consumption, gospel of, 39–40, 48–49, 96, 99–100
  Conyers' work hours proposal, 46–47, 247n42
  five-day week, 58, 64

four-day week, 187–88, 195, 220–21
Great Resignation, 122
Haymarket incident, 30–33, 235nn57–58
healthcare crisis, 15, 231n34
holiday leave and paid vacations, 24, 25, 236n88
hybrid work, 160
labour movement in, 47, 50–51, 60, 126, 155, 252n20
leadership for shorter work hours, 95–97
leisure movement, 33
Mexico, comparison to, 82
postwar baby boom, 48, 60, 100, 239n175
right to disconnect, 144, 155–56
right-to-work provisions, 50, 239n187
scientific management and, 34, 93, 94–95, 97, 245n8
shorter work hours, Depression, 40–46
shorter work hours, end of activism, 47–50, 51, 60–61, 100, 241n20
shorter work hours, nineteenth century, 25–34, 63, 234n21, 234n43
shorter work hours, twentieth century, 34–40, 46–51, 98–99, 236nn95–96, 236n108, 237n116, 237n120
work hours, cross-national comparisons, 21, 22–23, 24, 34, 37, 58, 65, 66–67, 233n10
Uruguay, 73, 74, 82, 83–84

vacation leave and paid holidays
Canada, recommendations, 206
cross-national comparisons, 24, 25, 53, 61, 65, 66–67
Europe, 242n5
Greece, 89
history of, 69–70
Mexico, 82
Russia, 87
Slovakia, 86
Thailand, 80
Turkey, 88
Uruguay, 83
U.S., 66, 236n88
Van Buren, Martin, 27
VDT (video display terminal) provisions, 112–13
Veal, Anthony, 12, 19
Venezuela, 73, 74
video conferencing technologies, 116–20, 170–71, 176
Vietnam, 73, 74, 75, 80, 124
Villareal, Melissa, 128
Vivo, 79
Volkswagen, 138

wage disputes, 27
Wagner Act (National Labor Relations Act, 1935), 44
Wales, 201
Ware, Norman, 32
Warzel, Charlie, 161–62, 177, 224
weekend, 67, 68, 69, 95
Weeks, Joseph (Weeks Report), 26
Wells, Victoria, 166
Whaples, Robert, 36, 233n3, 236n108
Woll, Matthew, 99
women workers
Bangladesh, 76, 81
computer technology and, 110
hybrid work and, 160–61
Jamaica, 85
protective legislation for, 37, 63, 66, 67, 68, 70, 76
South Korea, 76
Sri Lanka, 76, 81
Turkey, 88–89
work hours, in U.S., 23
Wong, Daniel, 150

work, evolution of, 211–12, 222
work hours
  approach to, 3–7
  agriculture and, 22
  consumption, gospel of, and, 39–40, 48–49, 96, 99–100
  Covid-19 pandemic and, 182, 212, 218–19
  cross-national differences, 23, *24*, 34–35, 37, 63–67, *65*, 70–71, 233n10
  educational efforts, 207
  "excessive" hours, contemporary, 72
  industrialization and, 22–23, 25–26, 75–76
  intensity of work and, 104–7
  landmarks towards shorter work hours, 67, *68–70*, 70–71
  leadership for, 95–97, 101–2
  1920s and, 91–93, 94–95, 98–99
  1920s vs. 2020s, 100–102
  O'Loughlin on, 217–22
  productivity and, 21–22, 28, 38–39, 58, 93–94
  scientific management and, 34, 57–58, 93, 94–95, 97, 205
  See also four-day week; Great Resignation; hybrid work; labour movement and unionization; overtime; right to disconnect; shorter work week; technology; vacation leave and paid holidays; *specific countries*
Work Time Reduction Center of Excellence, 213, 225
workaholism, 11, 96–97. *See also* overwork
working to rule, 129
work-sharing, 41, 47, 61
World War I, 36–37, 58, 91, 94, 205, 246n27
World War II, 44, 46, 47–48, 64

X (formerly Twitter), 167, 171–74
Xiang Biao, 123
Xie, Irene, 195

Yalnizyan, Armine, 129
Yip Wai-yee, 78, 79–80
Yoon Suk Yeol, 76, 77

Zee.Dog, 190
Zoom, 116–20, 170–71, 176

About the Author

Jon Peirce is a labour and social historian, essayist, playwright, and memoirist who lives and writes in Gatineau, Quebec. In 2011, he retired from an eleven-year career as a labour relations officer and researcher with the Professional Institute, a public service union. Prior to that he was, among other things, a newspaper reporter and editor, English professor, industrial relations researcher and writer, and industrial relations professor. He's long been active in the Ottawa literary community, serving for many years on the board of Ottawa Independent Writers. When not writing, Jon is actively involved in community theatre in both Kanata and Wakefield and enjoys cooking, swimming, long walks, good conversation, and progressive politics. He has three adult children and one grandchild. His most recent publication was *Plague Take It: A COVID Almanac by and About Elders*, which he co-edited with Ann McMillan, and for which he was principal author. He has also published an industrial relations textbook, an essay collection, and a novella about tennis and romance.